SHOT GUNNING

SHOT GUNNING

THE ART AND THE SCIENCE

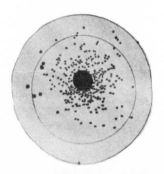

BOB BRISTER

Foreword by Grant Ilseng

WINCHESTER PRESS

TO SANDY

TARGET DRIVER, PELLET COUNTER, COMPANION,
WIFE, AND PARTNER . . . WHO HAS LEARNED MORE
THAN SHE EVER WANTED TO KNOW ABOUT
SHOTGUNS.

Library of Congress Cataloging in Publication Data

Brister, Bob.
    Shot-gunning.

    Includes index.
    1. Shot-guns. I. Title.
SK274.B64   683'.42   76–48642
ISBN 0-87691-184-X

Published by Winchester Press
  1421 South Sheridan
Tulsa, Oklahoma 74114

Printed in the United States of America

6 7 8 9 — 85 84 83 82 81

CONTENTS

FOREWORD

In 1956, a game warden friend of mine mentioned that the new outdoors editor of the *Houston Chronicle*, who'd just moved to the city from the piney woods of East Texas, was one of the best field shots he'd ever seen, and with a little coaching might make a champion at trap or skeet.

I promised I'd help the young man any way I could.

At the Oleander Skeet Championships at Galveston that year there was a special 50-target event for sportswriters covering the shoot, and Bob Brister showed up late—I expect on purpose. It was obvious he had never seen a skeet field and didn't even know which house the bird came from. I think for fear of being embarrassed, he didn't even bring a gun.

I introduced myself, handed him my old Model 12 and told him those targets were a whole lot easier to hit than doves or ducks. His first shot went off almost before the bird got out of the house. I'd forgotten to tell him my trigger had been honed down to a very light pull, and it went off before he was ready.

But he smoked the next target, and from then on all I had to do was stand behind him and tell him how far to lead the bird. He broke the next 49 straight and won the trophy.

What Brister could have done in clay-target shooting, if he'd ever gotten really serious about it, nobody knows. But his heart was in hunting, and also about that time live-pigeon shooting got started along the Mexican border and with his field-shooting experience he was a natural.

I don't know how many times he's made the All-American TAPA pigeon team, and I've watched him take trophies at trap, skeet, box-bird shoots, columbaire shoots, the Southwest Quail Shooting Championship, and just about anything that's done with a shotgun. We used to have an annual powder pigeon championship in Houston, a clay-target game similar to crazy quail, and Brister either won or placed in it every year. When our Greater Houston Gun Club installed an international trap field, he broke 100 straight, practicing for the final U.S. team tryouts, which is the only straight anybody ever shot on our international field.

In the 20 years I've hunted with him and shot competition with him, no matter whether the game was geese or clay pigeons, I could always count on two things: Brister would be hard to beat and he would also be changing guns, swapping stocks, testing loads, or experimenting with something the whole time.

I remember one big pigeon shoot; he was wood rasping the comb of his gun to make it shoot lower and somebody asked how many birds he'd missed to be hacking on such a beautiful new gun. He hadn't missed any, but said he didn't like the way he hit 'em, that he was shooting high. The next day he won the championship and was right in the middle of every bird.

When I heard some of our gun club members talking about a 16-foot-long moving target used for studying shot strings, I didn't even ask who it belonged to. Who else would go to the trouble of changing a 16-foot-long piece of paper after every pattern? But Brister has an inquiring mind that just doesn't run down.

If anyone is capable of writing this book, I believe he is. He's one writer who has lived what he writes about. And if there is anything he hasn't tried with a shotgun, I don't know what it is.

GRANT ILSENG
Houston, Texas

PREFACE

It has been written that shotgunning is a slapdash sort of thing, its use more an art than a science. Indeed the vague public conception of the "scattergun" is just that—pellets so scattered about that far less skill is required than with a rifle. Yet watching a bearded, muscled young man named Dan Bonillas, deep in concentration, relentlessly smoking fast-moving clay targets shot after shot, hundred after hundred, with the small, tight pattern of a full choke, it becomes obvious that there is also precision to the shotgun.

Each time the gun is opened, smoke curls up from cartridges evolved after years of research into the chemistries of powder and plastics, each shot a controlled explosion, firing within milliseconds of the ignition period of the one before it, and that is only part of the science of the shotgun.

An old master respectfully shoulders a fine double, and it becomes a living thing of grace and fluid motion, reading the myriad variables of angle, speed, and directional changes of birds in the wind to literally paint them from the sky. And that is the art of the shotgun—the most popular firearm in use in America.

As human populations increase, and big-game species become harder pressed for habitat, the use of the smoothbore will become more significant to the sport of hunting and thus to the continuance of the rights of Americans to own and use firearms. The majority of Americans now working hardest to uphold those rights are hunters.

The book is written out of respect for the shotgun and toward a clearer understanding of how it can be more efficiently used for the good of the game, the hunter, and the shooting sports.

Since I am neither artist, scientist, ballistician, nor even a very good nitpicker, no claim is made that my tests of patterns, performance, or shooting methods are to be taken as gospel. For acceptable statistical validity, thousands more tests would have to be run, requiring years for an individual to accomplish.

What we have here are *indications*, one man's attempt to find out new things about a very old firearm. The most significant findings would seem to be the addition of a new dimension to consideration of the shot string and what it means to clean-killing effectiveness with modern loads. In this respect, I am indebted to the counsel and assistance of many authorities, some shooters and some who work within the industries that produce the guns and ammunition. I have tried to be more reporter than investigator, although it is impossible to be one without the other.

Winchester-Western, Remington Arms Company, Ithaca Gun Company, and Federal Cartridge Company all contributed data, photographs, and in some instances ammunition for use in the tests.

I am particularly grateful for the assistance given by Tom Roster, brilliant young ballistician and professor at the Oregon Institute of Technology, who has produced handloads that surpass the performance of any previous shotshell load, and in doing so may have contributed impetus to the trend toward efficiency rather than sheer numbers of pellets put into the air.

I am also specifically thankful for the ballistical computations and computer material, along with technical insight, contributed by E. D. Lowry, former ballistician for Winchester-Western and now an independent consultant in Bellingham, Washington.

My personal and professional thanks to William B. Horn of Federal; Neil Oldridge, Ed Barrett, John Linde, and Wayne Leek of Remington; and also to Rod Van Wyk, John Madson, Ed Kozicky, and William E. Talley of Winchester.

Finally I must thank the gentleman who gave me my start in competitive shooting and who wrote the foreword to this book. Grant Ilseng, recently inducted into the Skeet Shooting Hall of Fame, is the only shooter in history to be named to the All-American skeet team and All-American trap team in the same year as an amateur, then achieve All-American status as a professional and in live-bird shooting as well. He has been a good coach and friend.

I do not expect every reader, nor even all these authorities, to agree with everything in this book. Nor is mention of any name or company to be considered agreement or endorsement of the material herein.

Since Major Sir Gerald Burrard compiled his classic *The Modern Shotgun*, toward the beginning of the century, little has been written of what actually happens to each pellet at that mysterious moment when a shotload reaches a fast-moving target.

I tried to find out. And as honestly and as best as I know how, I have photographed and reported this aspect of the art and science of shotgunning.

The reader can interpret the results as he chooses.

BOB BRISTER
Houston, Texas

1

LEARNING TO SHOOT

Susan Welton, a pretty teenager with brains, happened to be at our house one day when I needed pictures of somebody holding a shotgun. Although Susan had never handled a gun of any kind, she agreed to help out. Like most beginners, she wanted to crane her neck over the stock and bend backward rather than forward, but in five minutes she was holding the gun properly. Then it occurred to me. Here was the chance to answer the question I've been asked so often all these years: How long does it take to learn to shoot a shotgun?

I'd always figured learning to shoot a shotgun could be done, if done right, in about two weeks, maybe less. Not with the kind of proficiency that wins medals or money, but adequate technique for getting some game and being safe around other shooters. Susan agreed to give it a try.

I handed her my backyard practice gun, a Daisy Model 99 BB gun with its sights removed, and she started plinking at a Ping-Pong ball in the grass. Susan is a right-hander whose left eye is dominant (see Chapter 8) and so had to learn to shoot left-handed, to match that master eye. But after an hour or so, she had her left foot forward, her body bending nicely at the waist, and she was getting close to that Ping-Pong ball in the grass. I told her to practice 30 minutes in the morning and 30 minutes in the afternoon, to try and see where she was hitting, and to concentrate on the target rather than the gun.

Next day she was hitting the Ping-Pong ball.

We then put up a couple of little NRA targets, and I had Susan lower the gun and wait for the command to fire. Then I'd tell her to hit the left target, the right one, or maybe the Ping-Pong ball. She didn't know which until the command came. What I wanted was to focus her mind entirely on the target, not the gun. That sort of practice eliminates the "aiming" or "gun fixation" that so many new shooters acquire without realizing it.

Susan wasn't hitting the paper targets or the Ping-Pong ball every time, but she was getting closer. I watched her mental "computer" start to take over, an inch at a time pulling the impact of the BBs nearer to the point of aim. Remember she had no sights; this was the sort of instinctive pointing the human body happens to be better adapted to than aiming.

You don't see a good quarterback line up behind the football and aim his passes; he throws them instinctively. So do dart players, spear chunkers, and pool sharks, the best of whom concentrate on the target rather than on their "weapon." But shotgun shooters have a tough time learning that, and the best way around it is to eliminate right at the beginning the source of the fixation—the sight. Many shooters have probably read about and maybe tried the BB-gun technique to learn or improve their shotgun shooting, but very few bother with removing the sights. A rifle with sights teaches how to aim, and that's the last thing a new shotgun shooter needs.

Susan practiced her 60 minutes a day, but I got busy and couldn't really work with her. On the seventh day she appeared with a handful of paper targets, the bull's-eyes full of holes, and a half dozen riddled Ping-Pong balls.

"I can shoot where I look," she said, "and that's when you said we would go to the skeet range."

She was indeed handling the BB gun smoothly and naturally, and why not? In seven days, 30 minutes twice a day, she had probably put

Opposite, above:
The start of an experiment; the author attempts to teach a youngster who's never handled a gun to shoot a shotgun in one week. Here teenager Susan Welton, with a sightless BB gun, shoots at a Ping-Pong ball in the grass.

Opposite, below:
Because head position is the shotgun's only rear sight, proper placement of cheek on stock is a crucial part of early shotgun teaching. Here the author adjusts his pupil's head position, which was done each shot until she realized the advantage of having it there, otherwise new shooters often compensate and learn to shoot fairly well with poor head position, a problem that can be difficult to correct later.

that gun to shoulder more frequently and pulled the trigger more often than the average hunter does in a couple of years.

We went to the skeet range and started out at shooting station number 7. The incoming (high house) target there is a relatively easy one, requiring very little forward allowance, yet it is indeed a moving target and the shooter can start to learn the value of lead and swing. For the first five targets Susan wasn't allowed even her BB gun; I just asked her to stand in shooting position, watch for the target, and point at it as if she had an imaginary gun in her hands. If her point was jerky, high, or low she could see it as well as I could and correct it.

Again the purpose was to force her to concentrate on the target rather than the gun, and in Susan's case (she'd never even seen a clay

Starting from low gun position, the student is told to shoot either left or right target, not knowing until the command which it will be. This teaches smooth gun mounting and helps eliminate aiming or gun fixation by focusing shooter's attention on target. Shot by shot, the student's "mental computer" begins to narrow the error of shot placement, instinctively and naturally.

After a week of practicing 30 minutes twice daily, Susan breaks her second skeet target with dead-center hit.

target before) to gain at least some idea of the angle and speed of the object she'd be trying to hit.

Then she was handed her first "real" gun, empty, and she got more dry-run targets. Each time she was asked to swing on the target, point right at it, then pass it and see a little daylight ahead of it as she pulled the trigger.

I was watching over her shoulder, and it was interesting to see that built-in computer start to function with the actual gun. She had been accustomed to a lightweight BB gun with a heavy trigger pull, but this was a Remington 1100 20-gauge lightweight, weighing considerably more and with a much lighter trigger pull.

The first time the target came by, Susan poked at it and snapped the trigger. She may have shut her eyes for all I know, figuring I'd sneaked a shell into that gun. But after that she gradually smoothed out and the big moment had come. I checked her ear plugs, told her that the noise of the gun would seem strange that first time, as if maybe the gun had exploded or something, because a shot sounds differently when it happens right there in your face, but not to worry.

I broke a couple of targets for her, letting her hear the gun shoot, see it function, and see how little it kicked me. Then I handed it to her, told her to call "pull" loud and clear, and the target came sailing for us. I wish I could say she hit that first one, but she didn't. She shot in front of it. I'd made the mistake of telling her too much about shooting in front of things and she'd momentarily overridden her computer, trying to make the gun shoot out in front. So I told her to point at the target, and only at the last second move a little in front of it.

She smoked it! Then she broke the next one. And the next one after that. So I told her to try the low house, the straightaway bird, and to rely on her computer—no lead for this one, just let the gun find the target and shoot when she felt like it.

She surprised me, smashing that target like lightning. The wind was blowing and the target had been an erratic one with a chip broken off as it left the house. Instead of going straight, it had veered to the right. But Susan demolished it instantly; she'd simply done as told, and let the mental computer find it for her. She broke the next low-house target, and it was obvious to me she could stand there and break targets at station 7 all day long.

I asked her if the gun kicked and a blank look came over her face. "I really don't know," she said. "I was thinking about the target and I don't remember anything except the gun going off but I don't think it kicked me, did it?"

Few instructors are fortunate enough to get a student like Susan.

She ran into trouble hitting the long crossing shots at station 4, and again because she is a better student than I am instructor. I'd told her she'd need more lead ahead of that target, and fouled up her computer again. The first shot she swung way out in front, stopped, and shot. This is exactly what almost everyone will do the moment the mind starts concentrating on how far out front instead of how to get out there properly. So I told her to start the gun nearer the house, swing past that target and right through it, and see a little more daylight than she'd seen at station 7. That one she shot behind. So I told her to do the same thing but see a little more daylight. She smoked it.

From now on, Susan can be just about as good a shooter as she wants to be. The gun shoots where she looks. All she has to do is practice enough to know where to look. It is no miracle that she learned to do this in a week, nor are any of the instructional techniques used on her either new or revolutionary.

The BB gun was the basic and most important link in the chain of learning because it offered the opportunity for a lot of repetition, a lot of shooting without recoil, and very little expense. Many shooting instructors, including the U.S. Army, have learned that the BB gun is the fastest, least-expensive way to develop natural shooting ability. (The Army's "quick-kill" technique of instructive shooting was used in teaching soldiers to get on target instantly in the jungles of Vietnam.)

Most students want to skip the BB basics and start out with a real gun. This youngster is leaning too far back, weight on wrong foot, attempting to cope with recoil, swing, and a great deal of new advice all at once. But such instruction is better than none. The shooter here was participating in a National Hunting and Fishing Day observance at Greater Houston Gun Club in Texas. Several beginners who attended that clinic are now fine shotgun shooters.

Yet most students (and teachers) want to skip what they figure to be a rather dull step and start out on the shooting field with a real gun. And that is very often when bad habits are formed that are difficult to break.

Before any computer can function—be it human or electronic—it must have a certain set of standards or data programmed into it, and for a shooter's mind to move the gun instinctively, it must be programmed from the start to hit dead on. Unless the shooter can put gun to shoulder and hit dead on, how can his mind know for sure where "ahead" or "behind" may be?

If head position varies from one shot to the next, the mental computer is thoroughly confused. And the easiest way to lick that problem is to deal with it from the start.

That BB gun in the backyard will refuse to hit a Ping-Pong ball if the student's head position is out of kilter. Head position is a shotgun's rear sight. So the student quickly gets the message and his head starts positioning itself properly. If it doesn't, the most significant step the instructor can make is to get that head straight, right from the start. If the shooter learns to compensate and get by with head craned over the stock or in some odd position, he could learn to shoot fairly well, but never truly well. It is much easier to learn the right way.

The only trouble I had with Susan was in that first lesson on head position, and I stressed it constantly, literally forcing her head into place with my hands until her eye was properly over the barrel. Once she got the idea, the rest was easy. (A new device, described in Chapter 7, can do wonders toward teaching proper head position.)

It is fascinating to watch that mental computer start to function as a student practices. At first the shots will go wide of the mark. The student sees this and starts to correct for it. A few dozen shots and the gun begins to point nearer the target. Without consciously changing a thing, the student finds the shots coming closer to the target. That's the mental computer starting to take over, guiding hands, arms, and torso muscles toward a common goal. But there is nothing weird about it; you learned to drive a car the same way. You didn't aim at the road, you learned by practice where the wheels were and your mental computer learned how to center them on the right side of the road, perceiving just how much turn of the wheel or pressure on the brakes got the job done.

Once it learns, the mental computer can do those things better than the conscious mind. If you want to test that out sometime, just get into a car (preferably one with manual transmission) and force yourself to concentrate on each motion required in driving. Tell yourself your conscious mind is going to let out that clutch perfectly, without a jump or slip and that when you stop you'll do it by conscious effort at pushing the brake pedal with perfect smoothness.

Chances are you'll get a lousy letoff on the clutch and a jerkier stop than if you'd been driving along thinking about something else. If you try that "conscious effort" long enough you'll find yourself getting worse, because you're getting tired.

This conscious overriding is precisely what happens to many shotgun shooters when they begin trying to improve their shooting. You'll see a shooter relaxed and having fun with friends out on the skeet or trap field, smoking targets beautifully. Then he gets into competition, tries to override the computer, aims rather than swings, and begins chipping birds. Pretty soon he misses, no matter how hard he concentrates. Concentration is a wonderful thing, stressed constantly by expert shooters and instructors. But concentration cannot substitute for learned reflexes and practiced movements, the basics of doing something subconsciously.

That's how Susan learned to shoot in a week. She shot the BB gun a lot of times. And the same system will work for anyone—but maybe not in a week, maybe not in a month, because not everyone has a teenager's reflexes, eyesight, and natural ability.

Once any shooter learns to hit where he looks as a natural reflex, the big battle is won. After that it is just experience and learning where to look, how much daylight to see ahead of that bird or target. When the computer knows, it will put the gun there long before you can tell it to so do.

By none of this do I imply that within one week Susan or anyone else can become an accomplished shot capable of proficiency on game. This requires practice and experience, which is difficult to acquire other than going hunting and learning the hard way. One of the fastest alternative ways of learning game shooting is by going to an English-type shooting school, where targets are thrown in cover and at angles that simulate actual hunting conditions. But there are very few such facilities in America, the best known perhaps being the Orvis Shooting School at Manchester, Vermont.

The Orvis establishment is patterned after the famed Churchill School in England, and instructors there can fit an individual with a gun to his measurements, and when he shoots, watch the load in the air (another old English gimmick that greatly impresses people). Most good shooting instructors can do that, whether English or not, because the shot string is visible as a sort of shadow, or disturbance of the air, easiest seen on an overcast day with a background of light clouds. Actually a good instructor doesn't need to see the shot in the air; he can tell by watching whether you shot over, under, ahead or behind.

Unfortunately, there are too few really top instructors. Two of the best I've known are All-Americans Grant Ilseng of Houston, Texas, and Fred Missildine of Sea Island, Georgia. Ilseng coached my first round of skeet, and many times helped me out of slumps on the live pigeon circuit. He now teaches at the Greater Houston Gun Club.

The only semblance of an English-type shooting school in the South, to my knowledge, is Fred Palmer's layout at Alpharetta, Georgia, near Atlanta. He has grouse butts built like those in Scotland, a quail walk, high tower (for throwing clays simulating high-crossing doves or ducks), and a trap range. He's also the first instructor I ever saw teaching the BB-gun method, although it had been done by Lucky McDaniel and perhaps others before.

I realize many shooters scoff at BB-gun teachers, or for that matter English-type shooting schools. And certainly I had no benefit of either while growing up shooting ducks, doves, and quail in eastern Texas. But since then, I have had benefit of the counsel and friendship of one of the greatest of all English shooting instructors, the late Norman Clarke of the Churchill and Holland & Holland schools.

From Mr. Clarke I gained respect for the concept of such schools and what their instructors can do for some shooters, many things, for sure, that cannot be achieved simply by shooting American-style trap and skeet. Learning to mount, swing, and fire a gun quickly at a crossing clay target in heavy cover is much more likely to adapt a man to quail or woodcock than standing with gun rigidly mounted on the trap range.

I am surprised that more gun clubs in this country do not set up some sort of field course, quail walk, or whatever might be called a tour through the woods with targets coming or going at unknown times and angles. Archery clubs use such courses to sharpen up their members before hunting season, and riflemen have their offhand silhouette targets to simulate hunting conditions. But shotgun shooters in America mostly learn in the woods on their own, the best way they can.

No matter what the shooting conditions will be, nor whether the student intends to be a hunter, skeet shooter, or international trap champion, it all starts at the beginning with being able to shoot where you look. I believe the fastest way to learn that is with the BB gun and a great deal of pointing and handling practice before encountering the distractions of recoil, noise, and redundant advice.

First the new shooter must know where dead on is in terms of his own sight picture and head position. When those basics are fed into the mental computer, the rest comes naturally.

2

SHOTGUN ETIQUETTE

Shotgun etiquette, other than at shotgun weddings, would seem to be a rather simple subject. But thousands of hunters who are excellent shots are terrible "security risks" and have never been told why they are not overly popular as hunting companions.

When to shoot and when to wait is an instinct acquired by experience, but it can also be learned by thinking in advance. The good shooter knows that if he is on the right side of a blind or bird dog and the bird swings to the left, then this is clearly not his shot. He should not shoot across another shooter, even if there seems no danger of hitting the other man. (Ever have the muzzle blast of a shotgun go off in your ear?) The question is, how far away is the other hunter safe, from sound and stray shot.

Many shooters believe light bird shot will not carry far enough to harm a shooter some distance away. Unfortunately, several small lead shot can stick together in one lump that will go farther and hit hard at a distance. The best rule is *never* to pull the trigger with a gun barrel pointing toward any house, person, dog, or other object no matter how far away it is. You'll miss some chances at birds, but you'll never shoot anyone either. Practice makes this a built-in subconscious taboo that can stop a trigger pull even before the hunter can think.

Never yell at, give instructions to, or in any way interfere with another man's dog. This confuses the dog but not its owner, who is likely to be sure, right then, he doesn't want to hunt with you again.

Although only one bird of this bobwhite covey went to the right, shooter on the right concentrated on that one bird to avoid shooting past hunter to his left. In excitement of such moments shotguns are often fired too near a companion; muzzle blast in one's ear can be injurious to the hearing. Such a practice is both poor manners and poor sportsmanship.

Many young dogs will flush birds, then compound the mistake by chasing them, and it requires restraint to keep your mouth shut and your barrel down. But that restraint is necessary, for many a dog has been shot this way. A young dog chasing directly behind a covey of quail or a low-flushing pheasant is beneath the bird, of course. However, it is also behind it, and since many shooters miss birds by shooting low and behind, the dog could very well run into the load of shot intended for the bird. Good manners here are simply not to shoot if the dog is anywhere near the line of flight of the birds. If the distance is great, the birdshot may not hurt the dog, but its owner may well hurt you.

In walking in on a pointing dog, or with the expected flush of a pheasant or some other game bird imminent, never put the gun off safety until the game has actually flushed. You could stumble and pull the trigger. There is nothing more disconcerting to other hunters than to hear the click of a safety go off, knowing then that the other man's gun is ready to fire. Pushing off the safety should be a part of mounting the gun for firing. It should not occur until then.

When dogs chase birds, as most young dogs will, make sure any shots taken are up in the air and well clear of the dog. Firing at low-flying birds, particularly cripples a hunter is trying to finish off, has resulted in pellets put into many a dog. Although some dog trainers purposely "sting" dogs with long-range shot to reprimand them, the practice is dangerous (a clump of even small shot could put out an eye) and at close range a shotgun can kill.

One of the most frequently violated of gun-handling procedures is loading and shutting the action with the gun pointed in an unsafe direction. This is only a momentary gesture, but if a man slams shut a double barrel or lets fly the action of an automatic while the barrel is even flirting past someone's foot or fine bird dog, other hunters in that group should immediately call attention to his mistake. A firing pin could be stuck or broken, projecting in such a way that the gun fires as it is closed. Unless this mistake is called attention to, it likely will recur. Often the hunter isn't even aware he's done it.

In recent years it has become increasingly popular to take wives, girl friends, youngsters, and others hunting who may have had little or no previous experience with shotguns. This can certainly add to the pleasure of an outing, but I do not believe an actual hunt is the place to start anyone with a gun. There is too much excitement, the experienced shooters are too likely to be preoccupied with equipment, dogs, etc., and the first few moments out of the car when everyone is loading up can be the most dangerous. The place to teach such funda-

Note the position of the lady's gun; should it discharge there could be one less fine hunting dog or perhaps husband. This scene was posed to show the danger of putting beginners in the field before they are familiar with basic firearms safety.

mentals as loading, unloading, shouldering, and pointing the gun are in the backyard (preferably with safe "snap caps" rather than live shells).

Supervised dry pointing and mounting of the gun for a few sessions every evening weeks before a hunt can work wonders with beginners. Not only do they feel more familiar with the gun, they stand less likelihood to mount it improperly and get painful bruises, nor are they so likely to end up disliking the experience. If a youngster can actually hit something his first trip out, he may be sold on hunting for life. If instead he is berated for some fault of gun handling (which he really wasn't responsible for in the first place), he's likely to be turned off.

Another major danger out hunting, as on the highway getting there, is alcohol. If someone has been drinking, he simply shouldn't be hunting.

Every hunting accident today has extra significance, affecting not only the hunter hurt, but perhaps all other hunters as well. Antigun groups love to present hunting-accident statistics in their attempts at

Supervision of youngsters is important; they get excited and can only absorb so many hunting and safety lessons at once. Beginners should start out hunting with only one shell at a time, and younger nimrods should be up front with an adult where they can be observed.

promoting antihunting legislation. Parents refuse to permit youngsters a chance at one of life's most pleasant and healthful activities for fear of their safety, possibly to a great extent because hunting accidents make front-page news while car or motorbike accidents are less sensationalized.

Here are some practical tips that could help protect you and reduce those grim statistics that hurt us all:

Never start a youngster hunting with more than one shell in his gun. Kids get excited, and after they shoot often forget that a double or autoloader is primed to fire again. After a few trips, when the shooter has proved his coolness under fire, he can be permitted more shells at a time.

If a simple single barrel with visible hammer is used as a first gun, make sure the beginner can demonstrate time and again proficiency at letting down the hammer from full cock to safe position. Sometimes, with hands perspiring or cold, the hammer can slip and the gun fire.

Whether hunting birds, rabbits, or deer, make sure *every* member

This classic mistake, posed for the illustration, is so obviously dangerous it requires little comment, yet it causes a few accidents every hunting season. No gun should be pulled barrel first toward the shooter under any circumstances, whether taking it from the case or pulling it beneath a fence. Loaded guns inside vehicles ask for accidents.

of the party has some blaze orange clothing, even if it's only a bright cap.

Should you hear some hunter brag about taking a "sound shot" at a grouse or quail in heavy brush, keep clear of him. He's an accident going someplace to happen!

Don't develop the habit of resting a loaded gun on your foot to keep it out of snow or mud, even though such practice is now commonly acceptable on skeet ranges where some shooters wear special leather pads on their shoes for the purpose. Unlike hunters, skeet shooters—when not actually on the shooting line—*always* have unloaded guns.

One of the most common shotgunning accidents involves one hunter popping up from cover to shoot just as another fires from behind him. Always know where the others are before the trigger is pulled.

Hunting from a vehicle, besides being unlawful in some states, is dangerous in that one hunter may jump out to shoot just as another fires from behind him. This happens most frequently to hunters riding

By walking in on a quail covey side by side, these shooters have greatly reduced chances of accident. Note that each has picked the bird to his side. Even with birds flying virtually together, practice at picking "your bird" ingrains the habit and makes it easier when big covies buzz up suddenly and switch direction in midair. No matter which way a bird started out, it is the bird going to your side at shooting time that should be taken. If that bird reverses field and turns into another hunter's zone let him go and find one going your way. Thus you will "double" less on the same bird with another shooter.

in the cab of a pickup truck who bail out to shoot just as someone in the back shoots.

After every hunting trip unload all shooting jackets, vests, etc., of shells. This will prevent the possibility next trip of perhaps a stray 20-gauge shell being put by mistake into a 12 gauge. When that happens, the 20 can drop unnoticed into the barrel, and next time the gun is fired it may blow up. This is one of the most common causes of gun bursts.

Another, even more frequent, cause of gun bursts (although it usually results only in a blown barrel at the end rather than an explosion nearer the shooter that could be catastrophic) is accidentally getting mud or snow in the end of the barrel. If for some reason you have stumbled, or perhaps made a long crawl getting within range of game, unload and check the barrel.

Most experienced shooters know these things, but for some reason many still do not realize the tremendous muzzle blast their guns have when fired too near the ears of companions. Every season it happens two or three times to me, and each time I wonder if my head is still there.

If a crippled duck is swimming off, no matter if you put him down, let the hunter on the other end of the blind finish him off—or at least ask his permission (and give him time to get out of the way) before you do the job.

Last, shooters, like drivers, should operate defensively at all times keeping both eyes open for that hole in the end of somebody else's barrel. Doing just that, sometimes in the nick of time, is why I'm still alive.

3

THE PUMP-ACTION GUN

Arguing over the best shotgun is like debating the virtues of blondes, brunettes, or redheads. Beauty is in the eyes of the beholder. But bedchamber ballistics are rarely posted in public places, as shotgun shooting scores are. Although our data may be qualified, we can at least make some observations.

The highly regarded best-grade English side-by-sides, with their famed broad sighting plane, fine balance, etc., have almost disappeared from contemporary major competition. To my knowledge no top title at skeet, trap, ISU-Olympic trap, or international skeet has been won in years with a side-by-side. But the side-by-side was designed to be a game gun, a field shooter's joy. And for that job it remains one of the finest ever created. It has certain field advantages unshared by any other design.

Nonetheless, Americans tend to assume that if one gun is good for skeet or trap, it must therefore be equally good for field shooting. We have been doing that sort of assuming for years, and trends in American field guns (by those shooters who can afford any gun they want) have followed quite closely the trends among trap and skeet models.

In the 1930's, autoloaders (everybody called them automatics), mostly of the hump-backed Browning-patent design, had been around for years. But the sleek profile and swift handling of the Winchester Model 12 pump, the Remington 31 (the ball-bearing corn sheller it was billed then) and the corn sheller's silky successor, the 870 pump, won the hearts of serious shooters all across America. (Europeans, meanwhile, were looking with distinct distaste upon what they call magazine guns as unsightly, possibly even unsafe, and boorish to boot.)

The pumpgun promoters had plenty going for them. The guns were strong, simple, and would function in a driving dust storm that would put any automatic out of commission. They could be fired, it was claimed, as fast and maybe faster than any autoloader. The late Winchester shooting professional Herb Parsons went around the country claiming his company's Model 12 would do things impossible with any automatic, and he would challenge anyone in the audience to match his speed with the slick-pumping 12. In one demonstration he

Which gun is best to some shooters means performance, others price. In England, where development of the fine shotgun was epitomized by a class of guns known simply as best grade London guns, this Purdey over-under would be considered by some to be about as best as a gun can get. It features select wood, three sets of barrels, fitted trunk case, and several thousand dollars worth of prestige on its nameplate, was estimated to be worth something in the vicinity of $20,000 in 1976, and could ultimately be worth much more.

In winning the Olympic Gold Medal at the most difficult clay target competition of them all, international-style trap, Englishman John Braithewaite chose an over-under Browning. Over-unders have won every medal in recent history at this form of competition, which often requires very fast, long second shots.

would throw up seven clay targets with one hand and then break them all before they could get to the ground.

But Herb was an honest man. When I asked him, he admitted he accomplished his remarkable performance by holding down the trigger and, as he put it, "pumping like hell." On the old Model 12 this could be done; with the trigger down, the gun would fire the instant the action closed. This was not exactly a contribution to safety and has been changed so that on modern versions the trigger must be released and pulled again to fire.

Herb's technique underscores that, although the pump action was, and is, very fast, it is normally just a tiny bit slower on the second or third shot than an autoloader. This can be proved rather quickly at a fast game requiring two shots, such as international trap, although plenty of expert pump shuckers can break doubles at American trap with no problem.

Although the relative speed of a pump compared with an automatic or two-barreled gun could be argued forever, there is absolutely no doubt in my mind that the average shooter can get off two accurate shots slightly faster with an autoloader or two-barreled gun than with a pump. He has no action to pump, no split seconds of racking the fore end back and forward again, to distract him.

But in ordinary field hunting, that split second required to shuck the pump action may, for many shooters, contribute to *more* accurate shooting. The reason is that most English (and many of the best American) shooting instructors teach a field-shooting system in which the gun is brought rapidly up to a moving target and fired the instant the butt touches the shoulder. In this way, the movements of mounting and swinging are utilized to provide a certain momentum of gun and swing, which helps eliminate stopping or checking the swing.

Some English instructors teach that even when two birds are passing over, and the first has been felled by this quick-mount-and-swing technique, the gun should actually be dropped from the shoulder slightly, then remounted and fired in precisely the same way as the first shot. I personally cannot see that such remounting is necessary, and I know I'd have a tough time getting all that done with a covey of quail in a high wind buzzing around my ears or a fast flight of high doves hitting 60 miles per hour over a feeding field.

But the point is that there may be a tendency, after the first shot is fired, to slow the gun and aim for the second shot, since the gun is already shouldered and roughly on target. This, in turn, could destroy the built-in forward allowance of the fast-swing system.

This brings us back to the pumpgun, and the reason many shooters can score better in the field, particularly on ducks and geese, with a pump than with any other action. In the process of pumping between shots, the shooter is temporarily brought off target and must make a fresh point with all the advantages of the built-in momentum of the second swing.

Despite years of experience with pumps (and when I shot only that type of gun, I could shuck one pretty swiftly), I found—as have so many others—that the trombone action is just a shade slow sometimes in the competitive live-bird ring, where a great many dollars may be riding on a quick, accurate second shot. Unlike field shooting, where the shooter can get back on game according to his own timing, com-

A classic among American pumpguns for its balance and handling, this Winchester Model 12 is the two millionth produced. Presented to former Texas Governor John B. Connally, it has a circular medallion of solid gold inset in the receiver commemorating the state and national titles Mr. Connally has held.

petitive live birds must be dropped in a small scoring ring and sometimes a tiny thousandth of a second in timing can mean a bird lost dead outside.

I switched first to an autoloader, then to an over-under. With both these guns I originally missed the pumpgun in one major way—I had a terrible tendency at first to throw the second shot right behind the first one, without reswinging or getting started again, as I'd had to do with the pump. The result was a great many tailfeathered birds and missed shots until I finally learned what was happening.

Does that mean that the pump is the best field gun? In some ways, yes. It is a tougher gun than an autoloader and less likely to break down or jam in the field. It will withstand blowing sand and dust. And it offers three or more shots (depending upon laws governing game hunted), and those extra shots sometimes mean a great deal where game is scarce or quail coveys have sleepers that get up just about the time the two-barrel shooter has his gun open to reload.

English gun authority Gough Thomas has called the pumpgun "eumatic," a word he coined to mean convenient, in the sense its design actually helps it do its job for you. He specifically referred to the gun's ability to start to pump itself when the mechanism is released (by pulling the trigger) and the way that recoil from the preceding shot actually starts the pumping hand moving rearward to operate the action.

Although "eumatic" is in no dictionary (and Gough Thomas is probably in no telephone book, since his real name is G. T. Garwood) the gentleman, as in most instances, is quite correct. The pump does start to work almost automatically to prepare the shooter for the next shot. And if you'd like to have some fun with friends not aware of this, make a small wager that you have a pumpgun that will pump itself automatically.

One of the most versatile pumpguns is Remington's Model 870 in 20 gauge with lightweight action. It can be had with 3-inch chamber for magnums, yet weighs about 6 pounds. The magnum action will accommodate standard 2¾- or 3-inch cartridges. The 870 is one of the largest selling shotguns of all time.

The pumpgun is the choice of many veteran waterfowlers because it will continue to function despite mud, blowing sand, cold, or even lack of cleaning. It is easier to load than an over-under or double in the confined quarters of platform blinds, such as the one shown, and will function with light, standard, or extra-heavy magnum loads.

This self-pumping can be proved rather dramatically on a rifle range or anywhere there is a bench rest with sandbags. Rest a 12-gauge pumpgun of normal weight with its fore end on a sandbag, insert a magnum load, then hold the gun only with its pistol grip (as you'd shoot a bench-rest rifle) and squeeze the trigger. The fired case should go flying out of the gun almost exactly as if ejected from an autoloader. The reason is that the rearward forces of recoil shove the fore end back, opening the action, and ejecting the shell. Obviously this gimmick works best with loads of heavy recoil.

This is at least a partial argument for those who claim they cannot remember to pump a pumpgun. In my own instance, constantly testing guns and switching from one to another in the field or at trap or skeet, I find it almost impossible *not* to remember to shuck a pump, for the simple reason it starts shucking itself for me.

Since I'm certainly no mental giant at remembering things, I believe almost anyone can quickly adjust to remembering to shuck a pumpgun.

4

WHY A TWO-BARRELED GUN

In recent years there has been an international turn toward the over-under. It may not have the soft recoil of an autoloader nor the multiple shot capacity of either pumpgun or autoloader, yet some shooters (and I'm one of them) favor the stackbarrel above all others. Before getting into whether the over-under or side-by-side is best, for the purposes of this chapter, we'll lump the two together initially as two-barreled guns and discuss how they compare with pumps and autoloaders.

One of the most practical advantages of two-barreled guns is having two chokes rather than one. A two-barreled gun with one barrel tight and one fairly open can offer a choice of choke appropriate to the shot presented. For example, the first shot at game is often at closer range than the second. Thus, an open choke gives the first shot more pattern spread at the closer range; the second shot gives a more concentrated full-choke pattern for the departing game. This situation exists when jump-shooting pheasants or quail or almost any game that will be farther away by the time the second shot is fired.

Since most modern two-barreled guns offer choke selection, either in the form of a selective single trigger or two triggers, the gun's tight barrel can be used exclusively for high, passing singles (such as doves or ducks) and the firing sequence can be reversed so that the tight-barrel shot is taken at approaching game (say diving ducks which rarely flare but tend to come whistling on past) and the second shot

In close quarters like this Louisiana quail and woodcock cover, the shorter the gun the less likely it is to be stopped in its swing by brush, and the two-barreled gun is approximately three inches shorter than a magazine gun of the same gauge and barrel length. Also, in heavy brush the third shot offered by an autoloader or pump may not be important; birds often are behind brush by the time a third shot could be fired. Short-barreled doubles or over-unders usually are well balanced and fast to point, a factor more important than firepower in situations such as these.

can thus be taken with the more open barrel as the bird is closer. Some expert dove shooters like to employ this system, because when properly executed the birds can be made to fall in front of the shooter rather than behind him in the brush where they may be more difficult to find.

But is the two-choke option really adequate compensation for the lack of a third shot? With most hunters I doubt that it really is, and I believe the reason so many are going over to the two-barreled gun is not the choice of chokes, but that like myself, they prefer the shorter, faster-swinging, finely balanced aspects of this type of gun plus pride of ownership of a fine firearm.

In competitive trapshooting, many doubles experts use the two-barreled gun for its dependability and speed; it is a little easier to get around to the second target than shucking a pumpgun and a little

The two-barreled option of one choke tight and one open led to the demise of these dove and quail. The selective single trigger of the Beretta SO-5 was kept on modified for these high-passing doves. When the dogs pointed quail, the selector was moved to improved cylinder for the closer shot at the departing bobwhites; the tighter second barrel came in handy on second shots, particularly with coveys that flushed wild.

more reliable to shoot than an autoloader, which could conceivably jam or malfunction. (Modern autoloaders, and shooters who have learned how and when to clean them, continue narrowing that gap.)

At skeet shooting, where the rules are more lenient toward malfunctions, the autoloader is more common than the over-under for reasons of lower recoil and lower price.

Although almost anything in the above could be debated, one thing cannot be and that is that the two-barreled gun—of equal barrel length—is a shorter gun overall than the pump or autoloader. This is because the latter guns have a receiver about three inches long that the two-barreled guns do not have. Thus, for example, a 12-gauge over-under or double with 28-inch barrels is about three inches shorter overall than a pump or autoloader with the same length barrel.

Another reason often cited for the superiority of the two-barreled gun is its fine balance between the hands. This is certainly true with almost any quality gun, but in all honesty almost any gun can be weighted and balanced to provide between-the-hands balance.

It has also been said there is a certain snob appeal to the two-barreled gun, and on some hunts and in some areas (particularly overseas) the man with a fine double or over-under is looked upon with more esteem than one with a magazine gun. But I honestly believe that the reason most shooters are now using two-barreled guns rather

With birds such as pheasants, which sometimes flush underfoot and sometimes wild, two chokes are better than one. The shooter here is using a Charles Daly over-under with its lower barrel bored out (from modified to improved cylinder) and the top barrel full, an ideal combination for an all-around field gun.

than pumps or autoloaders is simply that the shorter guns feel better and they hit better for them. And that is by far the best reason of all.

Side-by-Side or Over-Under?

Proponents of the side-by-side double claim that the eye is naturally drawn to the center of the broad sighting plane between the barrels and that canting or twisting of the gun is easier observed, less likely to occur, and means less to pattern placement if it does occur than with the over-under. They point out that the side-by-side barrels offer less wind resistance and thus tend to be blown about less and swung easier against a strong crosswind.

Some purists are so emphatic in their determination that the side-by-side is really the only gun, that one writer with sentiment coloring his typing stated that the over-under was suited only to shooters with eyes set in their head 8 rather than 00. To me this makes about as much sense as suggesting that cars with the steering wheel on the left are suitable only for left-handed drivers.

But there are some very solid points to be made for the side-by-side that are not always mentioned. One is that the relatively unsupported barrels of a side-by-side (as opposed to the relatively stiffly supported barrels of a superposed) have more downflip and tend to shoot lower. This in turn means that the typical side-by-side can be stocked straighter, with more barrel visible to the shooter—and without shooting excessively high—than can the over-under.

To put it another way, over-unders naturally tend to shoot higher than side-by-sides, and when enough down bend in stock dimension is put into an over-under's stock to make it shoot dead on, there is the tendency to increase the gun's natural tendency to kick upwards into the cheek. In recent years builders of over-unders have become more aware of the importance of straight-back recoil and have compensated for the high shooting tendency by raising ribs on the barrel. This is true with many trapguns, and permits a straighter stock without overshooting.

But this can, in some cases, work the other way around.

Despite the general belief that all classic English writers have been totally in favor of the side-by-side, Major Sir Gerald Burrard, in Volume I of his famous *The Modern Shotgun*, stated: "There are some sportsmen who find that a very straight stock bruises their faces but who cannot shoot with more (down) bend. Such should try an over-under gun, and they find their troubles are removed."

In that same chapter Burrard states: "In ordinary (side-by-side) guns the tendency of the barrels to shoot apart (impact to not quite the same spot) is more pronounced than in over and under guns, because in the case of the former the lateral jump causes the right barrel to shoot to the right and the left to the left. But in over and under guns the jump acts in the same direction for both barrels."

Burrard did not consider this to be much of a problem, however, and neither do I, because well-made doubles or over-unders can be expected to impact very closely to the same spot. Over-unders in general have the tendency to impact a few inches higher with the top barrel than the bottom, and many side-by-sides shoot a tiny bit to the right with the right barrel. Of much more significance, I believe, is the lateral jump to which Burrard refers.

I had heard for years the argument that it was easier to get back on target for the second shot with an over-under, because firing either barrel of the side-by-side had the tendency to pull the gun in that direction, thus getting temporarily out of line with the target. I never paid much attention to it, and have never found it to be a problem in shooting any of the many doubles I've owned.

The most graphic illustration, however, of this lateral jump ever provided me came, of all places, from one of the most devout disciples of the classic side-by-side. Cyril Adams, of Houston, Texas, owns a fine collection of side-by-side doubles and has had many guns custom built. On one occasion, he had a pair of .458 rifles made up for a friend, one of them side-by-side, the other over-under. These guns were built by the world-famous Borovnik of Austria and were beautiful examples of the gunmaker's art. Their significance in this instance was that these powerful "elephant guns" had terrific recoil (as do all .458's I've fired) and because of this added recoil it was easier to determine what really happens when an over-under is fired compared with what occurs when a side-by-side is shot in the same circumstances.

There was simply no contest. The side-by-side .458 upon firing jumped laterally to the right and had to be brought back to the mark before a second shot could be dispatched. The over-under just held in there; it jumped up more than the side-by-side, but came right back down on line with the target.

Since few shooters will be aiming at elephants with their side-by-sides or over-unders, this has bearing only in that there must be, even with cartridges of lesser recoil, some jumping aside to be considered in

The classic side-by-side double, shown here in downing driven grouse on a Scottish moor, seems particularly suited to incoming and departing targets, possibly because its broad sighting plane is better oriented to vertical than horizontal alignment. And in shooting driven birds, one does not fire at 90° crossing birds without risking blasting one's companion in the next shooting butt. Although few clay-target competitors use the double, some of the world's finest game shots prefer it.

Ennio Mattarelli, Olympic Gold Medalist at trapshooting and designer of the Perazzi over-under, is well aware of the advantages and disadvantages of the stack barrel. Partially to permit straighter stocks (and thus less recoil), he designed the very high rib now adorning the MX-8 and MT-6 models, but for European-style live-pigeon competition—where shooting high is an advantage—he favors the straight rib shown on the engraved masterpiece he's holding. When asked which design (double or over-under) is "best" (the Perazzi firm can build both) he answers: "It is the over-under that wins."

getting back on target with a side-by-side double. I doubt it makes nearly so much difference in trying for a quick left and right on driven grouse with light loads as it would trying to put the second shot right behind the first at a departing clay pigeon with heavier, faster, Olympic-type traploads.

The two-barreled-rifle example was also included because one of the arguments of proponents of the side-by-side double has long been that this must be the best (and least recoiling) double gun, otherwise African rifles would always have been over-unders. I don't believe that it can be deduced that simply because the English (or anybody else) built a gun a certain way, that way had to be best. Yet Burrard, Gough Thomas, and many other English authorities have pointed out that the over-under was actually being made before the side-by-side, and thus if it were better, why didn't the over-under prevail? Thomas, whom I consider the dean of living authorities on the shotgun, remains English. In his famous *Gough Thomas's Gun Book* (Winchester Press), he makes the point, as did Burrard, that development of the modern over-under was primarily "the search for something new."

Thomas also takes pains to point out that the side-by-side survived another significant phase "during the trap shooting of live

Nuria Ortiz of Mexico City, one of the world's best women shooters at Olympic or International skeet, uses the over-under, as do most other champions at this fast and difficult game.

pigeons in the latter half of the century." He goes on to point out that bets were heavy on the live-bird contests, and that the winners used side-by-sides. He also points out that the famous All-American trapshooter Herb Parsons used a side-by-side.

I mention these points because they are so sadly outdated today. No winner of an Olympic medal at trap or skeet in many years has used a side-by-side. Everyone has used an over-under. For years the side-by-side also held its own in the world championships of live-bird competition, particularly on the Continent. But in the past few years the top winners have been predominantly over-under shooters.

This is intended to prove nothing other than that if we are to cite success in the fields of competition, live birds, or clay birds, we must at least be as current and fair about it as possible. And at this time, the single sighting plane is running far out front in widely published competitive results. The principal reason, I believe, is that it offers a more precise sighting plane. But precision in terms of sighting plane is a highly debatable matter that depends upon the gun (size of the barrels), the background, and whether vertical or horizontal precision is most important.

For example, one of my favorite bird guns (when carrying is likely to consume more time and energy than shooting) is a British Webley & Scott 28-gauge side-by-side double. With such small gauges, a single barrel or over-under can be easy to lose against a background of brush. But looking down those little 28-gauge double tubes offers a quite visible sighting plane. The sighting plane of a double 28 is roughly the same as offered by a wide-ribbed single of over-under 12 gauge. Also, most upland birds hunted against such backgrounds normally offer rising targets which makes the vertical precision of the side-by-side's sighting plane significant, whereas on doves, ducks, or clay targets crossing against a clear-sky background, the single sighting plane (with its emphasis on horizontal precision) might be better.

The winningest shotguns today are those with a single sighting plane, whether the action is that of a single-barreled trapgun, single-barreled autoloader at skeet, or over-unders at both those games as well as live-pigeon competition. But bird shooting in the field is neither trap, nor skeet, nor competitive pigeons. And for that reason, the debate will never be settled except by each man behind his own gun. If he believes in his side-by-side double, and gets more game with it, then that should be the gun he shoots.

Gough Thomas, discussing the pointability of over-unders, says that many of his readers who have switched from a side-by-side to an over-under have been troubled by the "off" eye seeing the side of the over-under and its lower barrel, whereas with the side-by-side "the dominant visual impression is that received by the aiming eye." In American vernacular, that would tend to say that the tendency to cross fire, or have the wrong eye take over, is more prominent with the over-under, and that when shooting with both eyes open it is easier for the proper eye to get the dominant impression with a side-by-side double.

Thomas makes a significant point in mentioning that at sports where the gun is already shouldered, such as trap or American skeet, there is less problem, because the dominant eye can be prealigned with the rib of the over-under. Although he did not say so, I would presume Thomas also feels that in the case of a non-mounted gun, such as in field shooting, side-by-side might more naturally come into proper dominant eye relationship easier and with less likelihood of the wrong eye seeing the side of the over-under.

This may very well have merit, although it must be mentioned that the fastest-pointing shotgun game of them all, started from the hip, is international or ISU-Olympic skeet. And the champions at that game are shooting over-unders.

All this will doubtless leave a bitter taste in the mouths of dedicated disciples of the side-by-side double who have observed that my personal preference for most shooting is the over-under and thus could logically deduce that I'm prejudiced beyond fair-minded appraisal. The fact is that my personal prejudice is in favor of the classic side-by-side double. I believe this is the most beautiful gun ever built.

Left:

Although the narrow sighting plane of the over-under is most precise against a clear background, it can be easy to lose (particularly with small-gauge guns) against the background of brush in which so much upland game shooting is done. This could be why the over-under is so popular with target games (all of which have or should have a reasonably good background) while the double with its wider, more visible sighting plane is often preferred by hunters in heavy cover. The narrow rib of the 28-gauge Browning pictured above could be difficult to make out against dense brush on a dark day after woodcock or quail. Although most shooters say they do not see their barrels, they do indeed point with them, if only subconsciously.

Right:

The broad sighting plane of the double, even in the tiny 28-gauge Webley & Scott pictured here, may be easier for some shooters to point against a background of brush. This is not only due to the width of the sighting plane, but to the fact that doubles downflip more and thus can be stocked straighter than other guns. This permits the shooter to "see more bird" without overshooting. Hunters accustomed to the flat sight picture of a single barrel often remark that looking down a European-stocked double gives them the illusion of looking up a hill. If so, it is an easy hill to see and to point with under conditions of poor visibility.

I delight in the sight, feel, balance, and swing of a classic English "best" gun. And someday I will have made up for me a fine double with a ventilated rib raised high enough so that I can utilize what I believe to be the precise pointing quality of a single sighting plane, yet retain the basic feel of the side-by-side. Such a gun would be an abomination in the eyes of a really devout side-by-side man, yet I believe it would be a compromise worth trying in competition.

I'm certainly aware that many side-by-sides have been made with vent ribs, but none high enough to raise my personal line of sight quite far enough to suit me or give me the extreme straight-back, low-recoil-effect stock I'd like to go along with such a gun.

In order to try and balance the books on this debate, I interviewed several of the most knowledgeable shooters of double guns in America, among them Billy Perdue of Mobile, Alabama. Perdue has one of the finest collections of side-by-side doubles in this country (I have no idea how many Purdeys for example) and his knowledge of the gun includes a lifetime of proof of the pudding. With side-by-sides of various gauges he has proved himself one of the finest field shots in America, and has won the coveted European Championship at live-pigeon competition twice, along with enough silver trophies to fill a small warehouse.

His carefully considered answers went as follows: "I use the (side-by-side) double at pigeons (European-style box birds) because the broad sighting plane is better oriented toward precise judgment of elevation; I can tell where I am (in elevation) better with a double than a single. And European-style pigeon shooting is basically a game of elevation; that is, elevation is where most of the errors are made.

"However, I believe in clay-target games, where vertical precision is so important, the single barrel may be more precise. There is no doubt in my mind I could shoot an over-under; I just happen to like the feel and handling of a side-by-side double, always have and always will. That's why I shoot one in the field, and why the entire matter is such a personal thing. The only qualifying remark might be that a really fine gun is needed by the double-gun shooter because I believe it may be more difficult in manufacturing to perfectly regulate barrels and point of impact of a double than an over-under.

"The main reason I shoot best-grade doubles," he concluded, "is that I get more birds with them."

5

THE MODERN AUTOLOADER

The modern gas-operated autoloader has multiple-shot capacity plus another advantage to which tens of thousands of shooters now bear testimony, one that may be a greater advantage than any claimed for the pump, over-under, or double. That is low recoil sensation, and the difference it can make in the shooting of some individuals is nothing short of spectacular.

Few hardnosed hunters will admit they even notice recoil. And it is a fact that in field hunting, where shots are well separated and often all too few, this kick is not a particularly significant factor to most of us. But many shooters suffer from recoil more than they realize; at least, their shooting suffers from it. Find a man who says he isn't bothered by recoil, put him on the trap or skeet range, and hand him shells one at a time so that he can't tell the difference when you hand him a dud shell. When the gun doesn't fire (and he thought it would) you may see some of the most unusual antics imaginable. In general, he'll shove his shoulder into the gun in anticipation of recoil, and very often will yank the fore end down at the same time.

The shooter, of course, has been doing these little numbers all along, every time the gun fires, but just wasn't conscious of them. Sometimes these various forms of flinches from recoil don't affect accuracy; sometimes they do.

But I firmly believe that any shooter will shoot better over a long period of time with a gun of low recoil than one of heavy recoil, all other things being equal. So the autoloader has a great advantage in reduced recoil, but how it accomplishes this seems to amount to a circumvention of the laws of physics. Rest assured the laws of action and reaction have not been repealed; the gas gun just spreads the recoil out over a longer period so there is less of a sharp peak—a shove rather than a smack.

I believe it is primarily this advantage that has made the gas-operated autoloader by far the winningest skeet gun in America, an increasingly popular choice at trapshooting, and one of the most popular game guns in general use in America. Although there may be more pumpguns out there (because the pumpgun has been around for so many years, and they don't wear out very easily), sales of shotguns in recent years have favored the gas-operated autoloader.

Many experienced shooters who've been soured by lack of success at keeping a gas gun going may argue those points. I'd be the first to agree with some of their gripes, since I've had gas autoloaders jam, hang, break down, and do about anything one of those pressed-parts beauties can do. But in recent years, learning the hard way from observation and personal experience, I've decided a high percentage of such problems are with the shooter rather than the gun.

The majority of hunters I've observed in the field will claim they clean their autoloaders regularly, and thus should have no malfunctions. But many times I've run a finger into such a carefully cleaned gun and felt a roughened, dirty, plastic-cruddy chamber. And the chamber, I believe, is the number-one source of trouble for the average field shooter.

This average field shooter may take the gun apart and clean the gas ports and piston, and he may clean the barrel so perfectly that looking down it reveals shining rings of concentricity. But the chamber is often forgotten. An ordinary barrel swab or cleaning patch or rag dropped through the barrel on a string does not clean the chamber. Neither does squirting in some form of aerosol-spray rust preventative.

If the chamber gets dirty or excessively roughened (it will often contain deposits of red residue looking suspiciously like rust) extraction of the fired hull is made more difficult and this produces problems. The least such problem is the hull that goes part way out and jams the action. The worst is when extraction is so difficult the extractor breaks, which it will invariably do when you are knee deep in weeds and/or doves and quail.

The best easily available substance I have found for cleaning gas guns is steel wool. Use it to dry polish the gas-port areas, then wrap it around a wire brush—or even a short stick if nothing else is handy—and twist and polish that chamber until it is slick and dry. Do that before each day's shooting (it takes only a few moments) and a great deal of your malfunction troubles should be over.

The low recoil sensation of the gas-operated autoloader makes it a natural for beginners who tend to be much more conscious of kick than seasoned shooters. Veteran instructor Grant Ilseng uses this 20-gauge Remington autoloader because its recoil sensation is little more than a fixed-breech .410 or 28 gauge, yet its pattern area and density is almost that of a 12 gauge.

I personally use a wire brush to knock the worst of the fouling out of a rusted or really dirty chamber, then wrap the brush with steel wool for a finer polishing job. Once the chamber is clean, and kept that way, periodic polishing with steel wool will usually keep it in good operating condition.

Don't get the idea that it is necessary to shoot several cases of shells to dirty up a chamber; time may be just as much a problem. One of the few bad things about plastic shells is that they react to handling (by some people, not all) in chemical ways that somehow leave a buildup of residue in the chamber that translates into that reddish substance sometimes called rust. The earliest plastic hulls were much worse than those produced today; certain chemical reactions occurred that would crud up a chamber in no time. And if left there any length of time, a roughened and trouble-providing chamber was pretty much a certainty.

Changes in plastics have reduced this problem, but it still persists. Neil Oldridge of Remington Arms Company tells me this mystery is still being researched, but that it does exist. And the way around it is to keep cleaning the chamber.

Winchester's machined-steel Super-X Model 1 autoloader was designed to get away from the jamming problem as much as possible, and it is a remarkably reliable shotgun. In the limited tests I've conducted, it functioned longer in dirt and sand than others. But almost any of the makes and models now on the market can be kept working under ordinary conditions by remembering the chamber. There are several devices on the market, one of them called the "Port-O-Swab," designed to get into the chamber without having to remove the barrel for cleaning. But unfortunately, that aforementioned product comes with a soft surface more like a powder puff than a steel brush. I've utilized the convenience of its offset handle design by wrapping the soft material with steel wool.

If nothing else, an extra stiff nylon toothbrush (which obviously can be carried in your pocket) makes a pretty fair tool for periodically polishing out an autoloader's chamber in the field and will also knock off the worst of carbon buildup and other deposits around the gas ports and along the piston.

One other device that I believe should be taken along hunting is that little detachable handle that opens the action of some autoloaders. For reasons of quick disassembly, this little gadget (which has been called much worse names many times in many fields) was in some guns designed to be removed simply by pulling it out. This works so well that sometimes it pulls itself out, and with your shot it may go flying off into the weeds someplace or worse yet, into the water below a duckblind. When that happens you are out of business because you can't open the gun to load it. Next time you're around the local gunsmith or sporting-goods store, ask to be shown the very simple procedure for replacing that operating handle, and then buy a spare handle and the spring that holds it in place. It's inexpensive insurance.

The best insurance against autoloader malfunction seems to be a slick, clean chamber and gas ports. Most shooters clean the barrel but forget the chamber. If inserting your little finger into the chamber reveals it to be rough (and perhaps leaves a little rusty-red residue on your finger) use a wire brush to thoroughly break loose the fouling, then wrap it with steel wool for a fine polish. The slicker and drier the chamber the better the gun should function.

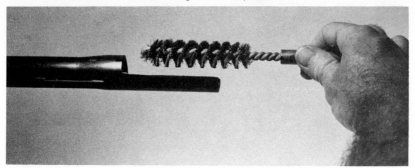

Some Model 1100 Remington shooters are now buying 3-inch magnum guns, and acquiring spare 2¾-inch barrels for use with light loads, the idea being that magnum action is slightly tougher and more beefed up than the standard action. But a word of caution on this. Do not use 3-inch shells in any 2¾-inch barrel, even if the action has "magnum" engraved on it . . . and do not expect the magnum action to handle light loads perfectly, even with a standard barrel. High velocities will work all right in the short chamber, but field loads may not. Some 3-inch chambered barrels (and actions) will function with ordinary high-velocity loads, but they weren't designed to do so dependably because there is a difference between the gas porting of the magnum barrel and the standard barrel.

Obviously it is a great advantage to own one gas-gun action that can serve as a heavy magnum duck or goose gun and then be converted to a light, fast-handling upland gun simply by changing barrels. Certainly the elongated action of the magnum will handle the short shells with plenty of room to spare. But when it comes to interchanging magnum actions and barrels, some shooters get confused. Remington has been sufficiently concerned about that to refuse to sell a 3-inch magnum barrel separately; the only way to get one is to buy the whole gun. This is obviously the company's attempt to eliminate potentially dangerous errors by dealers, consumers, or anyone else who might accidentally or unwittingly put a 3-inch magnum barrel on a 2¾-inch action.

Browning's Model 2000 gas-operated autoloader has an action long enough to accommodate 3-inch hulls, and the company offers spare 3-inch or 2¾-inch barrels that will interchange on the same action.

The Super-X Model 1 Winchester with machined-steel parts and computer-designed gas system proved the most reliable autoloader in the author's testing. It continued to shoot when dirty and digested quite a bit of blowing dust before finally failing to eject an empty hull. The model shown is the trap version with Monte Carlo stock.

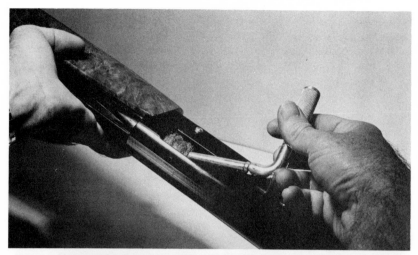

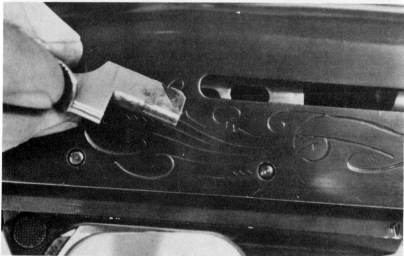

Above:
The *Port-O-Swab* is a chamber-cleaning device that can be inserted at almost any angle into any pump or autoloader without removing the barrel and can be wrapped with steel wool to properly dry-polish the chamber. This device folds into a package small enough to be carried in a shirt pocket; it's good insurance between rounds of trap or skeet or when field shooting is hot and heavy.

Below:
The detachable little gadget shown here is called bolt handle, charging handle, and various other names by different autoloader makers, and much more colorful names at times by owners. Designed to be removed by being pulled straight out of the slide assembly, the handles sometimes come out all by themselves and may be lost in heavy cover. A spare is good insurance.

At the time of this writing, Roy Weatherby was working on a patent application for the gas-operated Weatherby Centurion setup that would permit the use of either 3-inch or 2¾-inch shells in the same action, but unlike Browning would contain a device that would prohibit a 3-inch shell from being inserted into the action when the 2¾-inch barrel was installed. It's my understanding that Weatherby gas guns of the future will come with actions long enough to handle the 3-inch shell and that existing actions can be modified to do so at the factory.

No discussion of gas-operated autoloaders seems complete without at least the attempt to put a little more salve on a very old and argued contention that bleeding off gas for operation of the action is bound to reduce the hard-hitting qualities of the gun.

I have carefully tested penetration of loads from the same box, one fired from a pumpgun (fixed breech, non-gas action) and another from an autoloader. Shot after shot, penetration is almost identical. It will vary (because the shells themselves vary slightly even from the same box) but the total of 25-shot tests, using the chronograph to measure velocity and penetration box to measure penetration, show no loss of hard-hitting capability by the gas gun.

The gas bled off to work the action is so tiny, and taken at a point far enough down the barrel, that the shot load has already received its start and basic energy. You can test that yourself by shooting into an old telephone directory and counting pages penetrated. But this simplistic explanation won't satisfy all those guys who continue to argue it is impossible for any gun to shoot hard without kicking hard.

Wayne Leek, Father of the Remington 1100, once explained the gas gun's operation to me, and if anyone can give a sufficiently scientific explanation, it should be a man who developed one. Here's what Leek said translated into layman's language: "Let's take a common

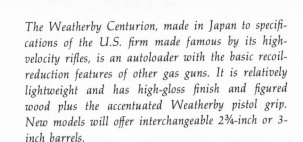

The Weatherby Centurion, made in Japan to specifications of the U.S. firm made famous by its high-velocity rifles, is an autoloader with the basic recoil-reduction features of other gas guns. It is relatively lightweight and has high-gloss finish and figured wood plus the accentuated Weatherby pistol grip. New models will offer interchangeable 2¾-inch or 3-inch barrels.

hunting load which we'll say would recoil against the shooter's shoulder with 25 foot-pounds of energy in a fixed-breech gun. We put that load into an 1100, and the shooter pulls the trigger. Before the load and gases leave the barrel to create full recoil force, approximately 10 foot-pounds of energy are tapped off at the gas orifice and stored into a moving mass not directly associated with the fixed gun mechanism, namely the action bars, breech-bolt mechanism, and action-bar sleeve. Therefore, at this instant, the shooter is getting kicked with 15 foot-pounds instead of 25."

My interpretation at this point is that the rearward-moving mass is temporarily postponing Newton's laws of motion in that whereas there is an opposite reaction to the action of gases moving out the barrel, it is occurring within the gun rather than impelling the whole gun to move backwards with 25 foot-pounds of energy. Obviously, however, Newton must sooner or later be paid back.

This is done, Leek said, as the mechanism moves rearward. When the action-bar sleeve impacts against the front of the receiver, five foot-pounds of the ten foot-pounds stored in the moving mass are put back into the equation and an instant later the breech bolt, still moving rearward, impacts against the rear section of the receiver, putting back the other five foot-pounds, thus satisfying Newton's Laws.

What really happens is that the shooter gets kicked three little times instead of one big time; the first kick coming with 15 foot-pounds of energy, the second with 5, and the third with the final 5. By the time the final foot-pounds arrive, the shooter is already recovering from the original 15 foot-pounds of recoil and does not notice them—at least, not nearly so much as he would notice the full 25 foot-pounds delivered at once.

I am much obliged to Mr. Leek because I can understand him easier than Mr. Newton. Although I thought I understood the basic

The Remington Model 1100 comes in every size from 12 gauge to .410 bore and is the largest-selling gas autoloader in the world; it is also the winner of more recent U.S. trap and skeet championships than any other autoloader.

method of operation of gas autoloaders, I was not precisely sure where Peter was robbed to pay Paul or when Mr. Newton got his full Laws of Motion back.

Certainly, various guns have various gas-recoil systems, and the reason I mention Remington's is that Wayne Leek explained it to me one day on an airplane returning from a hunt in New Mexico, and thus obviously I could not have been sitting that day beside Jim Tollinger (who developed the simple, effective gas systems for Ithaca's Model 51 and Big 10 Magnum) nor the computer which to great extent developed the highly sophisticated Super-X Model 1 Winchester. I certainly was not sitting beside the original inventor of the gas operated action because that was Mr. John M. Browning in 1889.

Actually all the new actions are good ones, all share great reduction in recoil sensation, and all share a common enemy in blowing

HOW A GAS AUTOLOADER REDUCES RECOIL SENSATION

Impulse stored in bolt mass

Impulse placed back into gun at bolt mass impact

———Normal shoulder force for fixed breech gun

– – – –Shoulder force with recoil attentuation in gas-operated gun

Here's a simplified version of a much more sophisticated sketch drawn by Wayne Leek to explain how a gas gun gets its recoil reduction. Looking from left to right and starting with the firing of the gun, the solid line shows the recoil curve (note the sharp peak) of a fixed-breech gun and the dotted line shows how the gas-operated mechanism spreads its recoil over a longer period of time to produce a gentle shove rather than sharp slap. The shaded area represents energy of impulse which the gas gun temporarily diverts into its moving mechanism and then, at far right, puts back into the "equation" of reaction to satisfy Newton's Laws of Motion. Note that after the fixed-breech gun has completed its action-reaction movement, the gas gun still has some reaction left to perform. But the shooter doesn't feel it because he is recovering from the larger recoil force that originated a split second before.

Despite its size (by far the largest autoloader ever made) Ithaca's Mag 10 chambered for 3½-inch 10-gauge magnum is a sleek, good-looking gun with almost unbelievably moderate recoil sensation. Shown with the fore end removed to reveal its simple but sophisticated gas system, the Mag 10 weighs 11¼ pounds and has an extra-full-choke 32-inch barrel.

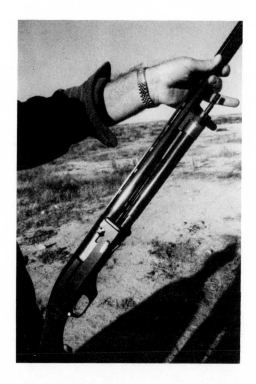

sand or dirt. Some shooters swear the old-style Browning and other non-gas automatics will take more punishment, dirt, etc. than the more modern guns, but I can remember all the years I shot those recoil-operated autoloaders and they too can certainly jam.

About all the shooter can do is keep the gun in its case when not in use and try and keep the action cradled in such a way that in carrying it there is some protection from his arm in sand-driving winds. I've wrapped the action with my spare foul-weather gear, or even a handkerchief, while waiting for the game to start flying. This has worked for me from Africa's Kalahari Desert to Mississippi River sandbars. I'm probably being too hard on the autoloader, because most of the time mine keep working fine.

But if your gun does get into the state that one of my oldtime duck-hunting partners called gritted up, a small can of WD-40 or some similar aerosol cleaning-lubricating spray may blow it out well enough to get it running again without disassembly when the ducks are moving. One of the best products for this I've found is called Browning Liquid Gunsmith. It cleans quickly and then evaporates leaving only a very thin film of oil. Too much oil is about as bad as too little, because it attracts grit and dust and invites the next blankety-blank hangup.

6

THE CASE FOR THE SMALL GAUGE

The greatest thing since sex and sipping whiskey, it might seem, is the trend toward sporty small-gauge guns, various virtues of which have been prescribed to cure just about everything from foot fatigue to senile swing. It has been written that because the small guns are lighter, they get on game faster, thus compensating for any disadvantages of long-range capability. And because they are lighter to carry all day, the shooter's reflexes are said to be a little less weary when his shooting opportunities finally occur.

Add to that a reduction in potential flinching from the heavier recoil of larger gauges and it might be concluded that for some shooters, the .410 would bag more game than the 12 gauge.

I severely question some such extrapolations of small-gun benefits, but since I hunt much of the time with a 28 gauge or 20 for doves and quail it is only honest to observe that the differences in ballistical capabilities of the larger gauge loads may be less important nowadays than the ratio of how much a gun is carried to how often it is fired. Also, most contemporary hunters do not have to subsist upon what they shoot, and if the little gun is more fun, why not?

Unfortunately, questions raised by shooters who are considering a switch to a small gauge are not quite that simple. How much harder is it to hit game with a 28 gauge or .410 than a 12 gauge of the same choke? How about the superlight 20 gauges now in vogue? How much in size of pattern does a hunter give up in exchange for less carrying

The .410, contrary to popular belief, actually has a larger pattern spread at close range than a 12 gauge, choke-for-choke, and this is particularly true with 3-inch hunting loads. Believe it or not, the little gun develops higher breech pressures (13,000 pounds per square inch compared with only 11,000 for a 12-gauge 3-inch magnum) and due to its long shotload relative to bore size the .410 deforms many pellets and scatters its load quickly. Some shooters take advantage of this characteristic and use relatively large shot on the theory that one or two No. 6 or 7½ shot will kill a quail and the .410's tendency to quickly open its pattern helps prevent tearing up game at very close ranges. But at ranges past 30 yards the .410's long, erratic shotstring is full of holes and may kill or cripple.

weight and quicker points at quail, woodcock, or grouse? How much range is given up for pass-shooting doves or decoying ducks?

About the only thing every gun book in my reference library agrees upon is that gauge has little or nothing to do with the size of pattern, this being, as English writer Gough Thomas puts it, "a function of choke rather than bore."

Most of the full-choked .410's I have tested with 3-inch hunting loads actually throw a slightly larger pattern spread than similarly choked 12 gauges with standard hunting loads in the same shot sizes, this being particularly true in the smaller sizes of shot used on dove

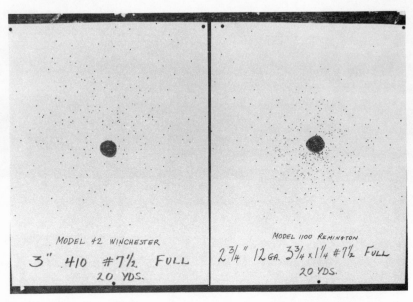

The overall pattern spread of this .410 pumpgun is clearly larger than that of a 12 gauge, both guns of the same barrel length (26 inches) and both choked full. Although contrary to the old idea that small gauges "hold their shot together tighter," many tests confirmed the opposite is true.

and quail. I'm sorry if this so totally disagrees with tradition, but I have a great many patterns made with moving targets to prove there is no law that says a .410 has a smaller pattern than a 12 gauge. The reason the contrary is often true is shot deformation. The 3-inch .410 has a very long shot column relative to the size of its bore, in effect it is a "mini-magnum" that deforms a relatively high percentage of its shot (inside its protective shotcup wad) at ignition and during passage through barrel and choke. Deformed pellets, in any gauge, tend to fly wide of the pattern and the highest percentage of deformed pellets tend to come from elongated magnum loads when the shell is loaded with relatively soft shot. Put very hard shot in a .410 and it starts to behave. But then, the shot in most hunting loads available today are relatively soft, a situation discussed at length in another chapter.

As a general rule, the spread of the bulk of a gun's pattern is more related to its choke than its gauge, all other things being comparable. Pattern density *within* the pattern is greatly favored by the larger number of pellets in the loads commonly used in larger gauges.

There is no way to prove precisely how much any shooter gives up by shooting a small gauge. Much depends upon how well he swings and points it. Some ladies and youngsters might be able to get more game consistently with a superlight, gas-operated 20 gauge than the finest double or over-under 12 gauge, because for them, differences in weight and recoil could overshadow differences in efficiency within the pattern.

There is, however, one data bank of statistical information that reveals how thousands of shooters, firing at thousands of identical targets from identical distances, have fared with the various gauges from 12 down to .410. This, of course, is skeet—and the National Skeet Shooting Association publishes each year the registered averages of its members. These averages, and the differences they reveal from one gauge to the next, give an indication of how much more difficult it is to hit with the little guns for shooters of average ability. Since we've specified "average" shooters, let's look at the average American skeet shooter who carries the classification of middle expertise called Class B. To be classified in Class B, a skeet shooter must have a registered average of roughly 80 percent hits with the .410, about 90 percent with the 28 gauge, 91 percent with the 20, and about 93 to 94 percent with the 12. So on that basis, we could assume that it is approximately 13 to 14 percent more difficult to hit skeet targets with a .410 than a 12 gauge. The 28-gauge shooter would be giving up only three to four percent between his little gun and the 12 gauge.

But skeet targets are broken at a maximum distance of about 25 yards, 21 yards being the average long shot taken as the target crosses the center of the field. What about longer shots that so often occur in hunting doves or spooky grouse or quail that jump well ahead of the dog?

A rule of thumb for killing efficiency at various ranges with various loads was some years ago established in a book called *Mysteries of Shotgun Patterns*. Although unfortunately no longer in print, this is one of the most authoritative and exhaustively researched documents ever done on shotgun capabilities. It was compiled by a couple of Oklahoma State University professors, Dr. George C. Oberfell and Charles E. Thompson, who with scientific precision conducted thousands of tests of patterns, penetration, and extrapolations of data derived from shooting live birds under laboratory-controlled conditions.

The most significant conclusion about gauges in that publication was: "It is the shot load that kills, not the gauge."

Oberfell and Thompson worked out their rule-of-thumb theory based on ounces of shot put into the air regardless of gauge, with, of course, all other conditions such as choke of the gun, pattern, and velocities being comparable. Since standard velocities of shotshells in common field loads are similar from gauge to gauge, I have found their rule to come close to being correct with perhaps the exception of the 28 gauge, which simply kills better than it is supposed to.

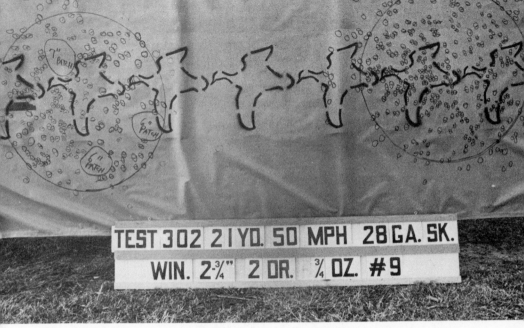

TEST 302 21 YD. 50 MPH 28 GA. SK.
WIN. 2-¾" 2 DR. ¾ OZ. #9

This comparison of a skeet-choked .410's pattern of No. 9 shot (left) and a 28-gauge skeet pattern of 9's (right) indicates how much more efficient the larger bore (and thus less shot deformation with the 28) can be on a fast-moving target even at very short range. These were fired with the moving target hitting 50 mph at 21 yards, the average speed and crossing distance of a skeet target. The .410 pattern contained large patches (circled in left photograph) while the 28 gauge maintained deadly density. This is the principal reason good skeet shooters average so much lower with the .410 than the 28; some shooters carry higher averages with the 28 gauge than the 20.

Ignoring the mysteries of the 28 temporarily, let's look at the O&T rule of thumb: The .410 with a half-ounce shot load is rated with clean killing efficiency (considering shot pellet size to be proper for the game hunted) at 30 yards. The 28 gauge is rated cleanly effective at 35 yards, and the 20 gauge at approximately 40 yards. The 12 gauge, with one and a quarter ounces of shot, was given a 45-yard rating. Since the 20 gauge with 3-inch magnum loads can throw one and a quarter ounces of shot, it could be considered closely with the 12 gauge, although being a magnum the 1¼ ounce 20 load is slightly slower in velocity and generally a bit less efficient in patterning than the 1¼ ounce 12-gauge load. Smaller gauges generate higher breech pressures and tend to deform more shot unless special hard shot handloads are used.

I once tried to explain all this to a lawyer friend of mine named Charlie who sorely wanted to convince himself he needed a light new gun. Since I knew he wanted to be convinced, and probably would be anyway, I suggested that since the 28 gauge is rated effective at 35 yards—and most shots at upland game are within that distance—he should do just fine with that little gun. And if, after carrying a light-

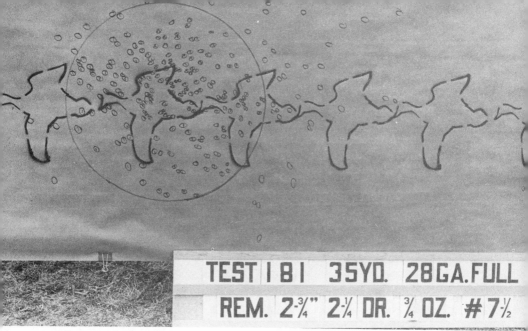

TEST | 81 35 YD. 28 GA. FULL
REM. 2¾" 2¼ DR. ¾ OZ. #7½

Although some shot stringing (flyer pellets at right) is evident at 35 yards, the left barrel of author's Webley & Scott patterned a remarkable 89 percent, certainly game-getting density at 35 yards and a target speed of 40 miles per hour. Although this tight-patterning barrel can, and has, killed many birds at 40 yards this is stretching the 28 gauge with factory loads; 35 to 37 yards is consistent clean-killing range on doves and quail and the little gun does well on decoying ducks at 35 yards or less.

weight 28 all day, he remained a bit better physically capable of swinging and leading a fast bird, he could conceivably even do better than with his 12 gauge.

Charlie glowered at me as only a prosecutor can.

"Now," he said, "I want to hear the other side of the case."

Since sundown happened to arrive at that precise moment, I mixed a couple of belts of branchwater while he rummaged around the gun rack and looked over some of the "shooting silver" trophies which clutter up the den and always need polishing when company comes.

"Southwest Open Quail Shooting Championship, 1972" he read aloud from one of them. "Hey, I remember that deal; there was a lot of publicity and a $1,000 prize and bird shooters from five states. There was some kind of quail walk with compressed air launchers hidden in the bushes and the birds came up in pairs flying like hell. Had to be dropped within a few yards to fall inside the scoring circle. I read about it. Bet you won it with a 28 gauge; nothing else could have been fast enough, right?"

I told him I tried a 28, a lightweight 20, and wound up winning with a 12-gauge Perazzi over-under that weighed nearly 8 pounds.

TEST 3|2 40 YD.   20 GA. FULL
FED. 3"   MAX. DR. 1¼ OZ. #4

This 3-inch magnum 20-gauge duck load, fired from a tightly bored Browning Superposed full-choke barrel, showed considerable loss to shot deformation and stringing. At 40 yards and 40 mph it put only 56 percent of its pellets into the 30-inch circle. However, with 1¼ ounces of shot, there remained obviously adequate duck-killing density at this yardage. Thus the lightweight 20 with No. 4 magnums can be an adequate duck gun with birds coming well within range, but computer readouts indicate the above load can be expected to bag only 80 percent of birds perfectly centered in its pattern at 43 yards; beyond that yardage bagging goes down and killing efficiency drops rather drastically. With smaller shot, such as 7½'s or 6's, clean-killing ranges are shorter still. Although occasional long shots can be made, due to a clump of shot striking the duck in a vital spot, much crippling accrues from stretching the 20 gauge in the belief that the word magnum is magic. For 20s not chambered for 3-inch magnums, the author recommends short magnum 6s.

"Doesn't prove that a good enough shot couldn't have won it with a 28 or 20, or even a .410," Charlie argued.

"Well," I said, "the runner-up was Sammy Lemoine of Ville Platte, La., and he used a 12-gauge over-under. The man who won the following year was Graham Hamilton who on his family's ranch near Cuero, Texas, permits guests to sample his fantastic quail shooting with nothing larger than .410."

"Aha," said Charlie. "The little gauge did win."

"Nope," I told him. "When the chips were down and the money was up, Hamilton won with a 1100 Remington automatic 12."

"That doesn't mean somebody couldn't have won with a little gauge."

"Well, let's take another form of registered competition where the contest is with live birds, and chips don't count. In all the years there has been a world's championship competition on live pigeons in Europe, with thousands of dollars at stake every shoot, nobody has won with anything smaller than a 12 gauge. And if there is anything that requires the most speed, and least significance of killing capability beyond 45 yards, it might be shooting at super-swift Zurita pigeons from 27 meters. The bird is usually out of the ring inside of two seconds. Speed is critical. But the winners all shoot 12 gauges; maybe somebody could win with a little gun, it's just that nobody ever has."

Charlie pondered. "How come your famous Oberfell and Thompson book didn't say that?"

"It did. It says: 'the smaller the bore of the gun, the lower the pattern efficiency will be, as a general rule, for consistent maximum efficiency.' "

"Hoo boy," groaned Charlie. "You gun guys can be ambiguous as Bible students; a Philadelphia lawyer couldn't sort out all the conflicts in what you claim."

"No conflict, just proof that almost anything can be proved with books or statistics," I told him. "But what really counts, whether it's gun legislation or gun ballistics, is what actually works . . . not what somebody thinks might work.

"Skeet targets, for instance, offer statistics but no reliable indication of a gun's game-getting capabilities. Skeet targets are shot from short yardages and known angles. Target chips count as much on the scoreboard as well-centered, smoked targets. But 'chipping' a live bird usually means a cripple."

"Sure," said Charlie, "and did you ever try and clean a skeet bird? Why did you mention skeet in the first place?"

"Because it points up some pretty big holes in what has been rewritten all these years about patterns and gauges. If choke, not gauge, were the *whole* story, then skeet scores should be as good with a .410 as they are with a 12. Both guns are choked 'skeet.' But even in this case 'pattern size' relates to 'effective pattern size.' And there is a big difference. Only the central portion of a .410 pattern is effective and sometimes it has holes. The fringe is ragged and thin. To break good scores a shooter must be either lucky a lot of the time or dead center most of the time. But with the 12 gauge, throwing a pattern covering approximately the same overall area as a .410 spreads its shot, the entire pattern coverage including the fringe area is dense enough to consistently break targets . . . which is why scores of 200 straight with a 12 gauge are so commonplace and 100 straights remain rather rare with the .410."

Charlie pondered while I pontificated: "Even if the total spread of shot from a small gun is the same as from a 12 gauge, the consistently *effective* pattern is usually smaller as the total payload of shot is decreased. This is particularly evident in pattern tests made on fast-moving targets with open choked upland guns. Indications are that the smaller the shot size and softer the shot the more pattern density is lost to 'shot stringing' on crossing birds. And any such loss hurts the little guns more than the big ones, because in many cases the little gun's pattern density is marginal to begin with. Thus shot stringing is still another reason . . . one you may not have heard or read of . . . why it's more difficult to get game with the smaller gauges."

"That's what I said from the beginning," Charlie chuckled, "it is more difficult, more sporting to shoot the little guns. But if you have a tight enough choke and do your part the 28 gauge will kill as far as a 12 gauge; the pellets go just as far, just as fast. You just have to hold it on 'em a little tighter."

"Will your new car go faster if you hold the steering wheel a little tighter?" I asked him. "Or maybe if you pucker up your mouth just right and hold real dead center on the road, will the car go farther on the same amount of gas?"

"Objection," said Charlie.

"Overruled. That is, until you at least take the time to go and test some guns the same way you'd test a car or anything else. Shoot some patterns with a .410 if you want your eyes opened. And if you don't believe the pattern board tells all that much about it, shoot some trap targets. I'll loan you guns in any gauge you want; pick the ones that feel best to you."

He went to the gun cabinet and immediately spied a 28 double. It was a sleek little Webley & Scott made in England, scaled down precisely from a 12 gauge with virtually every part in perspective. It had tattletale wear around the edges of the action, where it has rubbed against canvas-faced hunting pants, and a few brush bumps not totally hidden by the hand-rubbed oil finish.

"You hypocrite," Charlie cried out triumphantly. "You have been using this gun. You have done so knowing full well it is less efficient. All the ballistical ballyhoo you have crammed into my cranium goes out the window when you pick up your little gun. May I pick it up?"

He did, and his face flushed as a musician's might at discovery of a Stradivarius violin in a junkyard.

He just kept throwing it to his shoulder, pointing at imaginary quail.

"I'll test this one," he decided, "and take your word for the rest."

He left and I began gathering up a stack of guns to take to the range, some of them overdue for pattern testing anyway. There was nothing special about them, just field guns with factory ammunition.

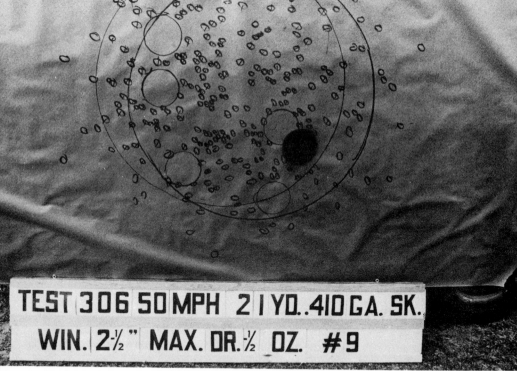

TEST 306 50 MPH 21 YD. .410 GA. SK.
WIN. 2½" MAX. DR. ½ OZ. #9

Here's another .410 horror story showing what can happen on a crossing target at skeet range and skeet-target speed. This was a handload containing ordinary bagged shot commonly used by reloaders, in a once-fired AA case and giving normal velocity. The patches circled are five inches, large enough for a clay target to get through. Although there is a possibility of one or two late pellets from the shot string to break a target occupying one of those holes in the pattern, they cannot be counted upon consistently to do so. The author believes one answer to this problem is that .410 skeet loads be loaded with very hard shot, even nickel plated, for competition. The best factory loads now available often have several patches in their patterns, but tests made with reloaded shells using extra-hard No. 8½ pellets robbed from traploads produced surprisingly dense and even patterns despite reduction in pellet numbers.

One was an old full-choked Model 42 Winchester .410 pump which has caused a few companions to raise eyebrows the way it puffs a dove or quail. And there was a Franchi over-under 28 gauge with a top barrel which will just about scalp a bird when the shot has to be taken close in heavy brush. The way the 28 smokes game I figured it probably would pattern tighter than a minister's morals.

No such luck. The Franchi did have a beautiful pattern, but it was still a 28 gauge and at 40 yards it had a few patches in it just as ¾ ounce of non-buffered shot will have when fired from most anything. The .410 with the identical load of ¾ ounces of shot in a 3-inch case threw patterns at 40 yards ranging from poor to pitiful.

I moved up to 35 yards, and the 28 gauge hit the pattern board so hard it jarred out one of the thumbtacks holding the paper.

At that time I couldn't be sure exactly why, but I had suspicions. And some time later when I got my 16-foot-long moving target, some of the first tests I did on it were with 28 gauges. Patterns were beautiful, and with tightly choked barrels there was very little stringing of shot, whereas full choked .410 patterns at the same yardage, with an almost identical shot load (11/16 of an ounce), strung out all over the board. Maximum .410 spread on the moving target, from the most divergent, flyer pellets, was 12 feet, and the basic pattern spread (where pellets began to be close enough together to kill or cripple a bird) was 7 feet, 5 inches. I couldn't believe my eyes. This was my old Winchester Model 42 pumpgun, the one with which I've killed so many quail and doves and shooting preserve pheasants.

I fired it again, this time with the target stationary. The maximum pellet spread (at 35 yards again) was slightly over six feet, or just about half as long as the shot had strung out with the target going 40 miles an hour. The basic pattern spread was 48 inches compared with 89 inches moving.

I fired several 35-yard 40-mile-an-hour tests with the tight left barrel of my Webley & Scott 28 gauge and carefully measured the spread. Maximum between flyer pellets was 54 inches, but almost all the pattern was concentrated within a basic spread of three feet. There was virtually no stringing of shot evident; the pattern was almost as perfectly round as if it had been fired with the target sitting still. In other words, that 28 gauge with that load had a short shot string, with most of its pellets arriving at the target at nearly the same time. Which perhaps helps explain why 28 gauges in general have developed such a reputation for hitting game harder and smoking targets better than they are supposed to.

I have tested 28 gauges since then, and anyone who believes he has a .410 which will shoot yard for yard, choke for choke, load for load with a 28 is welcome to test it out on a crossing target at 40 miles an hour. For that matter, I have yet to see a .410 that will shoot with a 28 gauge on the still pattern board.

Neil Oldridge of Remington Arms Company (where quite a few pattern tests are made) told me there are two mysteries in shotgun ammunition he cannot fully explain. One is why the 28 gauge is so highly efficient for the shot load it throws and the other is why the 12-gauge pigeon load of 3¼ drams of powder and 1¼ ounces of shot will pattern beautifully in almost any barrel.

Apparently the 28 standard load and the 12-gauge pigeon load are both balanced loads in terms of the length and weight of shot column relative to bore diameter and other factors.

One generalized assumption might be made that any time too much shot (or too long a shot payload in the barrel) is shoved out too small a hole (barrel diameter) there is a decrease in efficiency. One way to make a 20 gauge better handle 3-inch magnum loads is to slightly overbore the barrel diameter. The same will also work in aiding a 12 gauge to handle heavy magnum loads.

Therefore, it strikes me (as it struck the English many years ago) that if a man wants efficiency from a sporting, small-gauge load (and not to tear up game birds shot at close range) one way would be to use a very lightweight 12 gauge and shoot very light small gauge shotloads in it. Many years ago the English developed a really tiny load; 12 gauge shells only two inches long. Those little mini-twelves are light to carry, pattern well out of a standard chamber, but do not have enough power to operate most 12-gauge autoloaders. They do definitely have enough power to take quail, doves, etc., at the yardages at which ⅞-ounce loads are effective in any gun.

A correspondent of mine from Winston-Salem, N.C., J. Stephen Lord, was kind enough to send me for testing some English-made Eley two-inch loads and also some handloads which Lord made by shortening ordinary Winchester Double A 12-gauge cases. The English factory loads and the handloads both contained ⅞ ounces of shot, which is the same shotload as Federal heavy 28-gauge load and same as the 20-gauge light field loads offered by Winchester, Remington, and Federal.

Lord's two inchers contain 16 grains of HiScore powder, a .200 over-powder wad, ⅜ inch filler wad, and ⅞ ounces of No. 8 shot. They produced 97 percent patterns from a full-choke barrel at 25 yards. These cute little shells would seem to have some appeal to owners of fine, lightweight 12-gauge doubles or over-unders who prefer the feel of their 12's but want less recoil and less weight of ammunition to carry. The ⅞ ounce loads are about the same as shooting a light 20-gauge load except that they kick even less from the 12 gauge. But it is doubtful if U.S. manufacturers would ever offer such a load for many reasons.

However, it is possible manufacturers someday will offer very low recoil one-ounce 12-gauge loads. Some trapshooters are already getting "20-gauge recoil" with handloads and slow-burning powders such as PB and SR 7625.

One of the best lightweight gun-gauge combinations available in the U.S., particularly in terms of versatility, is the featherweight 20 gauge over-under with 3-inch chambers which with the lightest field load is about the same as shooting (and handling) a 28 gauge, but which can be loaded up to near 12-gauge performance by inserting 3-inch magnum shells. There are several superlight 20-gauge gas-operated autoloaders on the market which weigh within ounces of

This classic little Webley & Scott 28-gauge double is scaled perfectly to dimension, weighing about 5½ pounds and throwing beautiful patterns and very short shotstrings as compared with the .410. Choked improved cylinder and full, with two triggers for instant barrel selection, it is one of author's favorite "carrying" guns and has proved deadly on doves and quail.

most 28 gauges and due to gas recoil reduction have about the same recoil effect as a 28 gauge with ¾-ounce load.

However, if the only gun I owned happened to be a 12 gauge I'd certainly feel no less a sport firing one ounce of shot through it than shooting one ounce of shot through a 20.

There are shooters who definitely can put more birds into the sack with a lightweight 20 or 28 gauge than they can with a heavier 12. But this is not due to gauge but to balance, weight, gun fit, recoil, speed of swing—or maybe how well the man likes his gun.

Pride of ownership is a powerful thing. If a man really loves his little gauge, just enjoys carrying it, swinging it, and even cleaning it, he just may get more pleasure and birds with it than he would any other gun. And that is what matters, so long as he can do so without crippling a lot of game.

That's what I was going to tell Charlie when he bought home my 28 gauge, but before I could get started he handed me a chilled plate containing a limit of doves perfectly plucked and ready for the oven with a little handwritten note:

"This is my test of the 28 gauge. These patterns were made at approximately 30 yards but have since been soaked in cooking sherry. To avoid stray pellets in the gravy I used 7½'s rather than 9's, therefore my hitting average is not eligible for this year's Skeet Review.

"P.S., I really didn't want to know the whole truth anyway. I had already ordered a new 28 gauge before I came to your house. But if you should ever decide on a divorce, what would you want for that little Webley?

"Your legal eagle, Charlie."

7

HOW
TO MAKE
YOUR GUN FIT

Bill Jordan's quick-draw exhibition tours across America have made him a living legend of chain-lightning gun handling. But to me he's living proof that any man can shoot almost any gun, provided the reflexes are there.

Jordan is a towering, long-armed Louisiana man who makes a standard shotgun look like a Mattel toy. One day we were hunting pheasants at an arms-company seminar where the only guns available were ordinary factory models and I asked how he could get along with a stock that fit him about the same as my pants would (they would strike him somewhere around the knees).

"Wal," he drawled in an accent as thick as Cajun coffee, "I reckon it's about the same as that ol' Border Patrol hat I was issued years ago. Damned thing felt like a bear trap on my head. I did everything but stomp on it and it never stretched an inch. But after about 20 years it started feeling fine; best I can figure, my head changed."

By just such a system many shooters adapt to shotguns; their heads change (in position over the barrel) until no matter how unusual the stance it begins to feel natural. Such shooters may have outstanding reflexes, and may even be the best shots in their hunting crowd. They may scoff at the need for any sort of special stock or rib, making comments to the effect that the problem of shooting is not the stock, but the "nut" behind it.

That is unfortunate, perhaps, because a shooter of such reflexes could probably be a terrific shot with a gun that fits. He may learn to scrounge around on the stock, raise his head slightly, crawl the stock forward, or whatever is required to hit game. But he can never be quite as precise and consistent as with a shotgun that comes to shoulder with head naturally and comfortably against the stock and that certain "locked-in" feeling, which means that wherever the shooter looks the barrel must follow.

I know all that because I grew up getting game with guns that for the most part didn't fit me very well. Once I accidentally got hold of a stock that fit and it was a brand new ball game. Shots that had previously required great concentration to make sure barrel and bird were in proper perspective could be taken as easily as pointing a finger.

Unfortunately gun fit cannot be discussed as simply as pants fit, because a gun that fits properly for trapshooting might be a poor fit for hunting or skeet, while the pants should suit all of these occasions. Therefore, before anyone tells you positively what gun should fit you, he must be asked "for what purpose?"

If the answer is run-of-the-mill field hunting, I doubt anyone could be much more competent than a representative from some English custom gun maker such as James Purdey & Sons, or Holland & Holland, or perhaps Ben Upson of the Orvis (English style) Shooting School in Manchester, Vermont. The English are experts at fitting for field shooting, while the Italians are probably the world's best at fitting for live pigeons and international-style trapshooting. The best fitters for American trap and skeet are American stockmakers.

All of this has to do with experience with a certain style of shooting. The typical English style (and a most realistic one for the field) is head erect, eyes level, gun coming to shoulder without much movement or canting of head to meet the gun. This is often accomplished primarily with "cast off," a slight lateral bend of the stock, which the English call "advantage," that simply puts the barrels where they belong beneath the master eye. Yet most Americans have learned to accomplish a similar effect with non-cast American factory stocks by bringing their heads over the gun, in effect slightly cocking the head in the direction of the stock and slightly forward. Watch an experienced American field shooter and you'll observe he cocks his head down and toward the stock slightly before the gun reaches his cheek.

How much he has to do this depends upon the gun and his own build, but with practice he learns just how much is required and does it instinctively.

I have been fitted by Norman Clarke to obtain my "proper" dimensions for a Holland & Holland, and by Harry Lawrence for a Purdey. Both said I was difficult to fit, because no matter what dimensional changes they made to the adjustable try stock, I adjusted to

Harry Lawrence of London, England, who custom-fits shooters who can afford it with the most expensive shotgun built today (the English Purdey) shows the try stock and measuring device he uses to determine precise stock dimensions suited to the shooter's build and shooting style.

them within a few points of the gun. This is true, I've found, of many U.S. hunters who grew up shooting various guns at various game.

Harry Lawrence works around this by fitting in a darkened room. He used little cartridge-sized flashlight devices long before they became available on the market (Orvis sells them under the trade name of Spot Shot for 12 or 20 gauge over-unders or doubles). When chambered into the gun, and the trigger is pulled, they project a beam of light where the barrel is pointing. Since the shooter cannot see the gun to subconsciously adjust his head for proper sight picture, stock dimensions can be altered on the try stock until the light hits precisely where the shooter looks. Obviously a gun that fits in the dark will fit in daylight, and may be easier and faster to point than any gun that shooter ever fired.

Unfortunately a custom-fitted Purdey translates into something more like a jail sentence—say about three years and $12,000. And even if it is built within that time there is no certainty that it will still fit. The shooter may have grown fatter or thinner or developed arthritis or bankruptcy by then.

Ennio Mattarelli, designer of Perazzi competition guns, checks stock fit for a customer in Brescia, Italy. Stock and rib are both critical points of reference, and Mattarelli is looking along the rib to see precisely how the shooter's eye lines up with it. Italian shooters believe in looking over the barrel more than Americans, who traditionally look down it. But the Italian system, once mastered, provides a clearer view of game if the shooter can remember to hold beneath the bird.

Also the gimmick of the flashlight beam is not infallible because it does not register such things as downflip of the barrels (which can make a double gun shoot significantly lower than the light beam went, particularly with heavy loads) and stock dimensions that work for a 30-inch double-barreled try gun are not likely to be correct for a 26-inch double or for an over-under of any barrel length because the shorter and stiffer the barrels (the over-under is much stiffer) the higher the shotload will be thrown.

The flashlight device, however, is a valuable tool in determining stock dimensions for lateral load placement, and vertical placement can be worked out as required.

If this sounds complicated, remember that is invariably the price of real precision with any firearm and also remember that there will be variances of the so-called human element no matter how precise the measurement. Norman Clarke, who served at both the Churchill and Holland schools in England during his long and distinguished instructing career, told me that no two gun fitters are likely to agree completely on dimensions for a given shooter. But either one probably would come closer than the man could be by attempting to judge gun fit for himself.

I'm inclined to believe there may be more virtue to self fitting than has been realized, because the only true test of shotgun fitting is the shooter, not the coach. The proof is in the hitting. This is why so many European custom gun builders, particularly those in Italy, do not use the try gun method but instead study the shooter, have him try several guns of different dimensions until they (and the shooters) can determine through actual performance which is best. I will take that kind of fitting any day to the show-room opinions of a stock tailor, and one distinct advantage of being fitted at a factory or shooting school is that it permits testing performance on the spot.

Obviously, however, most of us cannot go to Europe or even the Orvis Shooting School at Manchester, Vt. for a fitting.

The time-honored old way to attempt to fit oneself is to shut both eyes, mount the gun quickly into shooting position, then open the master eye to see how it is aligned with barrel or rib. But unless the shooter is quite expert at gun fitting he may not recognize a slight twist or cant of the barrel, or even for sure how well the stock elevation suits him.

A new way I've been studying is made possible by a device called Accu-Point, a product of the W. R. Weaver Company. The Accu-Point is not to be confused with the much larger, scope-like Weaver Qwik Point device; the newer one is a slightly oversized front sight that

The Weaver Accu-Point sight is an optical device that permits the gun pointer to see a bright red dot only when the eye is looking properly down the gun's rib. By practicing mounting the gun at home, the shooter can quickly learn how—and how not—to get head, eye, and gun together properly. Otherwise he will not see the red dot. If the gun's stock is too high, or too low, the Accu-Point will make the problem obvious.

shows a fluorescent red dot only when the shooter's head is perfectly aligned with the gun. Raise your head an eighth of an inch, or cock the head too far to one side, as so many beginners tend to do, and there is no red dot. Within a few moments the shooter can see whether his comb needs raising or lowering or perhaps some cast-off or cast-on. A good gunsmith or stockmaker can make the changes, and in extreme instances the stock can be bent with hot oil (a common procedure done by Pachmayr Gun Works and a number of other stock makers). This stock bending is much less expensive than having a new stock made for a fine gun, particularly a sidelock action or one with well-figured wood. It is accomplished by softening the wood with hot oil, then making the bend very gradually.

Although the standard Accu-Point is designed to be screwed to the gun's rib as a permanent sight, the company makes a magnetic model designed for demonstration use by salespeople. This magnetic model is in my opinion a fine fitting device because it can be used on different guns, and also because I personally prefer a more conventional and less unsightly front bead sight. Some shooters may find they can hit better in the field with the Accu-Point, and if so they should have a permanent installation. Some shooters have been helped by it at trap and skeet where guns can be premounted and properly aligned before the target is called for. But in any case, the shooter must strive not to become mesmerized by the bright dot, and to focus eyes upon target; sight fixation is a bad thing for a shotgun shooter. My own observation has been that in quick-mounting field use the red dot of the Accu-Point is of minimal value to most good shots. And since it is taller than most front bead sights it will tend to slightly lower impact.

Because of this lowered impact, a shooter who has fitted himself with the Accu-Point, or used it to perfect his gun-mounting and stock-cheeking movements, will in effect be fitted to a slightly lower shooting gun than the same gun with its ordinary front bead sight. But this is no serious problem in field shooting. What it means is that a gun so fitted will shoot a tiny bit high when the Accu-Point is removed, and that is usually more an advantage than disadvantage, particularly on upland game and long crossing shots at waterfowl when gravitational drop of the shot load becomes a factor.

The shooter most likely to benefit by a permanently mounted Accu-Point is one whose gun previously shot high for him. If performance is not improved, or is adversely affected, the device can be removed and replaced with a conventional sight although its small screw holes must be plugged.

Let's say you have acquired use of a magnetic-based Accu-Point (no screw holes) and you find that you're having to raise your head

To understand the changes in your gun's stock that may be necessary to fit it to your face or figure, it helps to know the nomenclature of the stock and its basic dimensions. To measure a stock for drop, place it on a flat surface (taking care to have the sight (F) beyond the end of the surface, otherwise it will throw off the rear measurements). The most important two measurements are (E) the comb area where the cheek touches the stock and (D) the drop at heel. These two dimensions regulate to a great extent whether the gun shoots high or low. The normal measurement at the comb (E) is 1½ inches for a hunting or field stock and around 1⅜ inches for a higher-shooting trap stock. One-eighth of an inch at this point can vary pattern-center impact half a foot or more at 40 yards. This area of (E) is where moleskin or some other type of buildup pad is used to convert a field gun into a higher-shooting trap gun or perhaps one better suited to fast-rising game such as pheasants or quail. The dotted line (C) is the proper means of measuring stock length, commonly called length of pull. Most field stocks are between 14 and 14¼ inches long. This length can be increased by addition of a recoil pad or spacers and shortened by cutting it off. But in changing the length, care must be given to the proper dimension at (B) which regulates the pitch of the stock. Cutting the stock at the angle shown by the dotted line at (B) would give the gun added downpitch, which sometimes helps in fitting buxom ladies and heavy-chested males. Most standard field stocks come with about two inches or so of down-pitch, but most trapshooters (who want a higher shooting, straight-recoiling gun) often prefer zero or even reverse pitch. The area (A) denotes the toe of the stock, which with heavy-chested shooters can be ground off (or cast off) to obtain relief from gun canting and other ills of having the stock toe dig into the pectoral muscle area.

slightly off the gun stock to see the dot. This is quite common with thin-faced shooters and is not good for performance. You should feel a slight amount of cheek pressure against the stock to help lock in with the gun for precision pointing. The easiest solution is to build up the comb (where your face touches the wood) with a self-adhesive pad. The most practical of these I have seen is the Convert-A-Stock Pad by Meadow Industries of Meadow Lands, Pa. A small strip of self-adhesive velcro is attached to each side of the stock; the pad then sticks to the velcro without putting gummy residue on the comb. Pad heights come in various thicknesses from 1/16 to ½ inch and are available in many gunshops and sporting goods stores. They also serve the additional function of softening recoil to the cheek. My wife, who tends to get sore cheekbones from shooting waterfowl loads in doubles or over-unders, has found the pads a great help. But on some guns it has been necessary to cut down the comb beneath the pad to prevent too high a comb dimension. Field gun owners who occasionally shoot trap will find these easily removable pads a great advantage; they can in effect convert a field stock to a Monte Carlo trap stock in seconds.

It is important to note that the higher pads of this type may make the gun's comb too wide and thus with fat-faced shooters create a potential eye-rib alignment problem. The most practical thicknesses are 1/16 and ⅛ inch when the need is primarily for cushioning or slight stock elevation.

The same comb elevation can be attained with inexpensive moleskin available at any drug store, but again care must be taken to increase height of the comb without significantly widening it. This is best done by applying a thin, very narrow strip of moleskin followed by subsequently wider layers and covered finally by a rather large piece to make sure the others hold in place. Three or four layers total of moleskin usually will do the job, and if the face must be forced down into the stock to see the right sight picture down the barrel, you've added too many layers. For a field gun (flat shooting) you should see the front sight and perhaps a tiny bit of rib or barrel behind it. For a trapgun you should see a bit more barrel. One old trapshooter's trick to test comb height is to have the shooter shoulder the gun, with cheek comfortably against the comb, and then stack two or three 25-cent pieces at the rear of the rib. If the shooter can just see the front sight over the quarters, he is quite close to having the proper comb elevation for trapshooting. Obviously some shooters use much more comb elevation than that, others less. The quarters merely offer an approximation of fairly standardized American trapstock dimensions, and give the beginner some idea of the difference between a trapstock and field stock. With a common field stock (best for most

A slip-on rubber stock boot, available at most gunshops and sporting-goods stores, is an easy way to lengthen a stock for a few dollars and can work minor wonders for the long-armed shooter. When heavy clothing is worn and the gun feels too long, the boot can be removed.

shooters for hunting or skeet shooting) putting two quarters on the rear of the rib would blot out the foresight.

Moleskin can be protected from weather (and also from looking dirty very quickly) by covering it with strips of extra-wide black plastic electrician's tape applied longitudinally until all the moleskin is covered. This provides a slick surface for the face and to some extent protects against moisture.

This is at best a temporary solution for stock raising, but it is one that can be quickly removed if it doesn't help. Residue remaining from the adhesive can be easily removed with lighter fluid. If a stock is found to need permanently added comb height, clear glass can be added by a stockmaker.

Perhaps more common than a need for comb raising is the need for comb lowering by heavy faced shooters or those accustomed to shooting humpbacked autoloaders or old doubles with a great deal of drop to the stock. If the gun is expensive, with good wood, comb lowering should be done by a gunsmith. If the shooter doesn't mind rasping or sandpapering a common stock, it is quite easy to do, removing a very little wood at a time until the gun comes up with just the front bead showing. Be careful in lowering the comb to maintain the same basic contours as the original; obviously if you simply cut down the top, the stock constantly gets wider until you run into what amounts to "cast on" or unduly wide comb that can cause the gun to shoot slightly to the left for a right-handed shooter or vice versa for a lefty. Some very fat-faced shooters will find they need to remove a bit of wood from the inside of the comb to get proper head alignment. This amounts to a form of poor man's cast-off but it can in some cases aid in proper alignment as well as reducing some recoil against the side of the face. Just remember that in working with stocks a very little bit of change goes a very long way; ⅛ of an inch can produce significant change in where the load goes 40 yards downrange.

When your sanding has achieved what you believe to be the right feel of comb against face, smooth the job with very fine sandpaper or steel wool until it seems slick to the touch. Then run a damp cloth over the wood and let it dry. This will raise the fibers in the wood, which can then be taken off with successive light rubbings of very fine sandpaper or steel wool. After several wettings and polishings the stock is ready for pore filling. There are many wood filler compounds available and all sorts of stain; the best products for gunstocks are those put out for gunstocks. Most sporting good stores have stock-finishing materials. After filling and staining and a final light polishing with ultra-fine sandpaper the final finish can be applied. Since most common U.S. guns come from the factory with some form of epoxy finish, this is the easiest type for matching the original finish. There are many such finishes available in aerosol cans, Williams being the fastest drying I have found. Apply several light coats, lightly sanding between each, until you achieve a slick, waterproof finish. It rarely will perfectly match the factory finish but will serve the purposes of most hunters.

Stock drop can sometimes be achieved without sanding or bending. Try a slip-on rubber stock boot. These add about ½ inch in length to the stock, and in doing so slightly increase the effect of drop at heel. Remember that a stock is lower the farther back on it your face is placed. So lengthening it, in effect, slightly lowers the comb. Long-armed shooters may find these stock boots a great aid in helping them stay with the gun on steep angle shots and in general may provide a more comfortable feel. Obviously those who get their noses banged when the gun shoots could stand more stock length, anyway.

If this helps, a gunsmith can add spacers between stock and recoil pad to get precisely the length you need. If ½ inch is not enough added length, you can fit cardboard shims inside the stock boot and lengthen it as need be. Once the proper length is established, however, a permanent spacer job should replace it.

I purposely leave my stocks on some hunting guns a shade short, using a stock boot for warm-weather hunting and taking it off when I'm wearing heavy clothing, which in effect increases stock length.

Heavy-chested shooters may find considerable advantage to grinding off about ⅛ inch or more from the toe (bottom) of the stock at the point where it gouges into the pectoral muscle. Test this by mounting

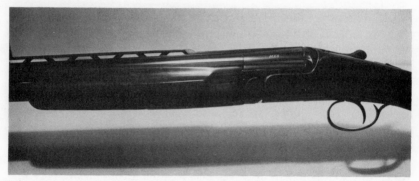

The step-up raised rib on this Perazzi MX-8 trapgun is designed to bring the shooter's eye quickly in line with target, and also to permit the use of a straighter stock (higher at heel) to reduce recoil. The higher the rib the lower the gun will shoot, thus a straighter stock can be used with the MX-8 type rib than with a flat rib. Simmons Gun Specialties now offer custom ribs of any height the shooter desires including the ultra-high "Olympic" used by champion trapshooter Ray Stafford. Remington Arms Company offers a step-up rib similar to that of the Perazzi on some of its new trapguns; extra barrels with such ribs will fit all Model 1100 trapguns.

the gun and swinging to the right (if right-handed). You may feel the toe of the stock dig in and start to bind your swing. This also can lead to twisting or canting the gun. Grinding off a little of the rubber recoil pad (rubbing on a rough concrete sidewalk will work in a pinch) gives the effect of what the English call cast at toe. To get the effect of a little cast-off for the entire stock, grind off a little of the inside of the recoil pad all the way from top to bottom, but always slightly more off at the bottom to prevent the stock digging in and twisting on angle shots.

Many shooters have a problem with the stock catching on clothing beneath the armpit in fast-mounting situations. This can be helped by grinding off the top of the recoil pad (the heel) so that there are no sharp corners or angles to the pad. Additional insurance against this problem (which has cost many a quail, woodcock, and grouse) is to paint the *sides* of the recoil pad and also the rounded-off area at the top with clear fingernail polish. Do not paint the portion of the pad that will rest against your shoulder; you don't want that part slick because you want the gun to stay securely in position at the shoulder during recoil. Guns with hard rubber buttplates (or even beautifully checkered wooden buttplates) often tend to slide down with the first shot and thus spoil the second. I personally like recoil pads on any gun, even .410's, not because of recoil but because the rubber holds

Many hunters who can hit with old humpback receiver autoloaders have trouble switching to other guns. The picture shows why. In front is a Browning AL-5, showing almost 3 inches drop at heel, as opposed to the more contemporary design of the Beretta AL-2 behind it, with only about 2¼ inches drop. The difference in drop means that the shooter of the Browning can hold his head erect and look straight down the barrel. This has some advantages for field shooting—especially for shooters long accustomed to it—but is not recommended for trap or skeet. The difference in comb height can also be seen clearly. If turned rightside up—or in shooting position—the Beretta would be seen to be much higher at the comb than the Browning.

better against clothing. Nothing can be more aggravating than a gun that sometimes slips out of the shoulder pocket slightly, particularly on high incoming shots.

One of the most common causes of missing is overshooting because the shooter, in the excitement of hunting, kept his head fully erect over a stock too straight for that head position. Sometimes adding a rib to a non-ribbed barrel, or raising the rib, will solve this. Adding a variable choke tends to make a gun shoot lower because among other things it raises the sight slightly. Sometimes simply replacing the factory sight with a larger one such as the Ithaca Raybar or Simmons "Grandpa" sight will lower impact considerably. This is because the shooter will tend to point with the highest projection at the end of the barrel, and the higher that projection the lower the gun will shoot. If you want to test that, or see perhaps how a variable choke would look on the end of your barrel, wrap black plastic tape around it enough times to create a blob the size of the choke device in question. A map tack with bright plastic head can be stuck into the tape to simulate a front sight.

I prefer a ribbed barrel to a plain barrel because I believe it helps a tiny bit in aligning with target, and also because I tend to shoot a shade high with a plain barrel on some pumps and autoloaders. The Poly Choke Company offers an inexpensive, lightweight rib, and many firms can add a metal rib of any height the shooter desires. I believe one reason many owners of fine doubles from Europe have trouble hitting with them at first is that the guns are either stocked straighter than U.S. dimensions or the shooter is accustomed to the single sighting plane of his pump or autoloader. Often the addition of a raised ventilated rib will make a double place its pattern more consistently where the shooter looks. It is easy to experiment and see whether a rib would help. A strip of balsa or some other easily worked wood can be whittled to the general configuration of the rib you have in mind. Paint it black and tape it on the gun to produce a dummy rib. For a foresight, use a map tack. These are available in any office-supply store.

Although such an arrangement may look clumsy, it will let you know very inexpensively whether a ventilated rib would help your shooting. If you arrive at the exact height of rib that works for you, send the gun to a rib installer with the wood in place and tell him to give you a rib of that height. Don Stark of Simmons Gun Specialties, Inc., Olathe, Kansas, says a high percentage of custom jobs come to him with a dummy rib in place; these almost invariably come from competition shooters who have learned to experiment and find exactly what they need. The field shooter can have the same benefits if he's willing to take the time.

Shooters switching from a humpbacked Browning, Franchi, Remington Model 11, or some similar autoloader frequently have troubles of overshooting with a new gun because they are accustomed to shooting with head erect to see over the rear of the humpbacked action. These shooters, unless they can learn to keep their heads down, may need an extra high rib to give them the sighting plane to which they are accustomed. Remington offers a high raised rib trap barrel that will fit standard Model 1100 autoloader field guns and just changing to this barrel can be the solution.

All of this pranking around with ribs, stocks, recoil pads, and the like is almost certain to draw derogatory comment from friends. But in working with the gun, pointing it, and experimenting with it, the shooter becomes more familiar with how and where it shoots.

Whether the gun is fitted to man, or man to gun, is less important than how the load hits the game.

8

CROSS FIRING

Ever make what seemed to be a perfect point and fail to cut a feather? Chances are you either lost contact with the stock (raised your head) or cross fired. Those two maladies account for more missed shots among good shooters than any I have observed. And I have been standing behind, and carefully observing, many a good shooter at the moment of a miss.

Cross firing is the reason otherwise good athletes sometimes cannot shoot a shotgun well, although they may be gifted at golf, tennis, or rifle shooting. What happens is that the wrong eye is doing the gun aligning, and when that happens the sight picture may look good but the target will keep right on trucking.

Many shooters don't even know which is their master eye, and some don't need to know because they habitually shut the off eye when shooting. This would seem a simple remedy, except that to shoot a shotgun with one eye closed is to give away some of the most significant reasons nature gave us two eyes. Humans have what is called binocular vision, in that the eyes are wide enough apart to provide a sort of natural triangulation providing depth perception and wide peripheral vision. Good race drivers and good shotgun shooters often have very good depth perception; it is a part of their skill because judgment of distance is so critical in either sport.

You don't see very many one-eyed airline pilots, or race drivers, but you do see many shooters throwing away a large percentage of what nature gave them by shutting one eye.

This is not to say that one-eyed shotgun shooting cannot produce championships; a few top skeet and trap shooters use only one eye. But at target games the shooter knows where the target will appear and at what distance it will be. The field hunter, however, must be able to judge distance precisely to be able to lead the target correctly.

Most of the top shooters at clay targets or game shoot with both eyes open, and a large percentage of hunters don't know for sure whether, at the moment of firing, they are using one eye or both. That is because they shoot naturally, just as they'd throw a baseball or squirt a water hose at a bush in the yard. Most of the time, I believe, they do those things with both eyes open. And this is where the trouble comes in with shotgun shooting. To line up a shotgun properly, the face must be down against the stock and master eye in line with the barrel. In doing so, the mass of the gun's action and barrel is placed partially in front of the eye doing the shooting, but the other eye, the off eye, is out there all by itself with nothing to block its view. Sometimes that off eye sees the target best and wants to take over.

Shooters fortunate enough to have what could be called a strongly dominant eye have no problem. But most of us have eyes quite similar in strength and dominance, and the off eye occasionally tries to do the pointing. This most commonly occurs when the shooter is tired, under added stress to win a shoot or bet, or when light is poor.

Worse off yet is the hunter whose dominant eye does not match his dominant arm. The dominant arm is perhaps a crude way of saying whether one is right-handed or left-handed. Quite a few people are right-handed but left-eyed, and may never notice any difficulty at bowling, tennis, or other sports; the body has learned to compensate. Eye dominance is also much less important with rifle shooting because most hunters close the off eye to line up the sights or look through a scope.

But when such a person of mixed dominance tries to shoot a shotgun with both eyes open, he must either crane his head completely over the stock (to get the master eye over the barrel) or otherwise somehow compensate for the gun's being mounted on the shoulder opposite the master eye.

So how do you know which is your master eye? The test is simple. Interlock thumb and forefingers (as shown in illustration) to form a circle. Do this with the hands at waist level and hold them there while you pick out some distant object small enough to be framed in this circle. Then with both eyes open and focused on the object, quickly bring up the circle so that it perfectly frames, like a peep sight, the object in the distance. Then shut your left eye. If the object remains centered in the circle, your right eye is your master

Many right-handed shooters with dominant left eyes attempt to compensate by canting the gun to the left (as posed here by the author), and usually crane their heads to the right over the stock, subconsciously attempting to get the master eye aligned with the barrel. Such shooters rarely hit consistently; canting or twisting an over-under can cause the lower barrel to impact to the right and top barrel to the left. A shooter who refuses all other remedies and continues to shoot this way would be better off with a single barrel gun which at least shoots more nearly the same place twice even when twisted or canted.

eye. If the object disappears from the circle you have a dominant left eye. Avoid focusing the eyes on your finger circle; always focus on the distant object. Otherwise you may see two circles and get a false reading. The reason for keeping your hands down, and quickly bringing up the circle is that the dominant eye will place the circle for you, just as it will point the gun for you.

Many shooters have so little dominance of one eye over the other that if they mount the gun to the right shoulder the right eye will take over and for a time seem to be the master eye, giving a correct sight picture over the barrel. But if in fact their left eye is slightly dominant, it is likely to take over occasionally.

So what if you are right-handed but left-eyed?

My wife had precisely that problem. So have a number of shooters I've taught. And if the shooter is a beginner, or anything less than a polished shot, I would unhesitatingly suggest learning to shoot all over again from the shoulder that corresponds to the master eye.

This is much less difficult than it sounds. My wife does everything but shoot right-handed, and she complained that mounting the gun to her left shoulder was impossible. But within three weeks she was mounting the gun to her left shoulder, shooting far better than before.

The trick was no magic, just repetition. For fifteen minutes a day, twice a day, I had her practice mounting an unloaded gun indoors, just taking the gun down and bringing it back up again into shooting position.

To make sure the master eye is aligning properly with the barrel, the indoors dry-pointing practice can be supplemented with backyard practice with a BB gun. The Daisy 99 Champion BB gun has a stock of more or less mature dimensions. Remove the front sight and follow exactly the same procedure I described in Chapter 1 in teaching my pretty young neighbor to shoot.

Switching from right shoulder to left, to coincide with the master eye, would be more difficult for a shooter who for many years has been shooting right-handed. It is not easy to change mounting procedures so solidly established, and for those experienced shooters there are other ways of getting around the master-eye problem.

Perhaps the most primitive answer is to learn to squint the off eye every time the gun is put into firing position, so as to force the eye over the barrel to assume dominance. Many shooters have been doing this for years and don't know it; I never realized just how many good shooters squint or even shut one eye at the last instant before firing until I began making telephoto-lens pictures of skeet, trap, and field champions to study their form. Many of them have both eyes open wide as they first view the target, but just before shooting, the off eye starts to squint. This is a rather natural and quite effective system in that it permits two-eyed evaluation of distance, angle, and speed of target, but at the last second makes sure the proper eye is looking down the barrel. This can be practiced indoors the obvious way, by mounting the gun and squinting or shutting the off eye each time stock touches cheek.

A better method is to keep both eyes open all the time, because nature is likely to open the off eye for you anyway, when the chips are down. Your body knows it can see better with two eyes than one. And when you are trying hardest to make a hit, it is trying its best to give you the benefit of maximum vision. This, I believe, is one reason so many shooters can do well when there is no pressure to win or when the game hunted is commonplace. But let a Greater Canada goose, or club championship, come into view and they miss.

Some trapshooters use a strip of metal or even cardboard taped or epoxied alongside the rib at the end of the barrel to blot out the off eye's view of barrel and front sight. If he points with the sight as even

Left:

A simple test to determine which is the master eye is to make a circle with the hands as illustrated. This circle should be formed with the hands at waist level, then with the hands down select some object snd focus upon it with both eyes. Then, quickly and without hesitation bring up the hand circle to center the object. Continue looking with both eyes focused on the object, then quickly close the left eye. If the object remains centered in the circle, the shooter's right eye is the master eye.

Right:

If the object seems to jump out of the circle and is no longer visible, then the left eye is the master eye. In conducting this test it is important to first view the object with hands down, then quickly move them up to frame it with both eyes open. Normally the master eye will center the object, even though both eyes are open. To attempt the test holding the hands high while framing the object can confuse the eyes and the shooter, possibly causing a mistake in determination of the master eye.

a vague reference, he knows he's pointing with the master eye. A most promising device for reducing occasional crossfiring is the Weaver Accu-Point which I discussed in detail in the chapter on gun fitting. It shows a bright red dot only when the eye is directly behind it. This means that the off eye sees no dot and if you point with that dot the master eye must be doing the shooting for you.

I realize many two-eyed shooters will say they never even see the front sight, and certainly English gun builder and shooting instructor Robert Churchill lectured that the shooter should not see the gun at all, but should concentrate on the game. I agree with half of that—the concentration on target.

But I believe Robert Churchill saw his gun the same as everyone else does. And if he didn't, why did he develop a highly visible tapered rib to give the illusion of long barrels for the short 25-inch barrels he so staunchly advocated? Sure he saw that rib, and the sight—but like most of us he saw it subconsciously rather than focusing upon it. An optometrist friend of mine says it is virtually impossible not to see one's gun barrel, at least subconsciously or as a vague image, because of the way our eyes function.

Most shooters who claim they simply cannot shoot with both eyes open probably decided this by looking down a gun barrel with eyes focused on the gun rather than the object to be hit. If anyone looks at a gun with both eyes open he is pretty certain to see two guns, a double image. But if he concentrates on focusing both eyes on the distant target, then brings gun up into firing position without changing focus to look at it, a remarkable thing occurs. He's seeing just one vague blur of a barrel. That is because his master eye is locked on the target and the gun coming up into peripheral vision is likewise seen best by the master eye.

One way to learn to shoot with both eyes open is to practice without firing. Start out in a darkened room and have someone shine a flashlight against a wall. Practice mounting and pointing an empty gun at that dot of light. Since you can't see the gun, you will learn to concentrate on the target. Then turn on the lights and continue to concentrate on target, mounting the gun into firing position and seeing the barrels only as an out-of-focus blur. That indistinct gun image is surprisingly precise; it is what most champion shotgun shooters have been pointing with all along.

There are other ways to lick the two-eyed shooting problem without special sights or gadgets on the end of the barrel. One of them calls for your regular shooting glasses and a tiny dab of petroleum jelly on your left forefinger. I'll give the instructions for a right-handed shooter; if you're left-handed, just reverse the procedure. First you'll need a good set of shooting glasses, and that means relatively narrow lenses that ride high enough on the nose to be clear of the cheek when the face is pressed down against the gun stock. The old-style round or oblong frames may be joggled or moved upwards when the cheek is pushed upwards by the stock.

With shooting glasses in place, mount the gun to firing position. Rest the fore end on something so as to free the left hand of its job of supporting the barrel. Make sure the right eye is looking straight down the barrel or rib, then shut the right eye. Immediately you will see the left side of the gun.

Focus on the end of the barrel. Then slowly, carefully move your left forefinger (with a dab of petroleum jelly on it) towards that precise spot on your left shooting glass lens that blots out the left eye's view of the end of the barrel. Only the shooter looking down the barrel can do this, because only he knows precisely how his eye sees the end of that barrel. When the end of the barrel is blotted out by the tip of the finger, deposit a dab of grease at that precise spot on the glasses. This produces a blurred area that should be made a little larger than your

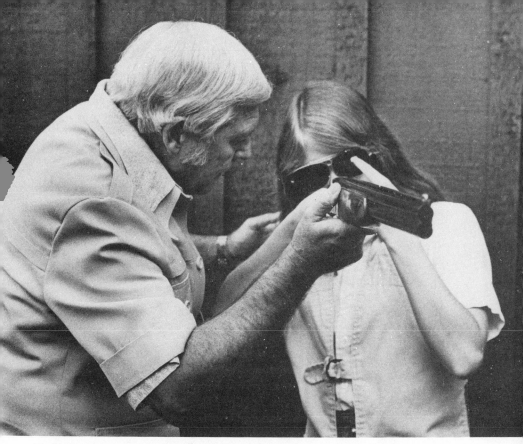

To blot out the off eye's view of the end of the barrel, a small piece of tape can be put on the shooter's glasses at precisely the spot where the left eye views the front sight. Here the author supports the gun while student Susan Welton places a dot of adhesive tape in position. The procedure is explained in the text.

fingertip. Then, keeping your head on the stock, slowly remove the finger. You will find that the greasy dot has blurred out the left eye's view of the end of the barrel.

Take the gun down and with both eyes open look through the glasses at some distant object. Strangely enough the "greasy dot" will not be in your way; it will be positioned high enough to be out of your central line of sight. You will still have the advantages of two-eyed vision.

Put the gun back to shoulder in normal shooting position with both eyes open. You may not be bothered at all by the dot on the left lens, but you will have an absolutely clear, single image of the shotgun's front sight. The reason is that the off eye has been blotted out at that precise place it views the end of the gun barrel, but only when the head is in shooting position. This means that you can view a target—duck, or quail, or whatever—with both eyes open, and when the gun is in shooting position, you won't cross fire.

With anti-cross-firing dot in place, the shooter's master eye behind the gun's barrel must do the pointing, and then the shooter can shoot where he (or she) looks. In field shooting, the dot is sufficiently high on the glasses that a hunter can view game with all the advantages of having both eyes open. But when the head is down in shooting position, the proper eye is forced to take over at the instant of swinging on game.

If you should decide to try this gimmick someday in the field or on the shooting range, but like most of us do not commonly carry petroleum jelly in your pocket, try rubbing your finger against the base of your nose. This will usually provide enough natural skin oil to blur the small area required. Hair oil or any sort of greasy substance will also work.

The greasy spot system is merely a temporary way of testing the procedure and providing added insurance against the occasional crossfire. If the spot bothers you, or doesn't seem to help your shooting after several trials, it can be cleaned off easily. But if the system does work it can be made more permanent by using a dot of adhesive tape, Scotch tape, or clear fingernail polish applied the same way you used the grease. A clear spot that sufficiently blurs the area is better than adhesive tape, because it is less obvious.

There is also a device called the crossover stock that does exactly what is implied. It permits shouldering the shotgun to the side you're familiar with, but has a dogleg bend to it sufficient to put the barrel beneath the opposite eye. The English have used custom-built crossovers for generations; nowadays the remedy is less expensive. A crossover stock for many standard pumps and autoloaders can be ordered from the Reinhart Fajen Company of Warsaw, Mo. Or most any custom stockmaker, including Bishop Stocks of Warsaw, Mo., can build a crossover stock for your favorite over-under or double.

These are strange looking stocks, and I would assume that at first they would require a bit of getting used to due to the changes in position of the gun and trigger hand. But I've seen a few shooters use them with accuracy; for them the "weird wood" was the beginning of a brand new ball game.

No matter how you go about it, the shooting eye must be over the shotgun barrel. Once it is, what you see is what you get.

9

RECOIL AND BALANCE

Shotgun kick, not to be confused with the simpler subject of recoil, is a complicated equation of gun weight, balance, stock fit, anatomy of the shooter, and even how much noise the gun makes. Any physics student can compute foot-pounds of recoil of a given gun and load combination, but how that feels to each shooter may be an entirely different matter.

It is generally known that a heavier gun usually kicks less than a lighter one firing the same load. But why do some guns kick so much more than other guns of comparable weight?

Newton's Third Law of Motion states that for every action, there is an equal and opposite reaction. If that is true, the load of shot pushed out of any gun would, by the laws of physics, have to recoil with that equal and opposite reaction. Yet kick varies with the shooter's reaction to it, and even to the way he holds his gun. The same force exerted rearward can come in the form of a shove rather than a jolt. I have in recent years become an authority-by-necessity on that subject. Before a surgeon's knife got my attention, I noticed little difference in firing a gas gun, pump, or double. But shortly after having cervical disc surgery I made the mistake of shooting a shotgun before the healing was complete. That shot I'll *never* forget; pieces of popped interior stitches worked their way out of my back for some time. For months after I'd flinch looking at a gun, and couldn't consistently hit the ground, much less a target. Fortunately the surgery turned out to be completely successful, and that flinching problem has gradually improved, but in making the many shots necessary for researching this book—at times as many as 125 consecutive shots through the chronograph at one sitting—I have relearned about recoil. One rather surprising revelation has been that the giant 10-gauge Ithaca Magnum gas autoloader, firing its 3½-inch howitzer shells, is a pleasure to shoot compared with 3-inch Magnum shells in a 12 gauge. In fact, even 3-inchers in a 12-gauge gas gun (1⅞ ouncers particularly) hurt me more than the shove of that very heavy, 11¼-pound 10 gauge. I'm inclined to believe that effects of gas-gun recoil reduction are relative in some progressive proportion to the amount of recoil. For example, with the 28-gauge gas gun, I can tell little difference from a fixed-breech gun. But as the gauge becomes larger, the difference becomes more—and with the 10-gauge Magnum there really is a difference.

Shooting an ordinary fixed-breech 10 gauge, such as the common European imported double barrels now floating around gun shops in this country, is to me a sensation very similar to being in a small car wreck. But shooting the Mag-10 gas gun, even with 3½-inch 10-gauge Magnum loads, is a breeze. My wife also shoots that gun with no other problem than lifting all that weight to her shoulder.

So there's much much more to recoil than just big or small gauge.

Wayne Leek of the Remington Arms Company provided me with a thoroughly scientific extrapolation of the complications of recoil phenomena which he separated into two basic parts. One is the action of the projectile material moving forward and the gun's reaction moving rearward. Second, there is the action (collision) of the gun against the shooter's shoulder, and the reaction of the shooter to the gun. This can really get technical because it involves the functioning of the gun as well as how the shooter feels the kick, but it is instructive, boiled down to layman language, because some of it is directly contrary to what most of us were told the first time we picked up a shotgun.

You were probably told to hold the gun hard against your shoulder; that if you held it loosely it would kick back much harder. I have found some verification of that a few times shooting international skeet when I didn't have time to get the gun all the way to my shoulder at Station 8 and took the recoil on the biceps of one arm. Yet the solid hold, or getting hard into the gun, can be taken too far.

Leek says shooters who hold their guns very tightly actually may not sense as much difference in recoil between a fixed-breech gun and a gas gun as do shooters who hold a gun rather loosely and absorb more recoil with hands and arms. The difference apparently is that the relaxed hold lets the gun move back more gradually, spreading out recoil. He also said that a recoil pad, several layers of clothing, or added

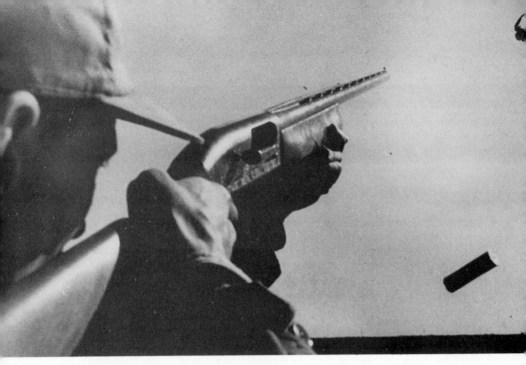

Despite the recoil reduction of a gas-operated autoloader, this shooter of heavy 1⅞-ounce 3-inch 12-gauge magnum loads has indeed been kicked. And he has reacted to it in fairly standard style, head momentarily jarred out of contact with the stock and fore-end hand pulling the barrel downwards. This fore-end flinch is something most shooters do not realize they have until perhaps a shell fails to fire or they snap on an empty chamber. Then they may find themselves doing all sorts of strange things anticipating recoil, the most common of which are shoving the shoulder into the gun and yanking downwards with the fore-end hand. In the instance shown here, the goose is felled regardless of recoil. But often a shot at another bird immediately following a sharp kick will be missed because the shooter's head is not back into proper position on the stock.

gun weight all work in something of the same way as the gas-recoil principle in that they spread the peak of recoil forces out over a longer period of time.

Grant Ilseng, one of the finest shotgun shooting instructors of all time, says that one of the best recoil reducers ever invented for the beginning shooter is a good set of ear muffs. The sensation of kick, he points out, is partly that explosion going off in your face when the gun fires, and the new shooter reacts to it because it's a new and sudden jolt to his senses. The experienced shooter conditions himself to it, but it remains a definite factor in his sensation of kick. The reason many veteran trap and skeet shooters wear ear-protective devices, aside from trying to protect their hearing, is to help prevent flinching. Reducing the noise gives the effect of less recoil.

Kick hurts a shooter's performance in many ways. If it jolts his head off the stock, the odds are the next shot will be a miss. If he sub-consciously begins holding his head off the stock, even slightly, to avoid a pounding of face or cheek, he is simply not going to hit well with that gun. Thus the effective kick of a gun may have little to do with the physics of recoil. It can be that the comb of the stock is slightly too high or too sharp for the shooter, and a few strokes with sandpaper can sometimes work more wonders than adding some miracle-cure recoil-reducing device. If a gun is perfectly balanced so as to recoil straight back, the recoil sensation will usually be relatively mild. That same gun, balanced so that its barrel jumps upwards with the shot, will tend to whack the shooter a sharp blow to the chops.

The easiest way around kick is to shoot a modern, gas-operated autoloader. With many shooters this reduction of kick amounts to about 30 to 40 percent of the jolt of a fixed-breech gun. Several youngsters I've helped get started shooting have been able to handle the kick of a lightweight 20-gauge gas gun as well as that of a .410. Since it is much easier to hit things with the larger gauge gun, a

Recoil reduction, or the sensation of it, gained from a gas gun is apparently pro-portional to the amount of recoil forces and gases to be worked with. The greatest advantage seems to be with the largest guns. Here the author's 125-pound wife Sandy shoots the biggest autoloader ever made, Ithaca's Mag 10 firing 3½-inch 10-gauge magnum loads. Her sensation of recoil was that it was not bad at all—it shoved rather than kicked. Yet most 3½-inch 10-gauge doubles or single bar-rels without gas attenuation generate fierce recoil.

Sound is a major factor in recoil sensation; earmuff-type protectors give the sensation of less kick, and some shooters use fitted earplugs (or cotton) inside their earmuffs to increase the effect. Hunters obviously cannot wear earmuffs—it would be a bit difficult to hear a duck calling or a quail getting up, but earplugs such as the "Lee Sonic" do not block out normal sounds but do help block some of the blast of the gun.

recoil-reduced autoloader is about perfect for starting out a new shooter.

Another way around recoil is to shoot lighter loads. Some guns that buck and bellow with high-brass loads are pleasant with field loads, and the loss in effectiveness is much less than is generally believed. But say you like maximum loads in a pump, over-under, or side-by-side double. What about the various recoil reducers that are advertised as being simple to install in the gun's stock?

Well, they do work. And so does lead weight. But balance enters

Competitive shooters constantly experiment with means of reducing recoil and muzzle jump. In this picture, Bill (Junior) Peale shows the lead weights taped to his Browning over-under to insure follow through at skeet. They apparently worked. He was runner-up to the high-overall champion at the 1975 world skeet championships.

here. Too much weight in the stock tends to make the gun butt heavy, and in a short-barreled action (particularly the over-under) it may cause a tendency for the gun to kick up rather than straight back. The Edwards Recoil Reducer, which I use in several of my guns, gets around this to a certain extent by adjustment. Turning the reducer clockwise or counterclockwise can deflect some of the recoil straight back and away from the shooter's face, but with some guns (and shooters) quite a bit of experimenting must be done before maximum effect is reached.

The supposed ideal point of balance of an over-under or double is at the hinge pin where the action opens. But this is not always true. I had one fine over-under so balanced that it kicked like a mule, until a few ounces of added fore-end weight tuned it into straight-back recoil.

To experiment with reducing the kick of a gun, it is not always necessary to invest a great deal of money or time. Most hardware stores carry plumbers wool or lead wool—simply shredded strips of lead somewhat resembling steel wool which can easily be compressed into crevices of the stock, fore end, or wherever it is needed to weight the gun.

Although it seems contrary to common sense, a long-barreled, heavy-swinging gun can be made to seem to point faster by weighting its stock. There is some sort of cavity in almost any shotgun stock; add the desired weight there and hold it in place by taping or packing with almost any sort of filler material. By changing the point of balance toward the rear, a long-barreled gun starts to swing more like a short one.

I cannot honestly recommend installation of too much weight in most field hunting guns for the simple reason that these guns will be carried more than they will be fired. Furthermore there is a slight slow up in shouldering a gun with its butt weighted. In general, recoil is much less noticed in the excitement of hunting than in the programmed repetition of target shooting. And, of course, a lot of the difference comes from that repetition—a target shooter may fire more times in one weekend than the average hunter fires in a whole season.

One of the worst things any shooter can do in determining how a gun kicks is to shoot it at a tin can, pattern board, or anything else that is not moving. For some reason, shotguns just kick much more that way. I'd rather fire 500 times at skeet, trap, or birds than once at a pattern board. Maybe there is something in the way the gun is held or in the rigidity of the body anticipating recoil with no fun attached to it that makes such shooting uncomfortable.

In general, a gun balanced slightly muzzle light will swing and handle better for hunting. But clay-target scores will be higher with a muzzle-heavy balance. The difference basically is that clay targets continue their original direction but birds do not necessarily fly that way. At trap or skeet it is a big advantage to have a gun that wants to keep swinging smoothly, and a muzzle-heavy gun is hard to stop once it gets started. But at birds, particularly upland game, there is often a need to stop and start in another direction when a bird abruptly changes course.

To get around such conflicts, some one-gun shooters balance their guns for trap and skeet by adding weight to barrel or fore end (to give muzzle-heavy balance) and then remove it for field shooting. Remington offers special weights for its lightweight .410 bore and 28 gauge

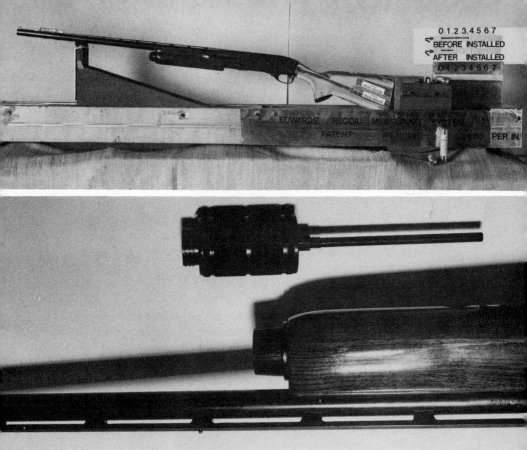

Above:

The most popular recoil reducer for shotgun stocks, the Edwards, consists of a small metal cylinder with a spring-loaded weight inside. The gun is resting in a recoil-measuring device built by Jesse Edwards, inventor of the recoil reducer, who claims the distance a heavy, moveable object is moved rearward by recoil forces is approximately 50 percent less than that of the original gun when two of his reducers are installed. The scale at top right shows the distance the device was moved before and after installation. Yet when tested in a pendulum normally used to measure recoil, Edwards reducers have shown little difference than the same amount of weight added to the gun. The difference, Edwards says, is that resistance of the shoulder is required to make his device perform properly. Some top trapshooters use two Edwards reducers, but the added weight (more than a pound) would make such an installation of dubious value for a field gun other than in pass-shooting situations.

Below:

Fore-end weights for lightweight, small gauge models of the Remington 1100 are popular with skeet shooters who want their small guns to more resemble the larger gauges in weight, and more importantly to insure smooth follow through. The weights shown, available from Remington, simply replace the fore-end cap which then screws onto the end of the weighted adapter. Removing this device can be done in seconds and the gun again becomes lightweight for field hunting.

that greatly help follow through at skeet but would make the gun feel like a fence post in the field. These are adapters that screw into the same threads as the gun's end cap, and can be removed in a few seconds. They not only put weight and balance forward, to keep the little guns swinging, but they add enough mass to give a reasonable approximation of the heft of the larger 12 gauge.

Double-gun owners can borrow a page from the golfer's book of tricks and use lead tape, a self-adhesive tape normally used to balance golf clubs. A strip or two of this stuff along the underside of the barrel inconspicuously adds weight wherever it's wanted and can be removed when desired. Many competitive shooters use this technique, in part to change the gun's balance, and in part to reduce the upjump of light-weight doubles and over-unders.

Probably the biggest advantage of weighting a gun is making one gun serve as skeet or trap gun and also field gun, changing its balance back and forth as desired. But be prepared to accept some ribbing from friends any time you experiment with a shotgun; they'll tell you it's not the gun but the shooter that needs improvement. Still, there are few champions who have not spent many hours customizing their guns.

In the matter of recoil alone, tens of thousands of dollars a year are spent by trapshooters on changing stocks and balance and adding recoil reducers of one form or another. All-American trappers Britt Robinson, Larry Gravestock, Gene Sears, and many others use *two* Edwards Recoil Reducers in their stocks. I have the same setup in several of my trap and live-bird guns, and one of the tricks of using the Edwards is taking advantage of its adjustability for direction. Turn it one way and the gun kicks away from a right-handed shooter's cheek; the opposite way adjusts it for a left-hander. Turn the two opposite each other and they work against each other virtually to nullify recoil. That's the setup I use for trap.

The Edwards reducer is a little metal cylinder with a weight and a spring inside. When the gun fires (according to the way its inventor Jesse Edwards explains it) the weight moves rearward, compressing air and also the spring that will ultimately move the weight back again. But in the process, when the weight moves back, something happens to recoil sensation. Without falling back too far upon Newton's laws of motion, there is an alteration of recoil peak when something within the gun (rather than the whole gun) can move backward as gasses leave the muzzle.

Yet if you measure the recoil of an Edwards-equipped gun in a pendulum, it likely will indicate about as much recoil as any other gun of the same weight. Edwards says the resistance of the human shoulder is necessary to make his device work properly.

Relative Recoil of
Modern Shotshell Loads

Gauge	Shell Length	Gun Weight	Powder Dram Equivalent	Shot Weight (oz.)	Recoil Energy (ft.-lb.)
12	2¾	7 lb. 8 oz.	3	1	18
12	2¾	7 lb. 8 oz.	2¾	1⅛	19
12	2¾	7 lb. 8 oz.	3	1⅛	21
12	2¾	7 lb. 8 oz.	3¼	1⅛	23
12	2¾	7 lb. 8 oz.	3¼	1¼	26
12	2¾	7 lb. 8 oz.	3¾	1¼	32
12	2¾	7 lb. 8 oz.	Magnum	1½	45
12	3	8 lb. 12 oz.	4	1⅜	32
12	3	8 lb. 12 oz.	4¼	1⅝	45
12	3	8 lb. 12 oz.	Magnum	1⅞	54
16	2¾	6 lb. 8 oz.	2½	1	20
16	2¾	6 lb. 8 oz.	2¾	1⅛	24
16	2¾	6 lb. 8 oz.	3	1⅛	26
16	2¾	6 lb. 8 oz.	3¼	1⅛	29
16	2¾	6 lb. 8 oz.	Magnum	1¼	36
20	2¾	6 lb. 8 oz.	2¼	⅞	16
20	2¾	6 lb. 8 oz.	2½	1	19
20	2¾	6 lb. 8 oz.	2¾	1	21
20	2¾	6 lb. 8 oz.	3	1⅛	25
20	3	6 lb. 12 oz.	Magnum	1⅛	28
20	3	6 lb. 12 oz.	Magnum	1³⁄₁₆	31
12	2¾	7 lb. 8 oz.		1 oz. rifled slug	28
16	2¾	6 lb. 8 oz.		⅞ oz. rifled slug	25
20	2¾	6 lb. 8 oz.		⅝ oz. rifled slug	15

The gun weights shown are average for each gauge. For a given load, approximate recoil energy varies inversely with gun weight. For example, to find the recoil of a 12-gauge 3¾-dram, 1¼-ounce load in a 7-pound gun, proceed as follows:

$$32 \text{ ft.-lb. (for 7½-lb. gun)} \times \frac{7.5}{7} = 34 \text{ ft.-lb. for a 7-lb. gun}$$

There are many other factors involved with shotgun recoil, significant among them the sharpness of angle of the barrel's forcing cone
and inside diameter. But that goes better with discussion of chokes,
chambers, and barrels, all of which are much less personal matters
than kick.

10

TRIGGERS, FLINCHES, AND LOCK TIME

Shooting a gun with a fine trigger is something like developing a taste for well-aged Scotch; you may wish you'd never known better, but trigger slack and soda pop will never be quite the same.

A good trigger simply makes a shotgun easier to shoot. It is one of the most important things about a gun, because things happen very rapidly during those critical microseconds when the mental computer is judging the speed, distance, and angle of a fast-moving target. To function at its best, the mind must know precisely when the gun is to fire if it is to tell the trigger finger when to pull.

Mass-production tolerances often allow for slack in the linkage between trigger and sear, excessive engagement between sear and hammer, and other mechanical meanies that combine to give relatively poor trigger pulls to a high percentage of guns in use by hunters. But if the hunter doesn't know that, and becomes accustomed to pulling through a long and squashy trigger to finally make the shot go off, he may get along fine. His computer has adjusted to a slow or heavy trigger sequence and if he doesn't shoot much he may never know the difference. Besides, he's probably read someplace that a shotgun shooter slaps a trigger rather than squeezes it as does a rifleman, so what difference would it make anyway?

The answer is to try a gun with a really good, crisp trigger. Slap it, pull it, squeeze it—it's still a good trigger and hitting seems to become easier as you begin getting used to it. That's because the good trigger is more precise, quicker, smoother.

The trouble with talk of slapping triggers is that many shooters equate that with yanking. To test results of that system, try shooting at a pattern board or something stationary and precisely hit it with the center of your load. This is rarely done well yanking.

Watch a shooter fire at game or clay targets. If he's a champ he'll be smooth about it. If not he may lurch into the gun, and yank it around considerably. One reason for that can be anticipation of recoil. But another can be the trigger. In general it has been my observance that the heavier the trigger pull, the more physical effort is required to pull it and the more that effort tends to translate into other physical movements by the hands and arms such as yanking down on the fore end at the instant of firing. The shooter in effect is manhandling the gun rather than controlling it with the graceful, almost artistic touch great shooters seem to share.

I cannot say what all the factors are, nor how much they matter. I have known hunters who never had the slightest idea what sort of triggers their guns had, yet who shot them very well. But I have known many more, and watched them come up through the ranks of pigeon shooting and clay-target competition, who suddenly began shooting better the moment they got hold of a gun with a good trigger.

Many times out hunting, someone has borrowed one of my guns and shot it better than his own; I've sold a good many guns that way to shooters who simply wanted that gun, no matter what the price. They always say it "fits" them. Yet most of the time, the significant difference between my gun and theirs was the trigger pull.

So what is a good trigger? I believe for hunting it is one of not more than four pounds for an average-weight 12 gauge, and maybe a little less than that for a very lightweight 20 gauge or smaller. A heavy trigger pull on a lightweight gun increases the tendency to yank the gun around in the process of pulling, and is much more noticeable than would be a heavy trigger on a heavy gun.

I could provide some tips for easily lightening trigger pulls for many standard pumps and autoloaders, but I'm not about to do so because if I did somebody would blow his foot off and say I suggested the idea. This is the problem the shooting industry has with its production guns; there is always the chance someone will fall down or drop the gun and it will go off. But a competent gunsmith can remove most trigger creep and slack and the gun should be as safe as it was before. With most ordinary pumps and autoloaders this can be done for a quite reasonable price. The best all-around pull weight I have found is about 3½ pounds; that seems to suit most shooters very well.

Trapshooters customarily use much lighter triggers than hunters, some so light I wouldn't want to shut the action very hard. All-

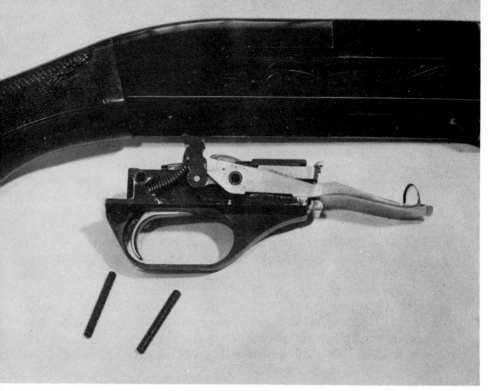

Trigger mechanisms can be easily removed from pumps and autoloaders by punching out retaining pins. This Ithaca Model 51 is simple but strong; it can be disassembled without special tools and has few moving parts.

American Larry Gravestock, who by the way is a trigger slapper and doesn't even touch the trigger with his finger until he's slapped it, was shooting a one-pound pull the last time I saw him. But that was for trap, not hunting, and Gravestock is his own gunsmith and a very good one. I certainly would not suggest anyone set a trigger at less than 2½ pounds because it probably will not stay that way. Trigger pulls often change due to metal contraction in cold weather, wear of parts, and other factors, and it is a good idea to test the pull periodically with a pull gauge. Oddly enough, many triggers get heavier, not lighter, with wear.

Much depends upon the metal of the trigger mechanism, how hard it is and how perfect the angle of hammer and sear engagement. With the proper angle, there can be quite a bit of engagement (which translates into safety against jarring off) yet a very good, light trigger.

I once saw a Perazzi that had been absent-mindedly left on top of a car when the shooter drove off. Although the gun was banged up a bit, the owner swore both hammers were still cocked when he finally found it beside the highway. In other words, that gun (which had a trigger pull of around 3½ pounds) would not have gone off had it been loaded, even falling from the top of a car and bouncing into a roadside ditch. That's the advantage of a good trigger to begin with, which some high-quality guns come with from the factory. But lacking that, a good gunsmith can make a good trigger even out of a pretty bad one.

Certainly a trigger does not have to be made in Italy or England to be good. The Miller Single Trigger, which many owners of fine doubles use to replace factory triggers, is one of the finest ever designed anywhere. I have two Model 3200 Remington over-unders that have factory triggers adjusted to provide about as fine a let off as any shotgun I've owned. One was perfect for me from the factory.

The 3200 is also the gun credited with having the fastest lock time of any production gun. In fact, it is claimed to get its load out the barrel before most guns fire. Lock time is simply the period between pulling the trigger and the firing of the shell. Some trigger mechanisms take longer (this is measured in microseconds) than others and in recent years many trapshooters have equipped their pumps and autoloaders with special speed-trigger assemblies of one brand or another to speed up lock time.

In shooting moving targets researching this book, I have tried to observe differences in forward allowances for guns with various lock times. I was able to perceive little or no difference. But then, this is a difficult thing to do because of the human element; I may have been faster or slower pulling the trigger on one target than another.

Whether a slow or fast lock time is an advantage or disadvantage, even if it is perceptible to the shooter, depends upon the shooting style used. In theory, an ultra-fast lock time would be an advantage for the sustained-lead shooter, because it would permit him to get by with a tiny bit less forward allowance ahead of target. But that speed could be a disadvantage to the fast-swing shooter who actually gets some of his forward allowance due to the elapsed time in which the

The Remington 3200 over-under, credited with the fastest lock time of any shotgun, is said to get its load out the barrel before some guns fire (assuming the triggers were pulled at the same time). The difference is only milliseconds.

gun barrel is passing and pulling ahead of target. Obviously, if the gun fires quicker, he would obtain less forward allowance from the interval.

Many trapshooters swear by their fast-lock-time triggers, and there is certainly no quarreling with their success. But in field shooting, I question the difference one way or the other.

I do believe there may be a perceptible difference between a trigger with a long and squashy pull over one with a crisp and sudden let off, because in effect the pulling of the trigger becomes a part of what is commonly considered lock time.

More tinkering with triggers is done, however, because of flinching than any other factor.

There are two entirely different forms of flinching. One we'll refer to as rifleman's flinch, although it applies to shotguns as well. It is the sort of flinch most shooters immediately think about when the term is used, because they have at one time or another flinched off with a rifle or handgun in anticipation of recoil. Making a trigger light and crisp can greatly reduce this tendency, which is why few competitive riflemen or shotgunners use a heavy or creepy trigger.

With a crisp, relatively light trigger, the shot is gone before the shooter has had much time to flinch from it. In general, the less physical effort required to pull the trigger, and the less interval of time between the start of pull and the firing of the gun, the less likely the shot is to be pulled off target. The lighter the gun, and heavier the trigger pull, the more the difference will be obvious.

But there is another entirely different type of flinching which we shall refer to as trapshooter's flinch, because that game is where it is most commonly observed. This type of flinch is not pulling off target, but simply a sudden and unexplained inability by the shooter to get off a shot. The target goes flying into the air, the shooter sees what he believes to be the correct gun point to break it, and he thinks he is firing. But the gun doesn't go off.

I can speak with authority on that subject because the first time it happened to me I thought the gun was broken. I was positive I'd pulled the trigger. But if my trigger finger had moved, it had not moved enough. There was nothing wrong with gun or shell.

I've seen that same kind of flinch happen many times to many shooters, sometimes rather spectacularly. A shooter will call for his target, lurch forward—sometimes taking an off-balance step or two toward the traphouse—but the gun doesn't fire. It is a weird feeling.

I have discussed this with several physician friends who are also shooters, and they seem to believe there is some sort of short circuit (layman language mine) between the order issued by the brain telling the trigger finger to pull and the actual nerve function that motivates the muscles to do the pulling. In effect, one portion of the brain seems to have overridden another; maybe the subconscious mind is refusing to be hit by recoil one more time or maybe that computer call to the brain was not sure about gun position and at the last instant cancelled the order to fire.

I believe the causes of this sort of flinching vary. Recoil may be the reason with one shooter, indecision the problem of another. But once it starts the shooter is in trouble. Sometimes, flinching will occur on the trap range and nowhere else. With other shooters, once this form of flinching begins, it will be a plague to field shooting, skeet shooting, or anything else.

Often laying off shooting for a while, and then resuming it with very light-recoiling loads (or maybe a gas-operated autoloader combined with light loads) will get around the problem. But more often it will merely postpone it. Serious trapshooters with a flinching problem usually wind up competing at clay targets with what is called a release trigger which is about as unusual as the problem that inspired it. With this trigger, pulling merely sets the trigger. Releasing it fires the gun.

Obviously release triggers take some getting used to, but they do (with most shooters) eliminate trapshooter's flinch, and that is why at a major trapshoot a sizeable percentage of shooters over 40 years of age will be using them. The device is not dangerous on a trap range when properly used, but I believe it can be dangerous anywhere there is the possibility of some other shooter accidentally picking up the wrong gun. What happens in this case is that he pulls the trigger, hears a click, assumes the hammer has fallen on a bad primer, and about the time he lowers the gun and releases trigger pressure it goes off. Perhaps for this reason no major manufacturer in America factory-equips guns with release triggers, but many gunsmiths make complete release mechanisms or trigger groups. An ordinary pull trigger can be converted to a release for relatively modest cost.

Fortunately most field shooters are never confronted by the release trigger, nor its reason for existence, and also fortunately for young shooters the problem rarely seems to arise until a shooter has shot a great deal or reaches the age of 35 to 40.

Some fine shots use release triggers at trap because they believe it is a smoother way of shooting that game. I've talked with many trapshooters who said they wished they'd started out with a release because their scores improved so dramatically once they got accustomed to the system. They also maintain that a release-pull trigger (release the first barrel, pull the second) is the fastest way to get off two shots with a shotgun, which it probably is. With a release-pull mechanism (such as Don Haldeman used to win the U.S. a gold medal at the

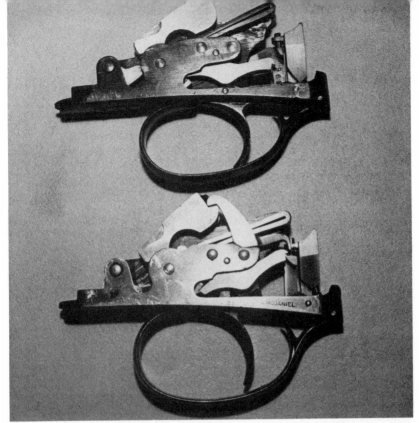

The release trigger (bottom) does not fire when the trigger is pulled. Instead the elongated finger at top engages the hammer, holding it until trigger finger pressure is released. Then the hammer is free to fall. Trapshooters afflicted with flinching install release triggers on pumps, autoloaders, and doubles. The assembly shown is a release conversion built by gunsmith B. McDaniel which interchanges with the factory pull trigger (above) in Perazzi Mirage, MX-8, and Competition models.

1976 Olympics) there are only two movements required (pull, release). A standard trigger requires three (pull, release, pull).

I have no intention of going any farther into this discussion other than to suggest that any gun with a release trigger either be kept in its case between rounds or clearly marked in some way to prevent the possibility of some other shooter picking up the wrong gun.

The old-fashioned double trigger is, in my opinion, still an excellent choice for field shooting with a double or over-under. The primary reason is instant barrel selectivity, but there is also a tiny lapse of time required to move the trigger finger from one trigger to the other that seems to give a split second more time to read the speed and angle of the bird and helps prevent throwing away the second shot before the shooter is really ready for it. As for speed, I believe I can shoot two triggers as fast as one, certainly as fast as I need to shoot them. Many of the top European live-bird professionals, as well as top guns at driven-game shooting in England, Scotland, Spain, and elsewhere, prefer two triggers and use them with lightning effectiveness. The Russian team I watched win the 1968 World Shooting Games at international skeet were also using two-triggered guns.

But most Americans believe they could never become accustomed to double triggers, and refuse to try. I'm inclined to believe most of them could get on to such triggers by firing a few rounds of skeet or trap (first shooting the target, then trying to instantly break the largest chip with the second barrel) and once accustomed to the system would prefer it. For example, in field shooting, when a high duck or dove comes over, the two-trigger man has to fiddle with no selector mechanism; he just pulls the rear trigger, which is his tight barrel. For closer shots he uses the front trigger. (The nearest thing to that for a single-trigger gun is the Remington 3200's selector mechanism which at the shooter's choice selects the over barrel or under barrel at the same time the safety is released.)

Double triggers are simple and in general less likely to malfunction than a single trigger. Years ago Browning offered guns that combined the two types of triggers. This could be called a double-single trigger, in that if one pulled the front trigger it fired the open barrel. Pulled again, it fired the tight barrel. Or the reverse; the back trigger fires the tight barrel first. Or, the shooter could fire one trigger and then the other. Sears Roebuck at this writing offers an over-under with such triggers.

Beretta, while being imported by Garcia Corp., came forth with a pivoting single trigger which if pulled at the top fired the lower barrel, and if pulled at bottom fired the top barrel. Of all the trigger systems I have tested, this was the worst. Yet in general, Beretta triggers are quite good.

Whatever trigger a shooter prefers, he should be familiar with it. And for the many hunters who now own one gun for ducks and another for upland game, it is wise to invest in some snap caps (or fired hulls to protect the firing pin) and snap the gun a few times to get familiar with the trigger pull before hunting. Under no circumstances should a shooter, unless he is a competent gunsmith, attempt to hone or file hammer or sear to make his trigger lighter. That is asking for trouble; it is a job for someone who knows what he's doing.

But if the trigger is a bad one, and it bothers the shooter, having it adjusted properly can be well worth the time and trouble. Many a bird is missed because the shooter flinched off and never knew it only because his trigger was too creepy, or too heavy, or both.

11

BARRELS, CHOKES, AND FORCING CONES

Somewhere it must surely be engraved in stone that a 12-gauge shotgun barrel must be bored with an inside diameter of .729″ or less, 16 gauge .670″, 20 gauge .615″, 28 gauge .550″, and .410 bore, .410″. This is basically how shotgun barrels have been made, and apparently will be made forever. Yet with the modern loads now being forced through those aforementioned barrels, none (perhaps excepting the 28) seem really the right size anymore to produce maximum pattern efficiency and minimum recoil.

Let's consider the 12 gauge, since it is the most common and also because it must digest the greatest variety of fodder—from heavy magnums to light traploads. When the old masters among English gunsmiths were developing the classic shotgun actions and designs that have since been adopted and modified into shotguns around the world, the loads for which 12-gauge barrel diameters were designed were very light, and many of the old guns had 2½-inch chambers rather than the modern standard of 2¾. Shells for these chambers usually carried an ounce or less of shot, and today's standard velocity English Eley Grand Prix cartridge still contains only 1¹⁄₁₆ ounces of shot, not much more than our standard 20-gauge load.

Yet the same basic 12-gauge barrel measurements, which so beautifully patterned those light loads in the old days, and will do so today, are now being asked to handle heavy loads of pellets that market hunters of old would have considered more suitable for a 6 gauge. In

At a glance this appears to be an ordinary 12 gauge, yet inside (at the muzzle and behind it) the barrels are larger than those of a 10 gauge. The Mauser-Bauer international skeet gun, like the German Rottweil Olympia and the Russian Baikal, has overbored barrels and jug chokes capable of greatly varied performance with different loads.

the 1870's, market hunter Fred Kimble recommended 1 to 1¼ ounces of shot for a 10 gauge and 1⅛ to 1½ ounces for an 8 gauge. Yet today's 12-gauge magnum is frequently fed nearly 2 full ounces of shot (1⅞). Even the modern 12 magnums, I'm sorry to say, handle such loads rather poorly. Pushing a heavy load of shot through a small hole is simply inefficient; it creates more recoil, deforms more pellets, and elongates the shot string.

If such heavy loads are to be used, would it not seem wise to increase the bore diameter of 3-inch magnum barrels?

Modern skirted plastic shotcup wads now permit considerable variation in barrel diameter, because the wad expands as required to seal off expanding gases and the shot charge is safe from disruption by such gases because it is encased in its protective shotcup. Loads of the past did not permit so much variance; if bore diameter were too large, gas could escape into the shot charge as it left the barrel and ruin patterns. This is one reason why so many guns, particularly older ones produced on the Continent, were severely underbored. Some are still built that way.

Loads of earlier days seem to be the only explanation for the abrupt, sharply-angled forcing cones seen in many modern guns that literally force the shotload into the barrel. With today's ammunition, all that I can perceive these severe cones accomplish is to increase pressure and recoil. The less traumatic and jolting a ride the shot

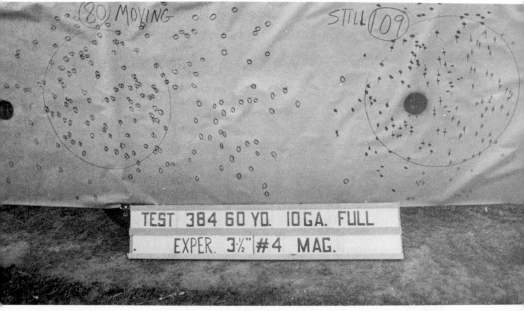

Value of larger bore size relative to shot load is shown by Tom Roster handload of 1⅝ ounces of shot in a 10 gauge. It patterned far better than 12-gauge magnums with the same payload, an amazing 74 percent at 60 yards. The 40 mph test beside it shows the inevitable shot stringing loss at long range, a pattern density of only 54 percent but still very good for 60 yards.

charge is given through barrel and choke, the less damage to pellets and to the shooter's face!

So am I suggesting 10-gauge barrels on a 12-gauge gun? Well, that just might make as much sense as 10-gauge loads being pushed through a 12-gauge gun. But the 10 gauge has a bore diameter of .775, which is too large to get suitable gas-sealing with 12-gauge plastic wads. And it isn't necessary to overbore that much to lower recoil and improve patterns.

Enlarging 12- or 20-gauge inside bore diameter by approximately .010 can work minor wonders, particularly in some doubles and over-unders of Continental origin that came across the sea with 12-gauge barrels measuring more in the direction of a 16 gauge choked down like a rifle. These guns share one advantage. They will cut down on consumption of shotshells because any time anyone pulls the trigger he will think twice before doing so again. They kick like mules.

But the belief persists that this must in itself be an advantage, that the harder a gun kicks the harder it must shoot. To test that hypothesis I chronographed an over-under that had the sharpest forcing

Experimenting with an over-bored barrel and Baker screw-in chokes showed dramatic differences in properly matching choke constriction to bore diameter. Tubes .698 (right) and .720 (left) apparently offered too much constriction. The .725 tube, which with an ordinary barrel would be a skeet bore, patterned No. 2 shot 80 percent at 40 yards and (as shown) 75 percent at 50 yards.

cone angle and tightest interior barrel measurements of any in my collection. I compared the velocities it achieved with velocities produced by other guns of more reasonable bore diameter. Then I tested for penetration.

There seemed simply no advantage to the tight barrel diameter nor apparently to the steep forcing cone. I sent that tight set of barrels to gunsmith Stan Baker in Seattle, who makes a business of back boring such guns, a job done with precision tools designed for the purpose. I asked for a slight overbore and reduction of forcing cone angle (in effect lengthening the cone).

When the gun returned it looked the same, but was an entirely different breed of cat—rather than mule. Instead of jumping up and slapping my cheekbone in recoil it was by comparison a kitten. And when I chronographed it, there had been no loss in velocity; in fact, there had been a small gain. In measuring its new barrel dimension, I noticed that Baker had shortened the choke taper, increasing its angle, and asked him why. He said he'd found he got the best patterns that way, and that the old idea of the elongated choke taper seems to require more constriction to get the same job done. He figures a short taper, which permits slightly less muzzle constriction, helps patterns by reducing shot deformation at choke passage.

I recalled hearing somewhat similar statements years ago from

A Stan Baker choke on an 1100 Remington 12-gauge barrel; note the slight bulge where the barrel has been expanded to accept the choke threads. Tubes are hard steel and are offered in nine constrictions for about $10 each.

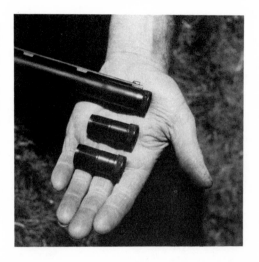

Harry Lawrence of Purdey's. He said that since many fine old Purdeys had 30-inch barrels, and the modern trend was to short ones, the company had done a great deal of barrel shortening and rechoking. He found that swage choking (in effect crimping down a short segment of barrel at the muzzle) gave as good or better patterns, with less constriction required, than a long, carefully tapered choke.

Nothing ever turns out to be completely new where shotgun barrels are concerned. For example, the radical contours of the now-famous Russian chokes (so called because the Russians made them famous by winning the world skeet-shooting championships with bulged-out, blunderbussed barrels) are now claimed to be new by some European manufacturers building barrels of this type for skeet shooting. There is no doubt (to me) that these strange chokes offer an advantage in skeet shooting because my tests show they elongate the shot string; skeet shooting is one of the few activities in which a long shot string is an advantage. Even a soft, deformed, or strung-out pellet or two will break a clay target at 21 yards.

In studying and measuring the contours of these strange-looking bulge-barreled guns, it is obvious that they did not just happen; this is more than just an expanded 12-gauge barrel. In fact, there are four different barrel dimensions in different places. But when you look at a simple diagram in this choke, what you are seeing is in effect a Cutts Compensator or perhaps more nearly a Lyman choke inside a 12-gauge barrel. The enlarged chamber is there, the taper back down to some choke constriction, then the flared or belled-out muzzle very much like a Lyman choke with its spreader tube installed.

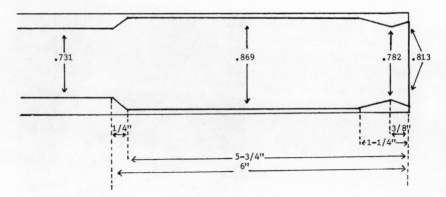

An interior look at the Russian choke shows what closely resembles a Cutts Compensator or Lyman Choke inside the barrel of an over-under. These dimensions were taken from author's Russian Baikal, but are similar to others. Note that true bore diameter is .731, slightly larger than standard in the U.S.; muzzle diameter of .813 is much larger than 10 gauge.

I will always wonder if the Russians, Germans, Italians, or whoever winds up claiming credit for this great advancement in skeet guns somewhere back in history did not watch some American in the 1930s winning with a Cutts Compensator. Or maybe, as in the instance of the invention of choke boring, the same basic idea came to different people independently in different parts of the world. Choke boring was invented by Kimble, or Greener, or Paper, or somebody named Smithsky—you can take your choice.

To me the source of a development is less interesting than what it does. And it doesn't matter to me how many others down through history may have overbored barrels. I wanted to see how my set done by Stan Baker performed. Pattern tests made me a believer. With a Federal pigeon load of 1¼ ounces of No. 7½ shot, the full-choke barrel averaged around 80 percent. With Winchester handicap traploads the pattern jumped to around 84 percent.

I thought about the poor patterns I'd been getting from so many heavy Magnum loads, and sent a 3-inch Model 1100 barrel to Baker asking him to really get radical and overbore it a little more than he'd ever done one and then install his Baker screw-in chokes so I could experiment with various choke constrictions to see what an ideal combination might be for the really heavy hunting loads.

The barrel came back overbored by .015, which Baker figures was a little too much and may have been, but with a choke tube that would, in a standard-bored gun, give modified patterns, the overbored job produced some of the best patterns I've ever achieved with 1⅞-ounce Winchester Super-X Double X Magnum loads of No. 2 shot.

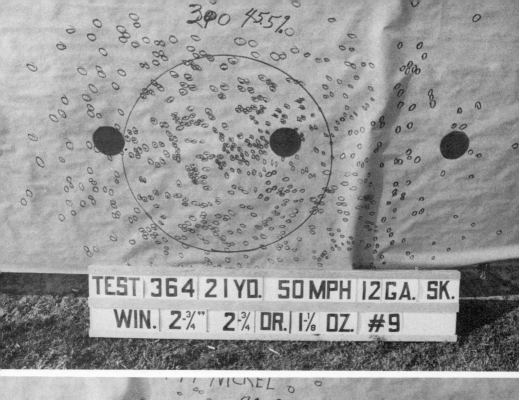

TEST 364 21 YD. 50 MPH 12 GA. SK.
WIN. 2-3/4" 2-3/4 DR. 1-1/8 OZ. #9

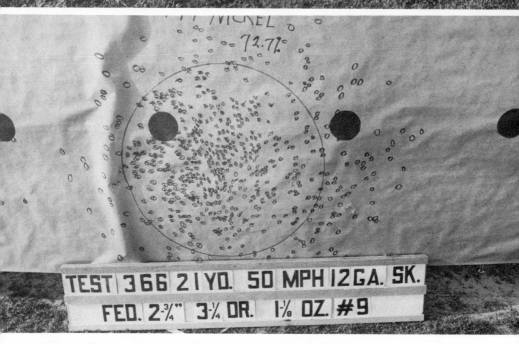

TEST 366 21 YD. 50 MPH 12 GA. SK.
FED. 2-3/4" 3-1/4 DR. 1-1/8 OZ. #9

Remarkable properties of the Russian choke were found by experimenting with various loads. With Winchester special skeet loads, which have no protective shotcup, the oversized choke provided a shot string almost one-third longer (top photo) and more spread than standard barrel. But when an international skeet load with shot collar and nickel shot was used (lower photo) the pattern tightened by 27.5 percent while a standard U.S. barrel varied only about 7 percent between the two loads.

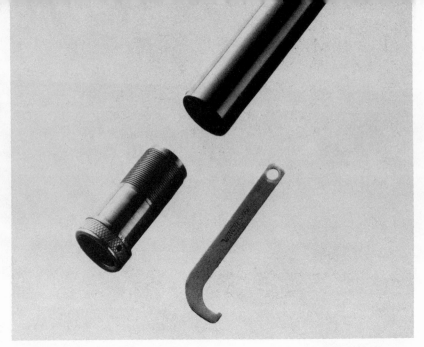

A forerunner of what may well become a new era of interchangeable, interior choking is the Winchester Winchoke, shown with the spanner wrench used in changing tubes. Interior tubes offer great versatility and more precision patterning than external twist type chokes. For anyone worried about potential choke damage from steel shot, here's an inexpensive answer. Replacement tubes cost only a few dollars.

I found there was indeed a drastic difference even in .005 difference between one choke tube and another. I tried Baker's tightest, the .690 tube, which would have given me the equivalent of tremendous overchoke or about .055″ constriction (.030 is closer to standard U.S. full-choke constriction). This did not pattern well, as expected, and the prettiest patterns came with tubes that gave between .020 and .030 constriction, the more open tube seeming to pattern better with 2's and the tighter ones a little better with 4's. This has been the case with my ordinary barrel (without chokes) but it was interesting to see just how much difference a little bit of choke can make. In one test, the pellet count of 2's jumped from 65 pellets in the 30-inch circle to 100 pellets by changing to a choke tube with only .005 less constriction.

Thus the overbored barrel did seem to handle Magnum loads more efficiently, particularly with choke tubes to find the right combination. I believe I went a little too far in overboring, because with some loads there was a slight loss of velocity between the overbored barrel and a standard barrel used for control purposes. But the loss was insignificant, and recoil reduction to me was quite significant.

Certainly overboring is not new. A friend of mine has an old Remington catalog that advertised a special long-range model of the

The first over-under to offer screw chokes in both barrels is the Perazzi MT-6. Nestled in a compact case no thicker than a briefcase, the author's MT-6 has seven choke options plus tool for swapping its instantly interchangeable stocks.

old Remington Model 11 (Browning patent) that was "specially overbored" for long-range performance in the 1930s.

Of all guns that would seem to need overboring, the .410 bore and 20 gauge (when used with 3-inch loads) would be high on the list. The .410 actually generates more breech pressure (13,000 psi) than a 12-gauge Magnum because its tiny bore and elongated 3-inch hunting load combine some of the worst ballistical problems of launching a shot load.

I have not tried it, but I would guess that careful overboring of the .410 would lower pressures and improve patterns.

The 20-gauge, 3-inch Magnum also could use some help, and in some guns has received it. Some years ago I tested a Richland Arms Co. double that had relatively mild forcing cones and slightly overbored barrels. It patterned better than any 3-inch 20 I've tested.

Overboring is not a panacea for all guns or uses; it would be difficult to improve on patterns now being achieved with standard-bore trapguns and modern traploads. But as shot load weights are increased, and shot columns lengthened, overboring seems to become a definite advantage. Tom Roster, in working up his super duck and goose loads (some of which I have patterned at a perfect 100 percent at 40 yards in my overbored gun) found that he got approximately 5 percent better performance with his barrel overbored to about .736 and forcing cones lengthened to 1½ inches.

So why don't manufacturers just make their 3-inch magnum barrels overbored to start with? Maybe the reason is added tooling costs,
or perhaps the feeling that there would not be enough accomplished to
justify "bastard" barrel measurements. But I know one thing for sure.
If I ever again fire a 1⅞-ounce Magnum load through a lightweight
pump gun, that barrel will have been overbored first. The difference in
recoil is significant. But if I were overboring such a barrel next time I'd
use only about .010 overbore rather than .015.

One thing I noticed about my present big bore is that I could get
full-choke patterns from a mighty big hole, even with the .725 tube installed, when using steel shot. That is significant because .725 means I
had the normal barrel diameter (at muzzle) of tight skeet choke—
almost wide open with plenty of room for those hard steel shot to get
through with minimal choke-passage pressure. Yet because of the
larger overbore behind it, I still got relative choke effect of about 20
thousandths, which is normal modified choking. Most modified chokes
will produce very nearly full-choke densities with steel shot.

Left:
*The gas-sealing effect of the modern plastic wad, clearly shown here with a Rem-
ington Power Piston, permits the use of overbored barrels without significant loss
of velocity or disruption of shot pattern. The shot remain within their protective
cup until well clear of the barrel. (Photo courtesy Remington Arms Co.)*

Right:
*A Stan Baker choke is shown here installed in the lower barrel of an over-under,
with both barrels slightly overbored to reduce recoil. This job can be done on the
Remington 3200 or Krieghoff, but not on guns with no space between barrels.*

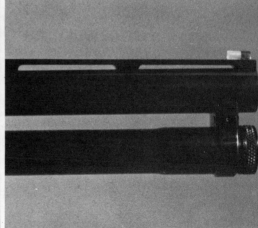

I would suspect that as shotshell technology makes possible heavier steel loads, which is now evident in new three-inch loads and heavier standard loads of 1¼ ounces of shot (rather than the old 1⅛ ounces) more consideration will be given to the muzzle diameter through which those heavier loads are pushed. It would stand to reason that choke expansion from the hard shot would be less likely from a less constricted muzzle. Again the easiest answer would be to overbore the barrel, leaving the equivalent of modified choke but overboring behind that choke sufficiently to achieve relative full-choke constriction. Tests I've done and reports I've seen indicate there is virtually no deformation problem from steel shot with modified constriction at the muzzle.

The whole matter of bore diameters and chokes is a relative one and measurements of the diameter of barrel at the choke mean little until one knows what's behind it. The old gimmick of using a dime to test for choke will work with some standard barrels. If the dime won't go in, constriction usually indicates full choke. If it barely goes in, the constriction is roughly modified. But any measuring of the choke, whether with dime or micrometer, can be misleading. Sometimes extra-tight constrictions (as with some old European guns) will throw loose patterns. And I've seen custom-bored barrels a dime would drop through that nonetheless produced beautiful full-choke patterns.

One day, years ago, I was inserting a dime into the barrel of a gun I intended to buy, and an old-time trapshooter came strolling down the firing line. "That test tells you two things for sure," he observed. "One is that you've got a barrel; the other is that you've got a dime."

12

CHOOSING CHOKES AND LOADS

Full choke is a demanding mistress; improved cylinder a forgiving friend. That's about as simple as I know how to put it, except that "friend" can have many connotations.

The term full choke is used not only to designate the amount of constriction at the end of a shotgun barrel, but also often to designate the percentage of pellets thrown into a 30-inch circle at 40 yards by that constriction.

The two are not necessarily the same.

With some loads, full-choke constriction (about 30 thousandths of an inch smaller than bore diameter) will throw modified or even improved-cylinder patterns and with other loads it will throw extra-full patterns. The quality of the ammunition, particularly shot hardness, nowadays has almost as much to do with performance as degree of constriction. And contrary to popular belief, more constriction does not necessarily mean a tighter pattern. Too much constriction causes patterns to suffer.

Tables showing how much ordinary barrels are choked to give various pattern percentages do not mean nearly as much as they once did. What does matter, more than ever, is patterning your own gun to see what sort of patterns it throws, at what yardages, and with what loads and sizes and hardness of shot.

One reason improved-cylinder choke is such a friend is that with proper shell selection it can be made to perform quite efficiently at the distance most game is taken, which is inside 40 yards. It is a forgiving friend because it allows more misjudgment by the shooter than do tighter chokes, which also will kill cleanly at the same yardages but actually may cripple more than the improved cylinder unless the bird is perfectly centered in the pattern.

Remember that at the ranges improved cylinder is most efficient (roughly 20 to 30 yards with a 12 gauge if the proper shells are chosen) pellet penetration and energy is still strong and fewer pellet hits of a given shot size are required to deposit clean killing energy into the bird than would be the case at 50 yards where the full choke is most efficient.

Let's turn that around and suggest there is more disadvantage to the full choke than is generally realized. This is partly due to the average gunner's rather vague impression of the spread of shot patterns. So much has been written of percentages that many shooters assume the spread of pattern and its percentage are directly correlated.

For example, a full choke is supposed to pattern about 70 percent or better at 40 yards, and an improved cylinder 50 percent or so at 40 yards. That's a difference of only about 20 percent, so the shooter may assume that at closer ranges he has only 20 percent less margin for error with the full choke than he would with an improved cylinder.

But shotgun patterns do not spread in perfect increments of range, nor does full choke spread its load at the same rate of dispersion as improved cylinder. For example, the bulk spread of an improved cylinder at 21 yards is about twice as large as the spread of a full choke rather than the 20 percent difference those chokes would indicate at 40 yards.

Trying to explain that can get complicated, but what it boils down to is that the full-choke shot string emerges from the barrel with its front pellets breaking atmospheric resistance for other pellets in the string behind it, which in turn will tend to stay in the area of least atmospheric resistance (in effect drafting behind the leading pellets much as stock cars do in a race). Thus, even a deformed pellet may stay in this area of protection and fly relatively straight for some distance before its abnormalities cause it to veer out of the pattern at some oblique angle. Thus the full-choke pattern stays quite tight for some distance while the load is under choke control, then begins to broaden rapidly once it does start to open up out at around 40 yards.

The improved-cylinder pattern, which exposes a higher percentage of its pellets to atmospheric resistance at the muzzle, spreads faster and in more direct ratio to distance. Gough Thomas explains this by suggesting the full choke stays tight, then spreads out suddenly, something like the bell of a trumpet, while improved cylinder spreads out as a rather constant cone. My wife, after a particularly tir-

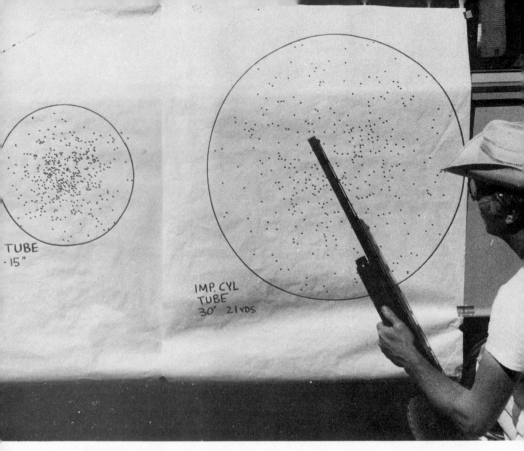

TUBE
·15"

IMP. CYL
TUBE
30" 21 YDS

Dramatic difference in pattern spread of improved cylinder compared with full choke at close range is observed by gunsmith Stan Baker of Seattle. Note that a bird at the edge of the supposedly sure killing 30-inch pattern of full choke at 21 yards could be fringed with only a few pellets, whereas the same degree of miss would provide an instant kill with the larger pattern.

ing day replacing test targets and tabulating data, suggested: "Just tell them improved cylinder goes to hell gradually; full choke all at once." However said, the significance is that at the distances at which much game is killed, between 20 and 38 yards, the improved cylinder is at its best, offering adequate killing density but at the same time a nice, broad spread to give the shooter more margin for error. Within that same critical yardage the full choke is mostly a tight cluster of center pellets surrounded by a ragged fringe.

The full choke's reign of superiority is considerably shorter in useful yards than the improved cylinder's. Between 40 and 50 yards, where the full choke shines, even the best of patterns (from ordinary hunting loads) begin to undergo a number of ills inherent to the smoothbore. Speed of the pellets drops drastically, and difficulty of judging forward allowance increases disproportionately to distance. The effect of air resistance is now being felt by all the pellets of the full-choke string and dissipation becomes progressively more dam-

Here's an example of how a duck that had not been given quite enough forward allowance would be crippled by rear-end hits with a tight choke (center circle), yet would be killed cleanly by a few more inches of pattern spread, providing pellets in the more vital area up front. Thus, full choke does not always "kill clean or miss clean" as is so often claimed.

aging to pattern efficiency. By 55 yards, with ordinary hunting loads, the full choke has become less efficient than the improved cylinder at 40. This is partly due to loss of penetration of pellets at that yardage.

So what we have here is one choke that is quite deadly for a distance of about 18 yards (from 20 to about 38 with most hunting loads in a 12 gauge) and another that shines for 10 yards or so with the same ordinary load. Moreover, in the improved cylinder's favor, the 18 or so yards where it is best happen to be the very ones where most hunters can, and do, take their game.

The question becomes whether the shooter is willing to sacrifice nearly 50 percent of pattern spread at the ranges he shoots much of his game in order to gain the 10 yards or so where the full-choke pattern is best—at a range where he may or may not be able to hit game.

The yardages and spreads here cannot be read as gospel because, as stated earlier, patterns vary greatly by the loads used. Also I have confined the discussion of choke constriction to the 12 gauge because

TEST 346   35 YD. 12GA.   I/C CK.
WIN. XX   2¾" MAX. DR. 1½ OZ. #4

A large margin for error, particularly above and below the 30-inch pattern circle, is shown by improved cylinder at yardage where tests have shown a high percentage of hunters kill their game, even ducks. The use of high-performance grex-buffered loads adds to the penetration capability of pellets around the edge of the pattern, because they are less deformed than fringe pellets from ordinary duck loads.

it is the most commonly used gauge in America. Actually, the same basic ratios exist with all gauges, the ranges simply being shorter with the fewer shot and less density of the smaller gauges, all other things being equal.

Modified choke is worth its own discussion. Some say it is neither fish nor fowl. I think it is very definitely fowl—perhaps the most versatile of all chokes if waterfowl hunting is to be done with the same gun used on upland game.

Modified choke can be made to open up and throw improved cylinder at 30 yards, although it will not open up much at 20 yards unless special brush loads or spreader loads are used. One way to open up a modified pattern is to shoot high-velocity loads. The increased velocity combined with the relatively soft shot in most hunting loads of No. 7½ or smaller shot tends to deform more pellets and open patterns slightly more than the same size and hardness of shot fired from low-brass or lower-velocity loads.

To tighten a modified choke to full-choke percentages, use the most efficient (hardest, least deforming) shot available. Nickel-plated shot are excellent but expensive. International traploads, or better yet pigeon loads, are great. If you can't find those, try a 3-dram factory trapload of 1⅛ ounces of No. 7½ shot and you will find that your modified has become full, throwing evenly distributed patterns of about 70 percent at 40 yards. This is because of the hard and efficient shot used in competitive traploads. This choke and load combination, by the way, is excellent on long-range doves.

For waterfowl, try a modified barrel and a buffered load of hard

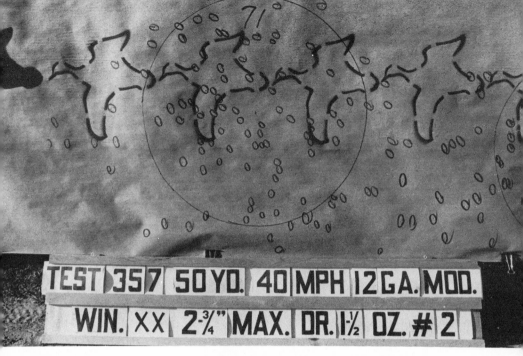

TEST 357 50 YD. 40 MPH 12 GA. MOD.
WIN. XX 2-¾" MAX. DR. 1½ OZ. #2

Modified choke has an unusual characteristic capability for tightly patterning heavy No. 2 goose loads, yet can be made to throw relatively open patterns with standard duck loads in No. 4 or No. 6.

shot, the tightest patterning factory load available at this writing being the Winchester Super-X Double X Magnum in No. 4 or No. 2 shot. Most modified barrels will pattern this load beautifully with what amounts to full-choke performance and a more even distribution of pellets around the edge of the pattern than a full-choke constriction will throw.

Try shooting an ordinary, non-buffered 12-gauge duck load (1¼ ounces of No. 4 shot) in your full-choke gun and count the pellets put into a 30-inch circle. Then shoot a Super-X Double X Magnum load of 4's from a modified barrel and count the pellets. Remember that pellets, not percentages, kill. You will see the more even distribution of the modified, and you probably will also have more pellets in the pattern than the full choke delivered with the ordinary duck load.

Modified choke has another capability rarely mentioned, and that is its ability to handle large shot very well. With No. 2 shot, modified barrels will normally put as many pellets into a goose at 50 yards as will a full choke. Some modifieds will handle 2's and BB's even better than full choke.

If you are after absolute long-range efficiency for pass-shooting both ducks and geese, the full choke is the one to use—not so much because it is any better with No. 2's or larger, but because it should (if fed the best load it will handle) kill a few yards farther with 4's or 6's than will a modified. But it is a matter only of a very few yards.

TEST 350 40 YD. 12 GA. MOD. CK.
FED. 2¾" 3¾ DR. 1⅛ OZ. #4 STEEL

Steel shot and buffered lead shot share highly efficient, tight patterns—so much so that some shooters may have difficulty hitting with them at medium ranges. Modified choke handles steel 4's with a higher percentage (this is crowding full choke) than most full chokes will handle standard non-buffered lead 6's.

Again it is a matter of what the hunter wants to sacrifice, and where he wants to sacrifice it. At the ranges where almost any good waterfowl load will kill ducks cleanly, 40 yards or less, the modified will certainly do the job and it will also kill cleaner if the bird happens to be fringed with the edge of the pattern than if the same bird were fringed by the same amount with a tighter full-choke pattern.

To be more specific, let's put shooter misjudgment into degrees of error. This is an important factor in the crippling of game, because even the finest of shots occasionally misjudge forward allowances, speed, or angle of the bird and either draw tailfeathers or put a few pellets into the bird's rear which will not put him down immediately.

An error of only ¾ of one degree in pointing the gun amounts to 1½ feet off center at 40 yards. Winchester's carefully tabulated tables of miss distances show that if the shooter mispoints a mallard by that amount with a modified choke (using the most efficient duck load now commercially available, the Super-X Double X Magnum load of 4's) the shooter could still expect to bag 45 percent of ducks so missed. There is that much margin for error in the fringe of the modified pattern with this load. But with a full choke, the shooter could expect to bag only 25 percent of ducks mispointed by 1½ feet at 40 yards.

The tables show further that if the shooter is absolutely perfect in his pointing with the modified barrel (and Super-X Double X 4's) he should bag 93 percent of his ducks, while the full choke would give him 100 percent kills. In other words, by using modified choke the shooter at 40 yards would be giving up only 7 percent efficiency if he were perfect, but he would gain 20 percent with a mispoint of 1½ feet. Certainly this can also work in reverse—a hunter who really misses badly may cripple some birds he would miss clean with a full choke.

Here's an example of the disadvantage of miss distance or margin for error in terms of crippling. With a tight choke, this duck would have been only tail-feathered, but with a slightly larger pattern he receives crippling pellets that may or may not put him down soon enough to be bagged. Expert shooters, often, with good reason, use the tightest chokes and loads they can find. The human factor cannot be overlooked in load and choke selection; miss distance is a two-edged sword.

Bear in mind that these tables are computed with a highly efficient load, and cannot be expected to be accurate with nonbuffered common duck loads, which throw considerably more open and less efficient patterns. It may be, with the present status of soft shot being loaded into common high-velocity duck loads, that the shooter's full-choke gun is actually throwing modified patterns to start with, and that using a modified barrel with these loads he would certainly be giving up more than 7 percent kills at 40 yards even if he perfectly centered his birds.

I am inclined to believe that the tables are significant, however, because shooters are getting smarter about their loads and their chokes and most are willing to admit that no matter how good they may be, they sometimes make a mistake or the bird makes a sudden directional change at the last instant. For these reasons I believe the average shooter will bag more birds with a modified choke than a full choke.

These are also the reasons why many veteran duck hunters have switched to modified, particularly for shooting over decoys. Some of them have learned to load their pumps or autoloaders with standard high-brass No. 4 or No. 6 (4's have proven best on big ducks in every scientific test I've seen) and then fire a standard Magnum 4 for the final going away shot after the birds are spooked.

In this way, the pump or autoloader is in effect gaining most of the benefit of a two-barreled, two-choke double or over-under; the first shots with standard, nonbuffered high-velocity load should give a rather broad pattern that is truly modified or maybe slightly more open than that. Then, when the shooter fires the Magnum load behind, he's in effect obtaining full-choke pellet density, provided he has carefully chosen a standard Magnum that patterns well in his barrel.

Perhaps I have overstressed the advantage of the Super-X Double X grex-buffered load, but it is the most efficient factory load I have tested. Right now other companies are in the process of developing loads that may equal or even surpass it, and when they do I believe waterfowl crippling losses will drop, provided shooters are willing to pay slightly more for high-efficiency shells to gain not only added

Here's proof of a rarely realized fact: Smaller gauge guns do not necessarily have smaller patterns. Much depends upon the load. All these patterns were from full choke, firing high velocity 7½'s. The 3-inch .410 (which deforms more shot) in this instance opens quicker and offers more pattern coverage at 20 yards than the 12 gauge. As range increases, the .410 pattern quickly becomes full of holes while the larger gauges retain adequate killing density.

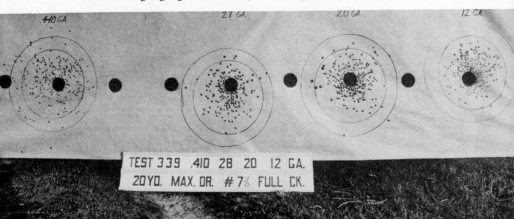

With skeet chokes and 9's, the 2½-inch .410 (right) has approximately the same pattern coverage as the 12 gauge (left), but the latter has much more density for longer clean-killing range.

clean-killing insurance, but more versatility for a single-barreled gun. The new super loads probably will cost more because of higher anti-mony content in the shot and the complications of loading buffering agents.

There is one factor that must be remembered about making a pump or autoloader shoot various patterns by varying loads. Shells do not fire in the same order they are inserted into the magazine. If you want to fire the broader pattern of a nonbuffered or ordinary load for the first shot, put it into the barrel. Then insert into the magazine the tightest or most efficient load, followed by another ordinary load. The last load put into the magazine will be first into the chamber after the initial shot is fired. In that way the shooter can have two modified-choke shots followed by the final full-choke from the most efficient load.

This discussion, of course, cannot be separated into merely talk of chokes or loads but most include both, because the end result is a combination of the two. I have tested a number of full-choked barrels with high-velocity 7½'s (a favorite of many shooters across the country for pheasant and even for ducks) and found that despite the advan-tages of the plastic shot collar and so-called modern ammunition, shot is now sufficiently soft in most loads that a full choke may pattern modified or even less with small shot. Yet large shot, even relatively soft ones, seem to deform less and thus the same barrel may throw full-choke percentages with 6's or 4's. Of six barrels marked modified tested in preparing this book, every one threw full-choke patterns at 40 yards when loaded with grex-insulated Super-X Double X 4's; two produced full choke with ordinary high-brass 4's. Remember also that shells from the same factory may vary considerably from one case to another.

Each man must pattern his own gun, using a number of loads, and soul-search a bit as to the distance at which he is getting his game. In general, large shot will kill cleaner as range increases. Stepping off yardage to a downed duck or pheasant is no true indication, because often the bird will have traveled some distance in the air after being hit. "Guesstimating" distances is difficult, and the common tendency is to overestimate the distance a bird was when hit, particularly a bird overhead. Human eyes are bad about misjudging tall objects. The moon looks small when it is overhead, but it is exactly the same size as that big, orange ball that came up on the horizon a few hours before. An overhead duck or dove also looks smaller, and thus many 60-yard kills are actually made at about 40 yards.

I suppose it is heresy, but I believe the average shooter going for waterhole doves, brush-country quail, and woodcock anywhere would get more birds with absolutely no choke at all. I know it has been written that without some choke pattern control is lost, and there are supposed to be donut holes in the middle of the pattern, and blown patterns, and all that. But it just isn't so, particularly with modern shot-protective wads.

In the thousands of patterns tested by Oberfell and Thompson for their *Mysteries of Shotgun Patterns*, the point is made repeatedly that the pure-cylinder choke (no choke at all) throws the most even patterns of all. That is, in layman language, the patterns have fewer patches or holes relative to the spread of the load. I do not fully understand all the systems of evaluation they used, but I do know that at 25 yards a pure-cylinder barrel will throw one of the deadliest game-getting patterns you ever looked at, more efficient at that yardage than a full-choke barrel at 50 yards. The Russians certainly proved that at 21 yards when their Olympic team member Eugene Petrov set a new world's record of 200-straight international skeet targets using a gun that was actually more open than a pure cylinder: It was belled out at the end to approximately .830, which means it was about .100 of an inch larger than pure cylinder and more like a blunderbuss. And if his pattern had any donut holes in it, they failed to show up 200 times in a row.

The value of just a little more pattern spread at close range, or the disadvantage of not enough of it, can easily be proved on a skeet range. Take out your modified or full-choke hunting gun sometime and see how many skeet targets you can break with it. If you're a

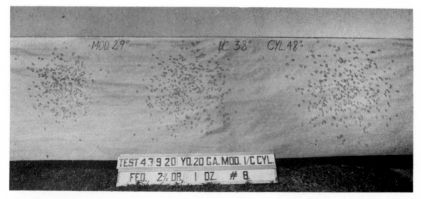

The advantage of cylinder bore (no choke at all) at close range is shown in its 10-inch-larger pattern spread at 20 yards over the improved cylinder, and almost 20-inch advantage over modified. Despite longstanding misconceptions, cylinder bore with modern loads does not throw blown patterns nor donut-shaped ones, but normally the most evenly distributed patterns of any choke.

champ you may break them all. But if you're an average shooter you're more likely to be embarrassed.

It has been my observation that most hunters are overchoked for the game they are after, and I've taken pains to prove that to my own satisfaction many times. I have one 30-inch barrel for an old Model 58 Remington that I've had reamed out to improved cylinder, and several times while hunting doves (particularly whitewing flights in Mexico where there is ample opportunity to miss) I have loaned that old gun to someone suffering a shooting slump. Since the barrel is marked full choke, they accept it readily and almost immediately begin getting game. Several have told me it was the hardest-hitting gun they ever shot. The difference, of course, was not hard hitting, but hitting. They were getting more pellets into the birds they had been fringing with a tighter choke.

One trouble is that everybody seems hung up on patterning guns at 40 yards, whereas most upland game is shot much closer. Try patterning a cylinder at 25 yards (which is probably farther than you can even see in a woodcock or quail thicket) and note just how dense and deadly that wide-open choke throws a load of 8's or 9's.

The fact is that upland hunters probably cripple more game by using too much choke than too little, by tailfeathering or fringing them with the tight choke. Doves and quail (the game most likely to be shot at with open-choked guns in America) are quite easy birds to kill if you can hit them. Very often two pellets will put a bobwhite down for good, whereas two pellets in a duck or goose is only likely to cripple.

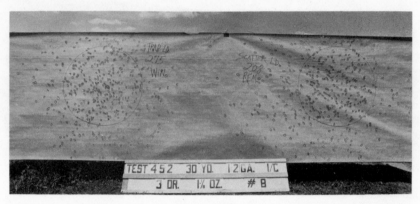

One way to increase pattern area is to use upland brush or scatter loads, the former offered by Winchester, the latter by Remington. Federal and Winchester offer special skeet loads of 9's that increase pattern spread about 5 percent over standard skeet loads, but may produce lead fouling in the barrel. Shooters using them should clean their barrels periodically with a wire brush. To tighten a pattern use traploads; they contain very hard shot, as is evident in the 275-pellet center density at left compared with 208 from a scatterload.

Doves are tough little birds, but not so much so as is often claimed. The hunter who tells you how tough they are, in terms of a puff of feathers he left floating in the breeze while the bird went on its way, hasn't tested the dove's toughness, only his tailfeathers. A dove is mostly tailfeathers and two or three No. 7½'s in his front end will usually put him down cleanly.

On manq trips to Mexico, South America, Africa, and elsewhere where weight requirements permitted me to take only one gun—or maybe I had to use whatever gun was available—I've used the improved cylinder a great deal. By that I mean I've shot a whole lot of game with an improved cylinder. In Botswana, Africa, where there are millions of doves and sand grouse, no bag limits, and a hungry mouth to feed for every shot fired, I've stacked up some sizeable piles of birds for the pickers and probably crippled fewer birds than had I been trying to center those dipping, diving waterhole birds with a tighter choke.

One of the most deceptive statements about the full choke (and it continues to be made constantly) is that it either kills clean or misses clean. Sorry, but it just doesn't work out that way all the time. The reason is that the full choke clusters so many of its pellets in the center of the pattern the edges are left ragged and thin. Thus, a hunter can be almost perfect on his lead and still cripple the bird, whereas if

Open chokes are at their best with small shot at close range. Here the 20-gauge cylinder bore is starting to get patchy with 7½'s at 30 yards but is still a more even pattern than that produced by improved cylinder. With 8's either pattern would have been more deadly at this distance.

he's had another two or three inches of pattern spread he might have registered a clean kill. This is the reason I believe so many hunters, particularly in the South, still hold on to their idea that No. 7½ shot is best for everything, even ducks. Many of them shoot full-choke guns, and there are so many 7½'s (so easily deformed and spreading so quickly) that the fringe area around the pattern is likely to be better endowed with pellets than had the load been 4's. But bear in mind that 7½ shot lose much of their penetration capability, and start to cripple badly on ducks around 40 yards. And when the guy tells you how many ducks he kills stone dead at 50 yards with his 7½'s, you can pretty much bet he was actually killing them inside of 38 yards. If you don't believe that, and don't mind sacrificing some spoonbill or other duck you may not intend to eat anyway, try hanging the bird from a limb, wings outstretched as if in flight, and step off about 45 paces (long ones to represent yards) and shoot at that duck. Then pluck him and see how far those 7½'s penetrated. What you'll find, I believe, is some 7½'s embedded in the bird's flesh (where it is easiest for you to bite down on them if you eat the bird) and very few penetrating far enough to kill cleanly. At that same yardage, 4's will usually plow on through and lodge against bone.

I'm aware of the old argument that it is easier to puncture a bird with the point of a knife than the blunt end of a pencil, which is the justification for the theory that small shot penetrate better—because they are smaller, get between the feathers easier, and offer a sharper penetrating edge than the more blunt area offered by a bigger pellet.

You can forget that one, unless you hunt birds by throwing knives at them. The penetration of pellets is basically a function of their retained velocity and energy, and larger, heavier pellets in general penetrate farther than lighter, smaller pellets.

In this discussion of chokes, miss distances, margin for error, and the like, we have been talking primarily about shooting game at ordinary ranges. For long-range pass-shooting of waterfowl—an entirely different subject—I can recommend only full choke and the tightest, most efficient pattern load available. Efficient loads string out less at long range and not only are capable of killing the bird being shot at cleanly, but are much less likely to cripple some bird farther back in formation with the tail end of an inefficient, elongated shotstring.

Majestic waterfowl deserve no less than the best.

Computerized Lethality Predictions
Percent Bagged at Aim Error (Degrees)

RANGE (YDS.)	(1° Aim Error is 25″ Off Center at 40 Yards)					
	0°	.25°	.5°	.75°	1.0°	1.25°
			Modified Choke			
30	100%	100%	95%	63%	18%	3%
35	99	97	87	54	18	4
40	93	90	75	45	17	4
45	82	77	61	37	15	4
50	68	63	49	30	13	4
55	54	50	38	24	11	4
60	42	38	30	19	10	4
			Full Choke			
30	100%	100%	99%	24%	1%	0%
35	100	100	90	25	2	0
40	100	100	80	25	3	0
45	100	98	68	23	3	0
50	95	86	57	20	4	0
55	82	72	46	18	4	1
60	67	58	37	15	4	1

Mallard ducks predicted to be bagged using 1½-ounce No. 4 Grex Load (Winchester Super-X Double X) used in Nilo Shotshell Efficiency Test (1972–73)

Here's an example of how higher velocity combined with softer shot produces wider, less dense patterns than a low-brass pigeon load with the same amount of shot. Hunters wishing to open up patterns can use the high brass, but low brass (in hard-shot pigeon loads) actually kills farther. Penetration tests in another chapter show that the less deformed hard-shot pellets retain their energy better at 50 yards.

13

SHOT
IN THE DARK

The average hunter in this country selects the brand of ammunition he believes best (or maybe the brand that happens to be on sale that day) and goes hunting with the assumption the shells will shoot as they are supposed to. If he has a full-choked barrel, he expects a full-choke pattern. Because he is an average hunter, he has never patterned a shotgun in his life. When he shoots, his shot is indeed a shot in the dark.

This hunter may be getting only a modified pattern from his full choke, and less than that if the bird he shoots at is crossing at a sharp angle where shot stringing is a problem. Or he may be getting a fine full-choked pattern because the particular load he bought was one of the relatively few hunting loads that survived the component cost crunch of the early 1970s.

What this cost crunch is mostly about is a substance called antimony, the principal ingredient used to harden shotshell pellets and make them pattern efficiently without excessive deformation. When the price of both lead and antimony skyrocketed in the 70s, producers of shotshells were caught in a crunch. If they continued to use sufficient antimony to make their loads pattern tightly, the increased cost would be passed on to the consumer. Yet rising costs of other components had already made shotshells so expensive that some shooters—particularly youngsters and low-income hunters—were in danger of being priced out of the sport.

What happened, at different times and with different loads as various factory runs were made, was that many American hunting loads went "soft." Pattern efficiencies dropped as antimony percentages were lowered to prevent more drastic price increases. There has been no attempt here, or anywhere else in this book, to compare or rate one brand of shotshell with others. Brand-name comparisons would be unfair, with the exception of certain highly specialized loads, because various lots produced by various companies differ considerably in shot hardness and it would be unfair to pick any one box or lot of shells to be compared with another.

The fact is that all companies were faced with the same dilemma. Six percent of precious antimony in a batch of shot can create very hard pellets that pattern beautifully, while a content of one percent can produce poor patterns. I have tested magnum goose loads of No. 2 shot that contained only half a percent! Yet the most important single factor in shotshell patterning is the roundness or perfection of pellets as they travel through the air en route to the target, and as stated above, that requires antimony.

The development of the modern plastic shotcup, or protective cup wad, alleviated some shot deformation caused by barrel contact, but nonetheless deformation of shot is still a major problem. For if the shot within the protective wad are soft, they can still be deformed during pressures of ignition setback, passing through the forcing cone, and in passage through the choke. The efficiency of the load then depends to a great extent on how many pellets were deformed, because the partially flattened ones will not fly straight, will retain less velocity and penetration, and on a crossing target may not arrive at the same time as the non-deformed pellets, thus, in effect, not really counting in terms of that pattern's central portion which is supposed to do the clean killing.

If all this sounds like a slam at the shotshell industry, it is not. The whole picture at the time so many hunting loads went soft must be put into perspective. This occurred during a period when the future of waterfowl hunting loads containing lead shot of any kind was much in doubt due to the controversy over lead-ingestion poisoning. The indications were that the U.S. Fish & Wildlife Service might ban all lead shot for waterfowl rather than just in hotspot areas of known problems.

Also during this same period it had become popular for shooting writers in major publications to advocate more open patterns for hunting of all kinds, and some tests by federal agencies seemed to show that most ducks were actually being taken at distances inside 40 yards. Thus, if the shooter could be given larger patterns (through the use of soft shot) and at the same time help hold down their ammunition

Not only are the wide variety of shotshell gauges and load weights within them confusing to the average hunter, there is little or no recognition of the importance of the shot themselves. In the foreground are three types rarely seen by most shooters; at right are square lead Desperante shot used for quick-opening patterns in Europe. The large shot are steel 4's and the small shiny ones nickel-plated, extra-hard 7½'s. The fired hull is a Winchester Double A trapload; the shot-protecting wad at right a Remington Power Piston. Left to right, the loaded shells are Remington's 3½-inch 10-gauge magnum; a grex-buffered Winchester 3-inch 12 gauge; a Canadian Industries Limited 2¾-inch superfast steel shot load (1,450 feet per second); a Rottweil (German) Brennecke slug; Federal ISU Olympic international trapload; Vigevano Italian live-pigeon load with nickel shot; a 2-inch 12-gauge English light-game load (Eley); Federal 3-inch magnum 20 gauge; standard high-velocity Winchester 20 gauge; Remington 28 gauge, 3-inch .410 gauge; and Winchester skeet load .410. Ounces of shot in these cases range from ½ in the short .410 to 2 ounces in the 10 magnum.

costs—why not? There was at this time widespread public belief that modern ammunition was patterning too tightly due to the protective shotcup wad.

One problem with such rationale was its basis upon pattern testing on the one-dimensional plane of stationary pattern boards. This did not take into adequate account the potential added loss of density suffered by soft shot on crossing targets at long range due to shot-string elongation caused by deformed pellets.

One significant means of checking overall pattern efficiency, however, was taken carefully into account by all the manufacturers. Competitive trapshooters quickly perceive whether they are getting shotshell efficiency or not. So antimony content remained high in their loads. Trapshooting is a prestigious sport for shotshell makers; if someone shooting Brand X wins the Grand American Handicap, other shooters and hunters across the country, who may never fire at a trap target, may be inclined to use Brand X hunting loads in the belief they are hotter, better, or whatever. Thus traploads have been so researched and improved they now are perhaps the most efficient shotshells in the world.

But by far the biggest market for any ammunition maker is the hunter, and the question was how efficient his loads really needed to be. If hunters were offered a premium-quality load, with nondeforming shot and longer clean-killing range, would they be willing to pay the price for the difference or even perceive the difference?

One manufacturer attempted to answer that question by combining high-antimony shot with powdered plastic granules sifted into the spaces between shot in the shell so as to cushion them against deformation. The result was a load that would put far more pellets of No. 4 or No. 2 shot into a distant duck, goose, or gobbler than any previous factory-loaded shotshell.

But did hunters beat a path to Winchester's door, trying to buy the new Super-X Double X Magnum loads with grex buffering? They did not. Years after its introduction, this premium load was still representing only a small percentage of sales of waterfowl loads by that firm. It is thus easy to understand the reluctance of other manufacturers to invest in high-antimony shot or expensive loading equipment for production of super loads. Dumping plastic or some other buffering agent into a shotload can improve its efficiency, but requires special equipment to vibrate the shell so the buffering agent settles properly. It is a troublesome and expensive process.

The foregoing were some of the explanations of industry people interviewed during researching this book. Some believe the average

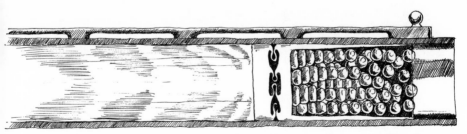

This purposely exaggerated illustration shows the rearward rows of pellets flattened by pressures of gas behind them and inertia of shot weight in front. Here the load is entering the constriction of the choke, but many of its soft pellets have already been deformed by setback forces at ignition.

hunter doesn't really care all that much and is better off with a broader pattern even if it does cost him some pattern loss. Others believe more hunters would buy premium loads if they were properly identified by packaging and their virtues made known better. The only thing everybody agreed upon was that antimony is the most expensive stuff since alimony.

I'm inclined to go along with those who believe the public somehow has not been made fully aware of the advantages of the super loads, particularly for long-range waterfowl and turkey, nor were hunters aware of the relatively poor performance of the standard loads they were getting. But the pendulum seems to be swinging back to better loads. Manufacturers are increasing the antimony content in standard loads, and every major manufacturer has been experimenting with tighter patterning, shorter shotstring super loads. I would like to believe this book may have some influence on this trend, because the moving target tests in it seem to point out clearly the added advantages of efficient shot not always evident in conventional pattern testing.

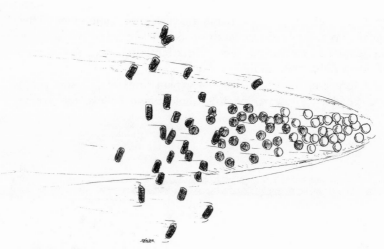

An exaggerated example of how flattened or partially deformed pellets, erratic in flight, leave the protective wake of the frontal pellets and encounter additional atmospheric resistance which slows them and causes them ultimately to string out behind the more perfect pellets up front. The more deformed pellets there are, the longer the shot string will be, the wider the spread of the load, and the less penetration peripheral pellets will have.

How much difference can a premium load make?

Well, in one of my tests I fired high-velocity No. 7½ hunting loads supposedly as good as money can buy from three full-choke test barrels, all excellent at handling No. 7½ shot. The stationary pattern average was around 60 percent, or about modified-choke performance. On the moving target the loads were worse; in several cases they strung shot sufficiently at 40 yards that the most dense area of some patterns was a patchy 45 percent. In other words, the hunter who fired that load at a pheasant under the impression he was using a full choke was, on a crossing bird at 40 yards, actually getting closer to improved-cylinder performance.

Then I took another box from the same case of shells, emptied the shot from them, and replaced the shot with No. 7½ pellets robbed from a popular trapload. The shells were then recrimped, the only thing changed being the pellets. At the stationary target, pattern percentages leaped to nearly 80 percent, an average of nearly 20 percent improvement. The difference was even more dramatic on the moving target. The soft shot load, remember, had strung pellets badly at 40

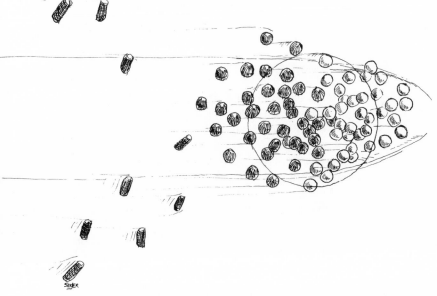

As the forward pellets break atmospheric resistance in a full-choke pattern, the pellets behind them take advantage of lowered resistance and gain on the leaders, much as stock cars draft behind lead cars in a race. This concentrates more pellets forward in the full-choke string, in effect shortening it by the time it reaches target. The exceptions are those pellets that have dropped back and spread wider (commonly called flyers), which may not arrive at the target in time.

This tight-patterning mixture is Winchester's hard-lead shot combined with white plastic granules called grex. When loaded into the shell, the grex settles between pellets, cushioning them against deformation and producing highly efficient patterns. But the process is more complicated and costly than standard loads.

yards and 40 miles an hour due primarily to deformed pellets that failed to reach the target along with the bulk of the load. But the same shell with high-antimony trapload pellets in it threw a beautifully round pattern at 40 miles an hour with an average center density between 70 and 75 percent.

Thus the difference, on a crossing bird, would be that the soft shotload was putting approximately 20 to 25 percent fewer pellets into the killing area around that bird than the hard shotload.

If this comparison is confusing, remember that 70 percent is commonly considered full-choke performance, and the high velocity load of No. 7½'s used for an illustration actually patterned only about 45 to 50 percent on the moving target. The soft shotload had lost density at the stationary pattern plate, and still more moving due to shot stringing.

It must be pointed out, however, that larger shot do not deform as easily as small shot, and thus the difference between true full-choke performance and patterning of soft shot No. 4's on the moving plate was less dramatic than the approximate 25 percent loss of efficiency of the 7½'s. But at longer ranges even big soft shot string out significantly.

The deformation potential exists throughout the spectrum of shot sizes, and created a great deal of discussion in 1975 among some members of the Sporting Arms and Ammunition Manufacturers Institute. There was talk of lowering SAAMI shotshell standards to 60 percent for full-choke performance. Since 70 percent had been considered full choke for many years, this talk of a 60-percent standard should be some indication of the soft-shot problem, and also provide a clearer understanding of what the modern shotcup plastic wad cup can, and cannot, do.

Left:

Proof that the industry is experimenting with more efficient loads is shown by this pattern. It results from an experimental Remington high-velocity shotshell with shot hardened sufficiently to produce patterns averaging 70 percent, the intent being to combine adequate margin for error yet retain true full-choke center density. Some loads produced during the mid-70s would not attain standard full-choke performance due to lack of antimony in the shot.

Right:

This excellent 80-percent pattern was produced by replacing the soft hunting load shot in a high-velocity Federal with hard trapload shot robbed from a Winchester handicap trapload. (The original load patterned only 68 percent.) Similar swaps were made between original loads of each major company, using hard shot from various traploads, and in each instance the percentage jumped dramatically indicating the problem was not with brand name nor high velocity, but merely in the shot itself.

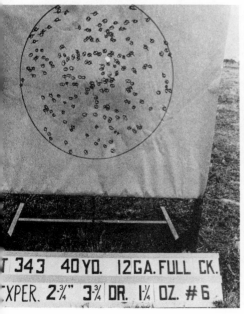 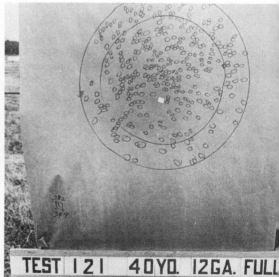

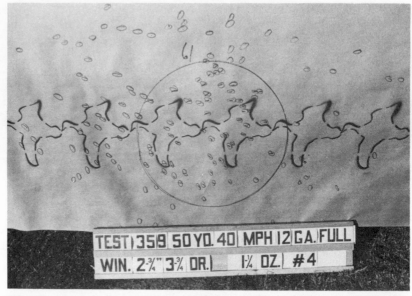

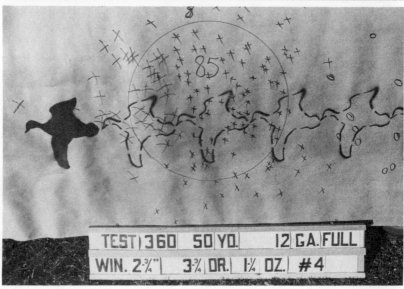

Increased stringing of non-buffered shot at 50 yards is shown with standard No. 4 high-velocity duck load which put 85 pellets (a percentage of 50 percent of its load) in the stationary pattern (test 360) after putting only 61 pellets at 40 miles per hour (test 359) for a 36-percent pattern. The loss in density was approximately 14 percent at 50 yards for this load, which had registered very little stringing density loss at 40 yards. These are actually quite good patterns for 50 yards; tests of the same loading in all three major brands fluctuated as low as 46 percent stationary at 40 yards.

Perhaps the soft-shot problem is an indication of the need for improvement in forcing-cone and choke design. The less traumatic the passage of a load through the barrel, the less shot deformation there will be. Some English guns made in the late 1800s with light loads of nonprotected, presumably quite soft shot were patterning better than modern guns handling loads with the highly touted shotcup wad. This is not the fault of the shotcup-wad system, which was a great breakthrough. But it does indicate the need for more study of barrel design and/or shot hardness and even means of shot production.

I have tested, for roundness and perfection, shot pellets from various loads made around the world. The better grades of Italian shotshells contained more perfect pellets than did most of American loads, one reason being they were formed with a different system than the drop-tower procedure (where molten lead is dropped from a tower through a sievelike device, which lets each drop of lead form in midair then be quenched into a ball as it falls into water).

There is, however, a limit to shot hardness obtainable with the tower procedure. Too much antimony in the shot will create nonround pellets with the tower. One method of helping common tower-produced shot form patterns with really high degrees of efficiency has been to plate them with copper or nickel or use buffering agents to cushion shot against each other within the shell.

The Italians have a method of making shot that can form lead pellets almost as perfectly as steel ball bearings are built in this country and apparently to a high degree of hardness. The Italian MB pigeon loads in size 7½ with nickel-plated extra-hard shot were the fastest lead shot loads chronographed in researching this book, some hitting 1,375 feet-per-second yet apparently doing so without excessive shot deformation, because they patterned beautifully.

With American shot and methods, acceleration of lead much over 1,300 feet-per-second often results in increased setback deformation which tends to open up patterns. But it must be noted that the best Italian loads are extremely expensive, and in no other country in the world can so many shooters afford basically good and dependable ammunition as can American shooters. Mass-production economies far outweigh the system's disadvantages.

Nor are hard shot and tight patterns the whole shotshell story. Soft-shot patterns give more margin for error by the shooter because they open up faster and larger. But such patterns also can give a margin for crippling if fired at game beyond their density capability. In this respect, hard shot have a very pronounced advantage; no matter what choke they are fired from, a decidedly shorter shot string is indicated on the moving target.

The modern plastic shotcup wad protects shot from barrel-scrubbing deformation, but not from ignition setback, forcing cone, and choke pressures. The "petals" of this Remington Power Piston (photographed with high-speed strobe) shows how air resistance is used to make wad drop back and permit shot to continue on their way. Note indentations in the plastic petals showing pressures exerted by the pellets being forced through forcing cone and choke. Hard pellets can resist such pressures; soft ones may deform, particularly rearward rows of pellets at the time of ignition. (Photo courtesy Remington Arms Co.)

My observation, after studying all the factors I can comprehend, is that a long shot string is simply evidence of inefficiency and a poorer load. Fringe pellets around the edge of the pattern may give the shooter some margin for error, but in the soft-shot loads these pellets tend to have less penetration than fringe pellets from a hard-shot load.

Deformed shot do not fly as straight as the rounder shot, and because they are not round and offer more air resistance they lose velocity and penetration power. Very often these deformed pellets will be the flyers around the edge of the pattern. I tested this by perfectly centering several shots into my penetration box, then carefully tabulating their average (mean) penetration. Then I purposely fringed the penetration box with edge-of-pattern pellets and checked their penetration. Some of the edge pellets from soft-shot loads had 10 to 15 percent less penetration than the less deformed center load pellets. With efficient hard-shot loads, there was little difference in penetration of edge pellets and center pellets.

Thus the argument that soft shot are an advantage to the shooter because they give him more margin for error must be looked at in terms of penetration and stringing as well as spread. The better error margin would be obtained with an efficient load in a more open choke. Modified choke, for example, gave essentially the same margin for error with hard shot as full choke with soft shot. But penetration of fringe pellets with the hard shot was better. In loads for quail, woodcock, or other game to be shot at short ranges (where penetration is no problem) soft shot are fine. Most shots are taken at going away birds in close cover and shot stringing is little problem at short range or at any range on a straightaway.

Many shooters would probably like to know which loads do contain soft shot, and would choose them if they had a choice. But in some parts of the country the belief persists that soft shot (such as the

A penetration box, located behind the pattern board, was used to compare penetration of central pellets of pattern with fringe pellets. Pattern sheet in front shows where pattern was centered, cardboard inserts numbered 1–25 and one inch apart measure how far pellets penetrated.

old drop shot) kill quail better than chilled shot. If hunters are a bit in the dark on their shotloads, they at least have a flashlight in the form of the reputation of the major companies, which is sure to be upheld in continuing improvement of loads. There is every indication that the shooter ultimately will have a clearcut choice between tight-patterning loads with hard shot (even though he may have to pay a premium for them) and soft-shot, quicker opening loads. There is already such a choice for 12-gauge upland shooters who know that in choosing a trapload they are buying tight-patterning, long-range ammunition, and in brush loads the opposite.

The handloader, however, is really in the dark. When he buys a sack of common bagged shot for reloading, he has no idea what the hardness will be. The term extra-hard shot, or derivations of that claim, can become a joke when one tests pellets even via the crude means of squeezing them with pliers.

Due to the high cost of factory ammunition, tens of thousands of shooters are now reloading. And many skeet and trapshooters use reloads for hunting as well as practice. Most good trapshooters use reloads for practice or 16-yard competition, but are reluctant to trust them at long yardage handicap because they believe their reloads are not as good as factory loads. That, of course, is true. But the big difference is not so much the reload but the shot within it. I have tested a number of brands of common bagged shot of various trade names and obtained patterns ranging from poor to fair. Then, on the same Ponsness-Warren reloader, with the identical powder charge, wad, and primer, I have substituted hard shot taken from factory traploads. Patterns jump dramatically. In fact, my handloads in some instances slightly out-patterned the factory loads from which the pellets came.

Most shooters probably would be unwilling to pay the price for hard factory shot, even it it were easily available. Winchester Lubaloy (copper coated) and Remington RXP shot are very hard and pattern well in reloads. But finding these hard pellets for reloading is not easy. Winchester will sell its Lubaloy pellets only in very large orders, which must come from a Winchester distributor. The only Remington RXP shot available to reloaders is No. 8½. Spokesmen for both companies said that so far there has been little demand for their premium shot. Federal, which uses very hard shot in its traploads and pigeon loads, presently offers no shot at all for the reloading market. Perhaps if enough reloaders request it, all of the companies someday can be convinced to sell hard shot through their normal retail outlets. Or perhaps reloading component firms will see the light and begin making some high-antimony shot. At present, however, few reloaders would pay the price for it; they'll buy the cheapest reloading shot they can find, then spend money working on barrels, wads, powders, etc. trying

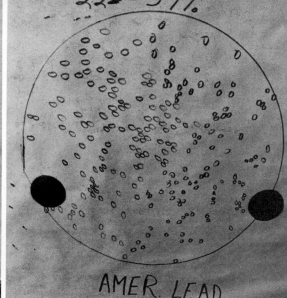

Left:

Shot pellets robbed from Winchester factory trapload, and reloaded in author's Ponsness-Warren machine (3-dram load Red Dot powder, RXP wad) produced beautiful patterns in once-fired Double A hulls. This one was better than some factory loads from the box the shot came from.

Right:

Common bagged shot, this from one of the best brands, produced much less dense patterns than hard factory shot when loaded with precisely the same powder, wad, and hull. Reloaders who blame their handloads for poor long-range performance should investigate shot hardness.

to get better patterns. They also, of course, then shoot factory loads in competition which further runs up the bill. A great deal of this, I believe, is the average shooter's lack of understanding of the importance of hard shot. But he can certainly satisfy himself about it in a hurry by making the same tests I did. Rob a few shot from a factory load, and run it through your reloader. You may not duplicate factory load efficiency, but you'll greatly improve the pattern over soft bagged shot.

Copper-plated shot of the less-expensive bagged variety (not Lubaloy) is very pretty to look at, but in my tests seemed to produce little or no better patterns than non-plated shot. The reason perhaps is that for shot plating to make much difference, the lead beneath it must be hard; simply putting a thin coat of copper over a soft pellet doesn't help it much.

Skeet shooters can get by with the cheapest of shot in the 12 gauge and 20 gauge because the soft shot will open up patterns nicely, and even though deformed will be adequate for breaking clay targets. But this is not the case with the smaller sizes, particularly the .410.

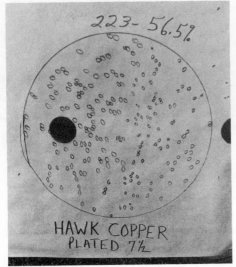

Copper plating does not seem to help patterning appreciably, unless the pellet beneath the plating is sufficiently hard. This, too, is a pattern from the same full-choke barrel that produced nearly 85 percent patterns from extra hard shot.

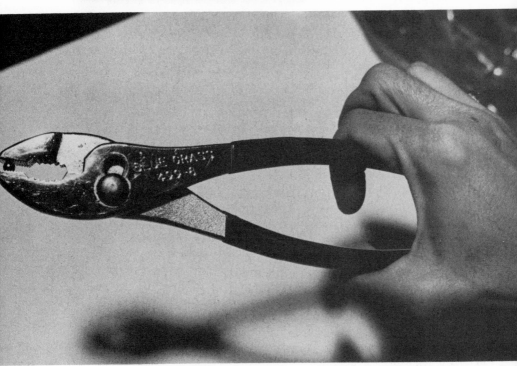

A crude but surprisingly revealing method of testing shot hardness is to squeeze the lead pellet with pliers, using only thumb and forefinger for sensitivity. Soft shot will flatten easily; good shot may require two fingers. Use hard shot from factory traploads for comparison.

With that little gun, consistent patterning is critical, and hard shot pattern most consistently.

Try robbing a few shot from No. 8½ traploads, or even No. 8 traploads, and load a few .410 rounds with them. You will not have as many shot in the load as with soft 9's, but the distribution will be more even, fewer pellets will be required to smoke targets, and on windy days you'll suffer less wind drift and pattern disruption. Hard shot .410 handloads in a 3-inch case are excellent in the field, better usually than factory loads which have been loaded with relatively soft shot.

Much can be accomplished by matching shot hardness, size, and quality to the specific job to be done. There is considerable evidence that with the present state of the art of shotshell manufacture, coupled with potential improvements in barrel boring, forcing cone and choke angle improvements, it may ultimately be possible to select the pattern desired merely by choosing the proper shell. At the time of my tests, any hunter could have (with his ordinary full-choke barrel) better than 20 percent more pattern density and quite comparable penetration at 40 yards by using a 3¼-dram, 1¼-ounce pigeon load rather than the heavier-recoiling 3¾-dram 12-gauge high-velocity load. Tests of Federal and Winchester hard-shot pigeon loads on still and moving targets confirmed the difference in long-range efficiency, and Remington's 3¼ x 1⅛ ounce international trapload with nickel shot outpatterned the 3¾ x 1¼ standard high-brass hunting load.

But until the shooter is willing to test his patterns, no matter what shell or choke he uses, he is simply firing a shot in the dark.

14

EFFECTS OF WIND AND WEATHER UPON SHOTSHELL PERFORMANCE

One of the finest wingshots I ever watched was an old-timer who had never seen a clay target and who cleaned his pumpgun on the same basis he took baths—once a season, whether needed or not. He knew nothing of ballistics in the written sense, but in his hands a gun became a living thing, reading the myriad angles, speeds, and directional changes of birds in the wind as easily as ballisticians read books.

Someone once wanted to bet that old-timer that by picking his shots he would kill 25 straight ducks. (The limit was 10 in those days, but the nearest game warden was more interested in dominos.) "Nope," the old man said, "you'd likely lose your money. I might make it on a still day, but on one of them sticky windy days I'd do good to get 20 out of a box. And real cold days is bad, too," he added. "A man's shells get cold and lose power."

Everybody laughed and that was that. But somehow I got the idea he wasn't joking about wind or weather.

Some years later I noticed most of the old-timers at European-style pigeon competition (box birds) would fire two shots into the ground each time before they called for the first bird. One of them, who had sort of taken me under his wing, explained why. "With most of us it's just insurance to see the gun is shooting, the safety isn't on, and to sort of get ourselves into gear before making a shot that could either win or lose the shoot. But by trying to center the pattern on something out there on the ground, the impact will show how much the wind is drifting the shot load. Those shots also warm up the barrels a little."

That old gentleman kept his gun and shells inside the clubhouse (for warmth) between rounds, and he firmly believed there was a difference between a cold shell and a warm one. Research now shows those old-timers knew what they were talking about. In 1973, John Madson and Ed Kozicky conducted tests of shotshell efficiency on 2,400 mallard ducks at Nilo Farms, Illinois. They found that the wind drift of the shot pellets was so severe at the longer ranges that they simply couldn't conduct comprehensive tests when the wind velocity was above 10 miles an hour, because they couldn't be absolutely sure of centering the ducks. This was true even with the duck strapped into a harness and the shotgun in a machine rest in perfect alignment with target.

I asked Ed Lowry, who worked on both the U.S. Fish & Wildlife Service's tests on mallards at Patuxent, Maryland, and the Nilo test afterwards, to compute for me some figures on wind drift for both lead and steel shot loads at ranges where such things count most—from 40 to 60 yards. He said that No. 4 lead pellets, the most common size used by U.S. duck hunters, will be moved 10 inches at 40 yards by a 14.5 mph crosswind, and No. 6 lead pellets will be moved 11.1 inches at that distance. At 60 yards, wind drift really becomes a problem, with No. 4's being moved nearly two feet (22.5 inches) and No. 6's more than two feet (25.4 inches). Smaller pellets would be moved even more. One reason why handicap trapshooters so often use No. 7½ rather than No. 8 shot at long yardage is that the larger pellets suffer slightly less wind drift.

Steel shot, due to its lower sectional density, is moved even more than lead. No. 4 steel (which compares in number of pellets per ounce and also in retained energy with No. 6 lead) is drifted 12.7 inches at 40 yards. At 60 yards, No. 4 steel pellets are moved 28.8 inches. No. 2 steel, which compares in pellet numbers and energy to No. 4 lead, is moved 11.4 inches at 40 yards and 25.8 inches at 60 yards. All of these distances are computed for a 14½ mile crosswind at 90°. There is a table at the end of the chapter giving distances for a 10-mile wind and comparing No. 4 lead and steel shot drift.

So how does a hunter compensate for wind drift on those strong-blowing days when waterfowl hunting is likely to be best? It is not quite so bad as it might seem, because wind is working on the bird as well as the shot load. For example, what might seem to be a straight-away or straight incomer is likely to be a sliding bird being drifted to some extent sideways by the wind, and he may in fact be sliding more than the shotload is drifting. No big problem here.

The downwind bird is obviously moving much faster than normal, so any drift of the load in the direction he is going is a help rather than hindrance.

The big problem is with birds flying into the wind. They may seem to be barely moving, and the shooter's tendency is to provide very little forward allowance. But the shot load is being drifted one way and the bird is flying the other. Here it is imperative to remember that although the bird's ground speed is slow, his air speed is probably not. Additional forward allowance should be given. It's difficult to do, but I've found it helps me to concentrate on trying to lead one of those slow-moving upwind birds about the same as I would as if he were flying at normal speed at that yardage. This helps compensate for drift of the shot load, but it's tricky because less compensation is required at close range than long range.

There is no formula for this, only experience.

There are, however, formulas for computing the difference in efficiency in shotshells at various temperatures. (This is shown in a table at the end of this chapter.) The differences may not seem to be much between 70° and 40° below zero, but in between there is quite a bit of difference in penetration and also a great deal of difference in patterning that is not shown in the table. For example, when lead and steel loads were first compared at Patuxent, Maryland, the steel load used contained only 1 ounce of shot, the same weight as in a standard 20-gauge lead load. Yet it killed ducks far better than ballisticians had expected it would (more about this in another chapter).

When similar tests were made later at Nilo, there was considerable questioning as to why the new and improved 1⅛-ounce 12-gauge load of steel shot did not perform significantly better than the 1-ounce load used at Patuxent. The mystery was merely that there was a 30° difference in temperature (Nilo was conducted in colder weather) and that difference translated into the equalization of a 1-ounce lead, and one with 1⅛ ounces of shot in terms of mallard mortality.

The difference, of course, applies to lead pellets as well. A high velocity 12-gauge No. 6 lead pellet at 50 yards will penetrate 1.81 inches (into 20 percent gelatin) at 50 yards at 70°, but only .94 inches at minus 40°. Since penetration of lead 6's (or steel 4's) becomes a critical factor at 50 yards, a difference of nearly 1 inch in penetration could mean the difference in killing or crippling with either lead or steel. Thus, for colder weather, the shooter would seem better off with larger shot. There is another reason for shooting big shot in cold weather; waterfowl that come through late in the migration are heavier feathered and more difficult to penetrate than early birds, and big shot wind-drift less in the howling winds that late-migrating birds often ride south.

Nominal Shotshell Performance at Varying Temperatures

SHOTSHELL LOAD	RANGE TEMP.	MUZZLE VEL. (ft./sec.)	ENERGY/PELLET (ft.lbs.) AT			PELLET PENETRATION (in.) INTO 20% GELATIN AT		
			30 YDS.	40 YDS.	50 YDS.	30 YDS.	40 YDS.	50 YDS.
12 Ga. High Velocity								
3¾ x 1¼ #6	70°F	1330	2.63	2.01	1.58	3.41	2.47	1.81
	-40°F	1240	1.83	1.35	1.00	2.19	1.47	0.94
3¾ x 1¼ #4	70°F	1330	4.77	3.71	2.97	4.59	3.44	2.64
	-40°F	1240	3.34	2.54	1.95	3.04	2.28	1.54
12 Ga. Standard Velocity								
3¼ x 1⅛ #8	70°F	1255	1.20	0.91	0.69	2.14	1.48	0.98
	-40°F	1180	0.83	0.59	0.42	1.30	0.76	0.37
20 Ga. High Velocity								
2¾ x 1 #6	70°F	1220	2.37	1.84	1.45	3.01	2.21	1.62
	-40°F	1125	1.61	1.19	0.88	1.86	1.22	0.75

Courtesy Winchester-Western

Effect of Wind on Shot Clouds
(Nilo Shotshell Efficiency Test, 1972–73)

FOR 90° WIND AT 10 M.P.H.

	40 YDS	50 YDS.	60 YDS.	70 YDS.	80 YDS.
#4 Steel	8.36″	13.21″	19.28″	26.80″	35.90″
#4 Lead	6.56″	10.38″	15.06″	20.71″	27.47″

Courtesy Winchester-Western

Patterns are also affected by cold and by altitude. As any airplane pilot knows, cold air is dense and warm air is thin. The resistance and/or density of air is what opens up a shotgun pattern; if one could shoot test patterns in a vacuum, a cylinder bore should give full-choke performance.

Thus, patterns will tend to be more open, and penetrate less, in very cold weather.

Patterns will tend to be tighter, and penetrate farther at high altitude because they are encountering less atmospheric resistance.

A gun that throws modified patterns at sea level may throw full-choke patterns at Denver, Colorado, or Mexico City.

All of which should provide some wonderful alibis for missing game. But in providing these, I must take away one. Like most shooters I had always believed that a crosswind would greatly disrupt a pattern, causing it to be full of holes. But according to Ed Lowry, this is not so much the case as might be assumed. "A crosswind does not disrupt a pattern in any way," he wrote me, "it just moves it over."

I cannot quarrel with a man of Lowry's credentials, but I have tested a great many patterns in South Texas wind and found some lowering of efficiency, particularly with steel shot beyond 50 yards. But I indeed failed to find any donut holes or other old wives' tales—and there goes another good excuse.

15

VELOCITY AND PENETRATION

Despite all advances in modern shotshell technology, a high percentage of hunters harbor antiquated notions about killing power contrary to capabilities of their cartridges. Two common misbeliefs are that small shot penetrate better than large, and that high-velocity loads are required for long-range penetration. Another is that soft shot kills better because it expands on impact and produces more shock to the bird.

Many believe magnums have more velocity and killing power per pellet than ordinary loads. This is the case with rifle magnums, which do as a rule offer added velocity and energy, but in shotguns, the term magnum merely means a heavier payload of shot.

The average muzzle velocity of the heaviest 12-gauge magnum load of 1⅞ ounces of shot is approximately 1,200 feet-per-second, or roughly 100 feet-per-second *slower* than the standard high-brass or high-velocity 12-gauge load with 1¼ ounces of shot. The magnum shotload would create dangerous pressures if moved at the same speed as the lighter load, and thus slow-burning powder and less violent acceleration of the load is required.

This is simple stuff, but quite sophisticated shooters persist in believing the old soft-shot theory. Here again we have what is basically a rifle complex. A full metal-jacketed rifle bullet will go through a game animal inflicting very minor damage, while a softer expanding-point bullet creates great shock. Thus, it is often believed that shotgun pel-

In preparing this study, the author fired velocity and penetration tests of virtually every gauge and U.S. shot load comparing standard and magnum loads, long and short barrels, 2¾- and 3-inch chambers.

lets should behave the same way. But shotgun pellets are round rather than bullet shaped; they move at much slower speeds than rifle bullets, slow down much faster due to atmospheric resistance, and are much lighter (buckshot excepted, obviously).

Thus the problem of shotgun pellets passing completely through the bird and wasting their energy in the air (as might a full-jacketed rifle bullet) is not the problem at all. At the range a shotgun pellet is likely to pass completely through a bird (provided the reasonably correct shot size for the bird is used), there is almost certain to be a sufficiently dense pattern and enough shock created by the pellets to kill the bird. The real problem with shotgun killing power is in delivering at a distance the full kinetic energy of pellets deeply enough to affect vital organs. The most important factors in achieving this are getting the pellet to the bird in a round and non-deformed condition, so that it arrives with full energy without having lost its punch fighting added atmospheric resistance created by flat spots or poor shape. Then the problem is retaining sufficient roundness for the pellet to penetrate most efficiently without excessive flattening at impact. The more the pellet flattens, the more resistance it offers against further penetration. It does little good to deliver shock to the feathers or skin of a bird.

I am convinced the old idea of soft shot shocking more originated with close-range hunters, probably quail hunters, who may indeed have bagged more game with old drop shot than with modern chilled shot. But the reason was probably not shocking power, but pattern spread. As soft shot deform, they open up larger patterns quicker, and thus can be an advantage in close-range quail hunting where almost any choke is too much choke.

Inside of 25 yards, the flattening effect of soft shot may indeed offer more shock to a thin-skinned bird such as a quail because at that distance adequate penetration is all but assured, regardless. But carrying that theory out to more distant yardages and tougher birds is a mistake.

Perhaps the most convincing demonstration of penetration significance comes from the most precise testing ground in the world, the competitive live-pigeon rings of Europe. More than 5,000 pigeons are shot at every weekend on the European pigeon circuit, with regular shoots every weekend in Spain or Italy. In Mexico, shooting goes on virtually year around.

Since shooters fire from carefully measured yardages, and birds must fly only 17½ yards from their point of release to reach the boundary fence (past which they are considered missed whether dead or not) it is obvious that much can be learned on the subject of which sort of shot instantly kill birds from various yardages.

If soft shot killed quicker and more efficiently, be assured that the live-pigeon professionals—particularly the Italians—would have created the softest shot on earth. Instead, most of the top professionals use the hardest shot they can find: extra-hard, nickel-plated lead. They may use softer lead to open up patterns at very close yardage (25 meters, or about 27 yards), but most stay with the hard nickel for their second or clincher shots. At yardages beyond 27 meters (just under 30 yards) most shoot nothing but nickel.

In 1976, after carefully studying the killing effectiveness of various loads, Winchester developed a new super pigeon load in No. 7½ and No. 8 shot. The chief characteristics of it were added velocity (1,265 feet-per-second compared to their old load at 1,194) and extra hardened shot that patterned 82 percent at 40 yards from a 30-inch barrel Perazzi, and 81 percent from a Model 12 Winchester—an increase of 11.6 percent over the previous Winchester pigeon load. Federal already had a hard-shot pigeon load in the same shot size, and Remington has extra-hard nickel-plated shot in 3¼ x 1¼ loads that some company employees have been using in the field for years. The Remington load is not catalog listed, but is available on special order.

There is no doubt the arms industry is now fully aware of the value of hard shot, and shooters smart enough to take advantage of some of the improved loads showing up on the market—rather than trying to save a few cents on cheaper shells—should observe considerable improvement in their long-range killing capability on anything from doves to geese. Some low-brass pigeon loads in size 7½ with hard shot actually cost less than high-brass loads, yet they pattern and penetrate better at long range because most high-velocity loads today contain softer shot.

This brings up another long-standing idea of shooters which is partly correct and partly untrue, the contention that adding velocity opens patterns and that reducing velocity tightens them. As a rule of thumb this idea is true. But it is not necessarily the velocity that makes the difference, it is the shot deformation. If shot are sufficiently hard to resist deformation at the higher pressures of high velocity, then they pattern about as well as the same shot at lower velocity. I tested this with the highest velocity loads I have ever put through a gun barrel and with the hardest shot of them all—steel.

Canadian Industries (CIL) made some experimental loads of steel shot several years ago apparently with the intent of increasing penetration by increasing velocity. To be able to do this with reasonable pressures, they loaded a very hot powder charge behind a light load of 1 ounce of shot (12 gauge) and obtained velocities said to be over 1,500 feet-per-second. I chronographed them at 1,450 feet-per-second, and thoroughly expected to see blown patterns with such velocity.

Instead those little loads patterned consistently better than 80 percent.

There is undoubtedly a slight pattern-opening effect from extreme velocity even with steel shot, but it is nothing like that experienced with lead. I tested some high-velocity lead hunting loads containing No. 7½ shot that were about as hard as most hunting loads produced in 1975 and early 76 and got 40-yard patterns around 68 percent from a full-choke Perazzi. With that same gun, but the shot replaced by extra-hard, high-antimony shot, the pattern jumped to 80 percent. The velocity was still there; the difference had been deformation.

I tested two basic loads, a 3¼ x 1¼ Federal pigeon load against a 3¾ x 1¼ Federal Hi-Power load, for penetration at various yardages. The high velocity (which, remember, had relatively soft shot) penetrated slightly farther than the low brass at 40 yards. But the same shells at 50 yards showed slightly less penetration than the low-brass, lower-velocity pigeon load.

Here again I am convinced the main difference was deformation. The high-velocity loads containing softer shot produced less-round pellets, and by 50 yards, atmospheric resistance had reduced many of them to less velocity than the harder, rounder pellets launched at lower velocity by the low-brass shell. Also, the faster an object is

Ultra-high-velocity steel shot load (CIL) pushed the Oehler chronograph to 1,452 feet-per-second with this shot, yet patterned 83 percent. Note tunnel through which shots are fired to be measured electronically.

pushed against atmospheric resistance, the proportionately faster it is slowed down by same. To take that one to the extreme, you can easily push your hand beneath the water in a swimming pool. But if you slap hard enough, the water will offer greatly increased resistance.

At very long ranges, the retained energy of pellets is much the same whether they were launched at 1,200 or 1,300 feet-per-second. The latest SAAMI tables of shotshell characteristics show that a No. 4 lead pellet launched from a 12-gauge full-choke barrel at a muzzle velocity of 1,330 fps retains 2.49 foot-pounds of energy at 60 yards. The same size pellet launched at 1,235 fps retains 2.32. Thus, nearly 100 feet-per-second at the muzzle is translated into only .17 foot-pounds of energy difference at 60 yards.

For bird shooters contemplating the advantages of high brass over low brass, a No. 7½ pellet launched at 1,330 feet-per-second (according to the new SAAMI tables) retains 1.23 foot-pounds of energy at 40 yards. The same pellet launched at 1,240 fps (approximately the speed of the new low-brass pigeon loads) retains 1.14 fps, or a difference of only .09 foot-pounds, a difference so slight I doubt a bird would know the difference. The comparison at 50 yards is .93 foot-pounds for the high velocity and .89 for the low brass, the higher velocity still retaining slightly more energy.

So how could I have obtained better penetration from low-brass pigeon loads at 50 yards?

High-velocity 7½'s penetrated an average of 13 to 14 cardboard squares in the penetration box at 40 yards, but dropped to an average of 7-card penetration at 50 yards. The low-brass pigeon load 7½'s had slightly less penetration at 40, but penetrated 8 to 9 cards at 50 yards, outperforming the high velocity at longer yardage by about 6 percent.

The difference was in shot hardness. The SAAMI tables were computed for shot of average hardness, approximately the same in high- or low-velocity loads. As stated earlier, most high-velocity hunting loads at the time of this writing contained relatively soft shot, while the special pigeon loads and trap loads contained hard shot.

Perhaps those retained energy figures will help explain to those who favor 7½'s for ducks why virtually every scientific test made on live ducks indicates 4's kill farther and cleaner. The retained energy difference of a No. 4 shot at 50 yards is 3.11 foot-pounds while a 7½ shot fired at the same high velocity (1,330 feet-per-second) retains only .93 foot-pounds. Obviously a very few hits with 4's at 50 yards will put more energy into the bird than a swarm of 7½'s.

Certainly it is also important where hits are made, and the odds are better that the larger numbers of smaller shot find a vital area. But if they do not penetrate sufficiently, and this is indicated in the tests that have been done, then they become vital-area cripplers rather than killers.

The old question of velocity and penetration relative to barrel length continues to be debated, but isn't really worth all the time spent on it. With the slow-burning powders associated with magnum loads there is a definite advantage in a long barrel, although 30 inches is plenty. As load weights are decreased, powder-burning rates can be

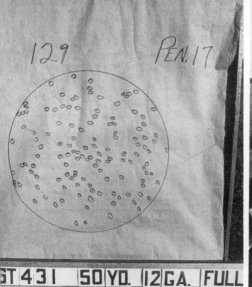

Left:
An excellent example of even patterning plus 17-card (duck-killing) penetration was this No. 6 lead load. High-velocity 6's of all brands in lead averaged 16-card penetration, about the same as No. 4 steel.

Right:
New Remington steel goose loads in No. 1 shot penetrated 100 percent of cards at 50 yards, dropped to a pattern count of 29 and penetration of 23 cards at 60 yards.

increased and short barrels become more proportionately effective. With light field loads, a 26-inch barrel is little different than a 28- or 30-inch barrel.

The belief that a 3-inch chamber reduces velocities and power of the 2¾-inch shells used in it seems to be more fable than fact, although in some guns the 3-inch chambers may pattern worse (or better) than in standard chamber. I've seen it work both ways. There is more difference in velocity between an improved-cylinder choke and full choke (the full choke has slightly more) than between the 3-inch and 2¾-inch chamber. None of these velocities are sufficient to matter much downrange.

To try and obtain a few figures for some other commonly asked questions, I made a number of tests on an Oehler chronograph with each load tested in strings of ten shots each. Since factory lots and brands vary considerably in velocities, these can be taken only as general indications.

The difference in velocity between a 3-inch 20-gauge magnum, with 1¼ ounces of shot and the same weight load in a high-brass 12

At 60 yards, Federal's No. 1 steel goose load showed very dense center, good penetration.

gauge was an average of 93 feet-per-second less velocity by the 20. The velocity loss from cutting back a 28-inch barrel to 22 inches was 59 feet-per-second, a part of this being the difference in choke. When the barrel was cut back, choke acceleration was lost because the barrel became a true cylinder. Returning the 22-inch barrel to full choke (with a Baker screw-pin .700 tube) added 17 feet-per-second, making the actual net difference in the short barrel 42 fps. The difference in velocity with standard magnum cartridges from a 30-inch barrel and a 28-inch barrel was 12 feet-per-second in favor of the longer barrel.

Tests of economy high-base loads against premium high-velocity loads revealed the premium loads had approximately 50 feet-per-second more velocity at the muzzle.

Contrary to widespread belief that tight chokes create more drag, and thus have slightly less velocity and penetration than open chokes, full-choke barrels consistently produced the highest velocity in every gauge and load tested although differences were slight.

A general conclusion based upon extensive penetration tests from 30 to 60 yards indicates the matter of muzzle velocities of shotshell loads is overrated, there being little difference in penetration (even with as much as 100 fps difference at muzzle) observed at the longer ranges where penetration becomes a problem.

16

STOCK
ANSWERS

Nobody bugs an expert rifleman because he has adjustable sights on his target rifle and maybe an adjustable scope on his hunting rifle. But for some odd reason, the shotgunner is considered a nitpicker if he tries to adjust his point of impact by varying his own rear sight, his stock.

Most of the top shooters work on their stocks until they arrive at the right combination. Trapshooters and live-pigeon shooters, both of whom compete for considerable sums of money, probably use up more bunion pads and moleskin (to build up stock combs) than do people with podiatry problems.

Most of the attention given shotgun stocks by hunters who don't bother with the competitive sports relates to ladies or youngsters—it is traditional to cut off stocks that seem too long for their shorter arms. Unfortunately, this is not so simple as it seems, because when a stock is shortened, it is also slightly reduced in drop; that is, the sight picture is raised slightly and so is the elevation.

Looking at a stock you wouldn't really believe that, because it seems to slope upwards out toward the end. But if you measure it on a flat surface, you'll find that the drop at the heel (end of stock) is more than the drop at the comb on a common field stock. And although it doesn't look it, the longer the stock is made (through addition of recoil pad or spacers) the more drop it develops and the slightly lower it should shoot. This means a great many youngsters and ladies with cut-off stocks have, in effect, high-shooting stocks.

The most overlooked of all are the heavyset man and the buxom lady. (Gun fitting among run-of-the-mill gunsmiths has advanced just about as far as tailoring of clothing would have come had it stopped with the sleeves.)

It is easy to take one look at a long-armed, lantern-jawed type with a neck like a whooping crane and deduce he needs a longer stock. But a heavyset gent with normal-length sleeves is told he's fine if the butt of the gun reaches somewhere in the general vicinity of his elbow when he grasps the pistol grip.

Trouble is that pectoral muscles (or ladies' bosoms) have nothing to do with elbows. And when a heavy-chested person mounts a shotgun, several problems can arise. One is that due to the pectoral muscle and thickness of flesh of the shoulder pocket, the stock may be slightly too long—at least in terms of arm-length measurement. But more likely to be a problem is the toe (bottom) of the stock digging into the pectoral muscle when the shooter attempts to swing (if right-handed) to the right or vice versa if left-handed. If the toe of the stock digs in and binds the shooter's swing, several more things happen. One is that the swing is slowed or stopped, another is that the gun may be twisted or canted, and yet another is that ladies in particular can get bad bruises from recoil in an area where ladies do not need bruises.

One of the mysteries of life is why shotgun stocks and the recoil pads that fit them continue to be made straight up and down when the human shoulder (or at least the pocket in which it accommodates the gun) slants at a distinct angle. It's an easy mystery to solve in economics; the builder of the gun doesn't know if the prospective shooter is right- or left-handed, and probably few shooters have complained much about it, anyway.

That was once the gun manufacturers' answer to left-handed bolt-action rifles and autoloaders. But shooters eventually did complain, and we now have right- and left-handed bolt-action rifles, right- and left-handed autoloading shotguns, and a few shotguns that come with stocks cast off for right-handed shooters. Yet this most important matter of cast off at toe continues to be largely ignored in the U.S., thereby perhaps bruising many a beautiful lady. Presumably fewer European ladies get bruised, because cast-at-toe is very common there.

What I'm hoping is that some enterprising builder of rubber recoil pads will come out with right- or left-hand models in which the base of the pad is flat to fit the gunstock, but the area that meets the shooter's shoulder is designed to provide relief through some sort of twisted shape that would at least get that digging toe out of one's pectorals. I've been plagued with that problem all my life, and have generally solved it by grinding away some of the toe of the recoil pad un-

The toe of this stock has been cast off to fit the natural curve of the shoulder pocket. The adjustment was achieved in this case with an adjustable Morgan Recoil Pad. It can also be done by offsetting an ordinary recoil pad, drilling new holes for the screws which secure the pad so that the stock toe is turned outward slightly. Slender shooters may have no need for this, but heavy chested shooters may find it greatly helps reduce canting on angle shots and lets the gun seat itself into the shoulder pocket more securely.

til it feels better. Another and perhaps more practical way, although it is more obvious in appearance, is to have a gunsmith offset the screw holes that attach the recoil pad so that the pad is angled more in line with the shoulder. This will give you a crooked-looking recoil pad, but most likely a straighter shooting gun.

There is an adjustable recoil pad commonly used by trapshooters called the Morgan Pad that can usually be found in gunshops catering to trapshooters. But the Morgan Pad is primarily designed to be moved up or down, not sideways, and getting much of an angle out of it (that will stay put) requires tightening the main adjustment screw with quite a bit of pressure. Probably the easiest way to get relief from toe digging is to have a gunsmith grind off the offending area of your rubber recoil pad until the gun feels and fits better.

Another item that often helps the heavy-chested man or buxom lady is a bit more downpitch, changing the vertical angle of the butt plate as it meets the shoulder. This can be very nearly as important as the lateral twist to get a good cast-at-toe fit. In general, downpitch is most needed by heavy-chested shooters or by those who wish the gun to come up into firing position pointed a little lower. By the same token, so-called zero pitch or even its extension, reverse pitch, is supposed to make a gun fit better for high-rising targets (such as at trap-shooting) and some say it reduces muzzle jump for them.

It is easy to experiment and see if pitch changes can make your gun fit better.

To increase downpitch, back out the screws holding the recoil pad. At the heel (top of the stock) insert several cardboard shims

Closeup of the rear of a Morgan Adjustable Pad shows interlocking metal "teeth" that permit the pad to be moved up or down (to raise or lower drop at heel) or cocked sideways (to provide cast at toe). The "cracks" in the pad are knife cuts made by the author to prevent the pad from slipping downward between shots. When pressure is exerted by the shooter's head downward against the stock, the slits in the rubber spread apart slightly to grip and hold. This can be important at international-style trapshooting, or live-pigeon competition, when shots are sometimes fired at steep upward angles with the shooter locked hard into the gun.

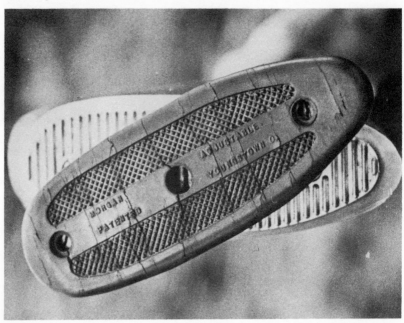

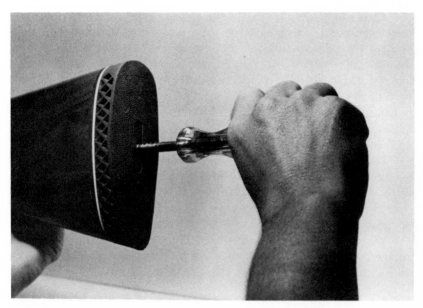

The Perazzi system of instantly interchangeable stocks makes one gun serve any number of purposes, from field shooting to competition, yet properly stocked for each. The stock-changing tool, an elongated hex-head screwdriver, inserts into an opening in the recoil pad. The stock can be unscrewed, and another replaced, in a matter of minutes.

(shotgun shell box tops make fine shims) and then tighten the screws again. This will reduce gouging of the toe of the stock by changing the angle at which it meets your shoulder. To reduce downpitch, or obtain zero or reverse pitch, do the same thing except at the toe or bottom end of the pad. If you find with your cardboard shims that one or the other makes the gun feel or shoot better, a gunsmith can make the job permanent. Just be sure to leave your shims in place so he can see by how much to change the angle. If pitch change doesn't help, remove the shims and you haven't hurt a thing.

The easiest way to experiment with stocks, other than with a professional try gun, is to beg, borrow, or buy a Perazzi. This Italian over-under offers instant interchangeability of stocks without the trouble of removing the recoil pad. The Perazzi has a small hole in the recoil pad (which usually cannot be seen since it is closed over by the resilient rubber butt plate of the recoil pad) and all the shooter must do to change stocks is insert a slender tool that looks like a hex-head screwdriver. The stock is unscrewed and another replaces it in a matter of minutes.

Changing stocks in this manner permits the use of one over-under shotgun for anything from field hunting to trapshooting and is particularly handy for shooters who must wear a lot of heavy clothing during cold weather (and thus need a shorter stock then). It is also handy for trapshooters who like a relatively flat shooting stock for 16-yard singles or doubles, but who want more elevation for long-yardage handicap shooting. Long-yardage handicap targets are broken at distances around 50 yards, and at that yardage the shot load starts to drop some, hence the need for more elevation.

For me the Perazzi interchangeable stocks have offered a chance to check all sorts of stocks on the same gun, a much more accurate method of determining what works best for which shooting situation than changing the whole gun. I now have about 15 stocks that fit one or more of my Perazzis (most will interchange with all of them) and I've tried straight grip (English style), pistol grip, short, long, crooked, straight, Monte Carlo, classic, rollover comb, Etchen grip—you name it,

Major trap and skeet shoots attract gunsmiths and gun dealers who offer custom, fancy, or spare stocks of various dimensions, some of which are usually available for testing on the practice range. At the Del Webb Handicap in Las Vegas pictured here, hunters showed up among the trapshooters searching for bargains in gun work and stocks.

Most shooters, with a little practice, can handle a stock longer than they believe they can, and usually attain more precise shooting once they master it. This candidate is being measured for a Pederson Custom Gun with one of that firm's adjustable try guns.

just about every sort of shotgun stock there is. Some of my stocks contain one Edwards Recoil Reducer and some have two; some have the heel rounded off (to reduce friction against clothing for fast mounting) and several are trap stocks with combs lowered to field or skeet dimensions (about 1½ inches at comb) to determine if the straight heel and low comb reduce recoil while helping prevent over-shooting at skeet or normal field shooting. I think they do.

From all these experiments, many of which have been tested on friends, have come some indications of perhaps general interest. One is that most shooters can handle a stock a little longer than they believe they can, provided they practice mounting it. I believe that with the slightly longer stock, one tends to stay with the gun a bit better (at least I do) and particularly to be more precise at long-range work such as pass-shooting waterfowl or doves. It is perhaps supportive of that statement that trapshooters, who must be the most precise of all shot-gun shooters, normally use considerable longer stocks than are usual for ordinary field guns. Two of the deadliest trapshooters I have known, All-Americans Larry Gravestock and Britt Robinson, both use stocks of around 15½ inches length of pull, which is about 1½ inches longer than the ordinary off-the-shelf hunting gun.

That doesn't mean I recommend such an elongated handle for a hunting gun, but it does lend some credence that a slightly longer stock helps keep the shooter down on his gun a little more than one that is too short for him.

For fast-mounting situations, such as close-cover grouse, quail, or woodcock, on the other hand, I commonly use shorter stocks, because they mount a bit faster and are less likely to hang up on clothing when the shooter must suddenly shoulder the gun from some odd angle in a briar thicket. I fully realize that students of Churchill and similar shooting schools may argue that if properly pushed out and mounted, a long stock can be brought quite swiftly to the shoulder. But in dense thicket things are not always completely cricket, and I like one I can get to my shoulder somehow before the bird is gone.

If you're a one-gun owner (and if so you must by now be thoroughly confused with what length of stock I am trying to say you should have) an inexpensive way around the problem is to make the stock the shortest length you think you'll need in heavy cover. (For an average-sized man the 14-inch factory length is really quite close to correct.) Then, for long-range pass-shooting of doves in warm weather,

Close-up of a try stock shows adjustments for comb height and length. Many custom stock makers now have such devices and the buyer can select the dimensions that feel best to him. With the experienced shooter, just as the experienced buyer of clothes, personal preference is important. The fitter cannot know how the fit feels, only how it looks.

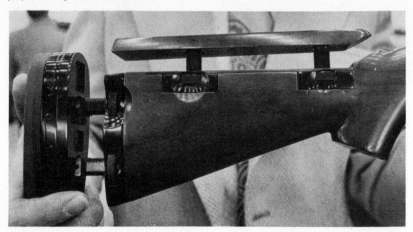

or maybe just to experiment anytime, slip on one of those little rubber stock boots that will lengthen the stock roughly a half inch. If that isn't long enough, or you want to experiment more, a few of our wonderfully available cardboard shims from the top of your favorite box of shotshells can be put into the boot, providing up to another quarter inch or so of length. This is a temporary thing, meant only to let you experiment with whether you can shoot a long or a short stock better. Once you decide, a gunsmith can, if you wish, lengthen the stock by adding spacers.

Those rubber boots for shotguns are quite handy. In cold weather, when you're wearing a lot of clothes, you take the thing off and the gun fits better. Otherwise you may want it on. It's just as soft as, but cheaper than, a recoil pad.

One of the oldest arguments in shotgun stock design is the advantage, or lack of it, of the so-called English straight grip—that sleek, streamlined beauty that makes almost any shotgun look better. Some U.S. shooters make a joke of the English stock, saying it puts wrist and arm in a bind, robs the trigger hand of control of the gun, etc. Yet if you read such English gun authorities as Burrard, Gough Thomas, and Churchill, you'll begin to believe the English stock is the only one ever carved worth carrying.

I believe the U.S., and English ideas both have sound basis; the big difference is in the shooting styles with which they are used. I have four Perazzi stocks that have had their pistol grips removed, converting them to English style. This can be done with relative ease on any gun by anyone who can work with wood. I've done several "temporary" jobs myself to see if I liked the feel of the stock before going to the expense of having it checkered and refinished.

What I've found is that all those European live-bird professionals

The classic English grip is slim, graceful, handy to carry, and has definite advantages in upland hunting. Almost any U.S. gun with pistol-grip stock can be converted to English style by almost any good gunsmith or stock maker. The factory model here, the Ithaca 280 English, is a relatively inexpensive and increasingly popular lightweight field gun.

The pistol grip gives the stock hand basic control over the gun, contributing to a smoother, more deliberate swing and less use of the forward hand. The author favors the pistol grip for target shooting, English grip for upland hunting.

who shoot the straight-grip English stock are not just yielding to tradition. One advantage they claim, and which I now believe, is that the wrist is indeed put into something of a bind, enough so that in mounting the gun the elbow of the grip hand is almost automatically pulled a little higher and the angle of mounting tends to pull the gun upward against the cheek. This provides a deeper shoulder pocket for the gun, and it just seems easier for me to keep my head down and with the gun when using a straight-grip stock. I cannot promise it will work that way for everybody.

The English grip seems a little more comfortable to carry and quick-point in upland hunting, and for me it tends to make the same gun (with otherwise identical stock dimensions) throw up to shoulder with a shade higher point. This can be an advantage shooting upland birds on the rise. It is definitely true that with the straight grip, the shooter has less command of the gun with the grip hand, and whether

Along the firing line at the Grand American trapshoot in Vandalia, Ohio, where some 17,000 shooters each August toe the line for the largest single participatory sports event in the world. Virtually every sort of stock can be seen with a high percentage of them in some way customized by the shooter. Trapshooters are most sophisticated about stocks; their sport is so precise it has been called "rifle shooting with a shotgun."

that is good or bad depends upon the shooter and the game. For clay targets I prefer the pistol-grip stock and I try to control the gun as much as possible with the grip hand. This makes for a smoother swing. A good skeet shot with a strong arm may be able to break 25 straight with one hand tied behind him. The fore-end hand is mostly a barrel rest.

But shooting fast-darting game is another story, and most of the top European pigeon shooters I have seen use their left hands a great deal in moving the gun. They make erratic, quick points perhaps, but pigeons are erratic, quick-moving targets. So are grouse, woodcock, and doves. It is quicker, I believe, to move the barrels with the hand out there on the fore end than with the hand back at the trigger.

The straight English grip forces more use of the fore-end hand, and whether that helps you point quicker on quail is just something you'll have to find out for yourself. If you're willing to sacrifice a standard field stock and remove the pistol grip, you'll know pretty quickly. The worst that could happen is that you'd have to buy a replacement stock, which, for most popular modern single-barreled pumps and autoloaders, is easy to come by and costs a lot less than buying a whole new English-type gun to find out if you like that stock style.

You might want to order a fancier stock, anyway, for the old field

This strange-looking contraption is a crossover stock designed to put the barrel in line with the shooting eye when the stock is shouldered to the opposite side. This is used by shooters who for years have shot right-handed, then perhaps lost dominance or use of the right eye. Rather than shoot left-handed, they use the crossover stock. These stocks are available as standard items from several U.S. stockmakers.

gun; it's amazing how classy an otherwise standard pump or autoloader can become with the addition of fancy wood from Fajen, Bishop, Anton, or some other stock maker. In most cases these stocks can be ordered without sending the gun; they'll interchange with the standard factory jobs. But on doubles or over-unders you'd have to send the gun and preferably go with it to be measured so the stock can be "tailored" to your needs.

In a standard, interchangeable stock, one of my preferences (particularly for the pump-gun shooter) is the Fajen Regency, which has a slightly emphasized pistol grip that looks (but isn't quite) like the famed old Etchen grip made famous by Fred Etchen and his sharp-shooting son Rudy, with whom I've enjoyed some pleasant days of shooting. Rudy believes that the exaggerated pistol grip, with its curve extended so as to confine the fingers of the grip hand, helps reduce flinching. His shooting is a great testimonial.

The accentuated pistol grip can be a distinct help in holding on to a slide-action gun through recoil-recovery and pumping phase, and lots of hunters like the better control it gives with any gun.

R. J. Anton of Waterloo, Iowa, has developed one of the most interesting stock designs to come along in recent years. It has twice won the Grand American Handicap and has been used by trapshooter Elgin Gates in a number of well-publicized achievements here and in Australia. Anton's basic design involves quite a bit of drop at heel (as much as 3 inches or more in some stocks) mated with a rollover Monte Carlo comb in line with the gun's rib. The result is a gun that comes up with the stock low in the shoulder pocket and the head supported in such a way that the shooter doesn't have to hunker down hard to get locked into shooting position.

Anton's observations of many years of stock fitting seem to mesh closely with the studies I've done of various stocks and people via the Perazzi principle of easy stock changing. "Lots of people have been canting their guns for years because their stock butts were straight but their shoulder pocket isn't straight," he explains. "They can get by with that with a single-barrel gun because when it's twisted very little changes, but when they twist a stackbarrel (over-under) it throws that under barrel off to one side and they miss without knowing why."

Some would argue with that, since quite a few top shots with over-under are also notorious gun canters. But theoretically Anton is correct, and the shooters have just somehow managed to compensate.

The biggest problem Anton has had to face in his low-heel, high-comb rollover stocks is that old bugaboo of upjump of the stock in coil. The more crooked the stock, the more the forces of recoil theoretically should whack upward into the face of the shooter. Yet I've shot several Anton-stocked guns (they all seemed to fit me surprisingly well) and none kicked any more than conventional stocks. Somehow, through manipulation of pitch, cast, or other dimensions, the gentleman from Waterloo has managed to research his way around the upjump problem.

17

HOW GOOD IS YOUR DUCK LOAD?

A couple of camouflaged customers in a Stuttgart, Arkansas, cafe at 4:30 one morning were pontificating upon the pleasures of long-range duck shooting. One said he had a 20 gauge "choked down like a rifle" that would kill ducks as far as any 12 gauge. "Just have to hold it on 'em a little tighter," he beamed.

When I asked what special barrel boring and handloading formulas he had used to accomplish this he looked at me blankly. "Just plain ol' high brass 6's or 7½'s," he said, "doesn't matter much. A little gun like that just naturally holds its shot together tighter than a 12 gauge."

How long can such tales persist? They have the same scientific foundation as the fable that toads cause warts, yet are still believed with almost biblical devotion in many areas of the country today. Unfortunately, some of those areas contain a great many ducks. And those ducks are the most important thing about this chapter. I can feel only slightly sorry for a man who has never patterned his gun, who has no idea how far No. 6's or 7½'s will retain clean-killing penetration. But I can feel extremely sorry for the ducks that man shoots at beyond the clean-killing range of his particular gun and load. And I can sympathize with all the shooters elsewhere who will never have a chance at those ducks that were crippled and lost—perhaps without the under-gunned hunter even knowing he hit them. In this respect, every hunter has a stake in what other hunters use on ducks.

Some readers will not like what this chapter has to say. But it comes as close as I honestly can—after hundreds of pattern and penetration tests and observing in person the famed Nilo tests by Winchester—to setting straight the facts on duck loads most commonly in use.

First off, it must be made clear that there is absolutely nothing wrong with the 20-gauge load of 6's touted by that Stuttgart shooter. In a full-choke gun, in the proper hands, it should cleanly kill about 93.4 percent of mallards that come over at 35 yards or less. A good hunter and duck caller can shoot his birds at that short range. And in some areas of the country, including Stuttgart with its beautiful pinoak flats and greenheads sifting down through the green timber, many ducks are killed at around 30 yards.

But if you recall, the man at the cafe was talking about long-range duck killing. And a great many shooters, from California to the Eastern Shore of Maryland, do not belong to the sort of duck club that presents to its members relatively close-range opportunities at ducks.

All those other guys (and there are thousands of them) either take shots at ducks at long range or get no shots at all. Unfortunately, it is often this shooter rather than the duck club member, who knows least about what his gun and load can be expected to do. I would bet my bottom dollar that man in the Stuttgart cafe was a skyblaster of the worst order, and I hope he reads this chapter. Because I can say to him, backed by the best data available, that at 55 yards his 20-gauge load of 6's (no matter if it was his daddy's gun and choked down like a rifle) will be crippling more mallards than it will be killing. In fact, it should kill just about 32.4 percent of the ducks perfectly centered in its pattern at 55 yards.

And how can I claim to know that?

Well, when Winchester tested 2,400 game-farm mallards rigged on a moving trolley to simulate birds in flight, the tests were conducted at precise yardages with full-choke guns scope-sighted and programmed to perfectly center every bird. The tests were done on a pellet-for-pellet basis to provide a data base of duck-killing efficiency that could be plugged into a computer to reveal the clean-killing capability of any load. All the computer would need to know, once that data base was established, was shot size, muzzle velocity, and pattern density from the gun. Other factors such as penetration, effect of pellets on the mallards, etc., were there. And within reasonable tolerances of wind, temperature, and air density, that computerized system works. At least, when tested on my moving silhouette targets of ducks, pellet hits indicating clean kills closely matched the computer's answers.

Unfortunately, much of the significance of the Nilo tests seems to have been overlooked in the squabble over steel shot, which was ac-

Firing various gauges and loads at a moving target offers information previously unavailable as to how loads actually reach the bird. The author's 16-foot-long target is covered for each test with a fresh strip of pattern paper. Some contain silhouettes of ducks which permit analysis of lead required, drop of the load at long range, and many other factors. By swinging smoothly on the front duck it can be determined (by measuring how far behind that duck the pattern strikes) the approximate forward allowance for a bird crossing at that speed, distance, and angle, and how the lead looks over the gun in terms of life-size duck lengths. Pellet distribution reveals how much of the load's pattern density has been lost to shot stringing and whether there are gaps or patches in the pattern.

tually only part of the data derived. Winchester never got the credit it was due for having come up with the first (extremely expensive) computerized lethality formula that could advise the ordinary hunter how his own gun and ordinary load of lead shot can be expected to do on ducks.

Winchester has not yet to my knowledge published a breakdown of its computations based on its Nilo data for the ordinary high-brass No. 4's and 6's, which the average duck shooter uses. Published charts from the Nilo tests showed performance of lead loads only in the Super-X Double X Magnum, which relatively few hunters use (but I am convinced more should). Also never published were comparative performances of the 16 gauge or 20 gauge on mallards or how ordinary lead 4's rate against lead 6's.

E. D. Lowry, who computerized the Nilo data before he retired from Winchester-Western, translated it for some of the common loads most hunters use. The findings agreed closely with a lifetime of observation of wild-duck shooting by myself and a number of guides to whom I have shown the table appearing at the end of this chapter.

This table shows predictions of ducks bagged (in terms of percentages) at ranges from 30 to 60 yards from various gauges and shot

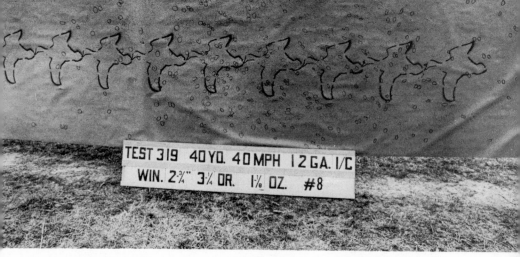

TEST 319 40 YD. 40 MPH 12 GA. I/C
WIN. 2¾" 3¾ DR. 1⅛ OZ. #8

Many shooters use small shot on the theory that the more the shot, the broader the coverage, and the more likely a vital organ will be hit. This photo shows how a load of small shot can string out and perhaps hit other birds not even being shot at. Since small shot lose penetration capability rapidly beyond 30 yards, it is likely that in this instance only one or two of the ducks shown here would be killed, while others would likely fly off crippled.

sizes. All figures are for full-choked barrels unless otherwise specified, and since all loads tested at Nilo were Winchester loads (and computers function properly only when fed a consistent diet of data) the performances shown are for Winchester loads.

All are high-brass cartridges loaded to approximately the same basic specifications of the Sporting Arms and Ammunition Manufacturers Institute, used by other manufacturers, so it can be assumed within reasonable limits that no matter what brand you shoot, the table will come pretty close to telling what your favorite load will do. Certainly some guns will pattern one brand better than another, and each man must find out for himself what works best.

A 20-gauge load of 1 ounce of 6's will kill ducks just as dead at 30 yards as a 12-gauge 3-inch magnum. How dead can dead be? But where do the major breakdowns in performance occur, at what yardage, and with what shot sizes? No. 7½ shot, although the preference of many shooters, penetrated so poorly at ranges beyond 40 yards that they were not considered in the Winchester tests (nor in my own) at long range. Inside of 35 yards, it doesn't matter much if the shot are 4's or 7½'s, but the small shot may offer a slight advantage in increased density at the pattern's fringe.

Almost any load will kill a high percentage of ducks at 35 yards, but the common 20-gauge high-velocity lead 1-ounce load begins to drop drastically in efficiency at 40 yards. At 35 yards a 20 gauge loaded with 6's was killing 93.4 percent (and with 4's 95.1 percent).

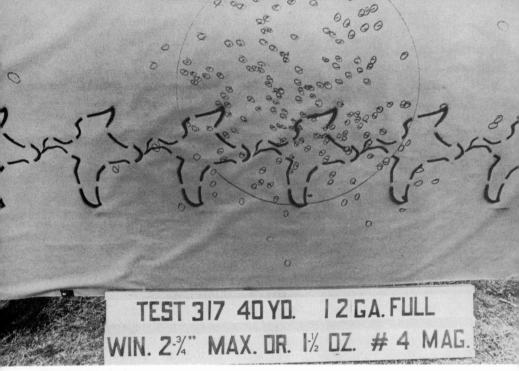

TEST 317 40 YD. 12 GA. FULL
WIN. 2¾" MAX. DR. 1½ OZ. # 4 MAG.

*This is the load used in the Nilo tests on mallards: No. 4 shot in the Winches-
ter Super-X Double X Short Magnum with 1½ ounces of grex-insulated shot.
The 78-percent pattern above, made at 40 miles per hour, shows only slight effects of stringing, even though it is considerably less tight than the 87-percent
stationary patterns registered during the Nilo tests. Note how few stray shot
struck other ducks on the target, bearing in mind that wild ducks do not fly nose
to tail in a row. With a tight choke, efficient load, and minimal shot stringing,
there is little danger of secondary crippling.*

But at 40 yards the 6's were killing only 79.4 percent and the 4's were
killing 83.7. Between 40 and 50 yards the standard 20-gauge load becomes a crippler; efficiency with 4's being only 53 percent and with 6's
only 45.5 percent. What that means is that if the shooter is absolutely
perfect, shooting a full-choked 20 gauge and high-brass, high-velocity
factory loads, he can expect to cripple or lose about half the ducks he
hits. Skyblasters take note.

Certainly this is not the fault of the gauge, because shot pellets,
not gauges, kill birds. Certainly custom 20-gauge magnum loads can
be produced which will kill at very long range. But this discussion is
based upon ordinary factory loads used by the majority of duck hunters, not super handloads, and if you'd like to estimate what your 20
gauge would do loaded with 3-inch 20-gauge magnums just glance at
the standard 12-gauge column in the table at the end of the chapter.
Standard 12 loads are slightly more efficient than factory 3-inch 20
loads, but the difference is not great.

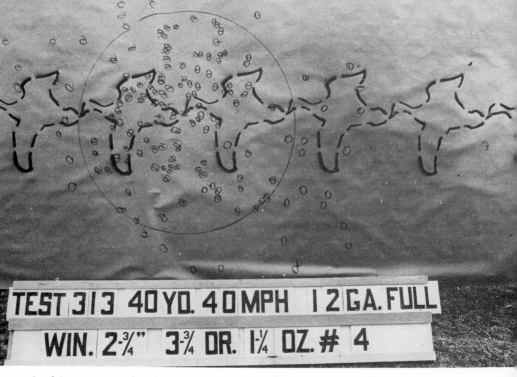

TEST 313 40 YD. 40 MPH   12 GA. FULL
WIN. 2-¾"   3-¾ DR. 1¼ OZ. # 4

As deformation of shot increases, so does loss of general pattern efficiency and loss of pattern density due to shot stringing. This load of No. 4 shot, without benefit of grex insulation against shot deformation, patterned only 68 percent, 10 percent less than the previous illustration. Although the standard high-velocity No. 4 load (1¼ ounces of shot) contains an average of 34 fewer pellets than the 1½-ounce Super-X Double X load, the photograph shows more pellets spreading or stringing out beyond the 30-inch pattern circle. This is still a good duck load, but not as efficient as it would be with either harder shot or with grex buffering.

Never get the impression that simply by using a 3-inch magnum 20 gauge you can kill cleanly at the same yardages (again with factory loads) as with the 3-inch 12-gauge magnum. In effect, what you've done with the 3-inch 20 is push a standard 12-gauge load out a smaller hole. The high-brass 3-inch 20-gauge magnum load has less velocity than the identical shotload in the standard high-brass 12-gauge load.

The term high brass is used because that seems to be the way many hunters seem to want to refer to high-velocity loads in comparison with standard-velocity or low-brass loads. The brass in modern plastic shells has nothing to do with it other than looks. For that matter, the word magnum does not mean the same in shotguns as in rifles. In rifles, magnum denotes higher velocity; in shotguns it means merely a heavier load of shot, which translates actually into lower velocity due to breech pressures that would at higher velocities be developed by the heavier shotload. Therefore, if you are shooting magnum duck loads, you are shooting slower loads, and this is true in any gauge. The difference in forward allowance, however, is not really significant, particularly if the shooter is accustomed to using standard-velocity loads in other hunting.

In terms of the Nilo data, 4's seem to be the best for ducks. But I'll admit that boggled my mind a bit because I have long believed No. 6 shot offered more chances for hitting a bird in the head than 4's, particularly ducks smaller than mallards.

My personal compromise preference has long been No. 5 shot. Unfortunately there is no data from Nilo or Patuxent on No. 5, and the Patuxent tests seemed to indicate 6's are best.

I doubt it is necessary to sympathize with shooters who for years have been cleanly killing their ducks with 7½'s and probably will continue doing so. Nor is the matter of shot choice laid to rest merely by plugging in a computer. Comparisons of 4's and 6's from the Nilo Lethality Model are merely computations, because no No. 6 lead pel-

Although a duck-killing load at 40 yards, this No. 6 shot load shows quite a few flyer pellets that will string out at longer range. Small shot deform more easily than large, even if both have the same antimony content for hardening. Also, 6's have less penetration than 4's. It has been established that between 40 yards and 50 yards, lead 6's drop off in efficiency considerably more than 4's, although the two shot sizes kill with almost identical efficiency at 40 yards when the same gun and shot load are compared.

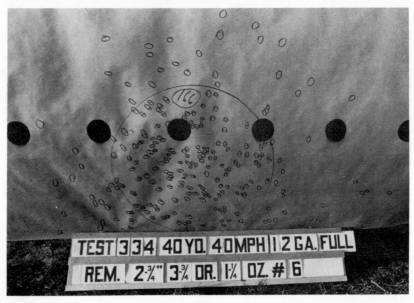

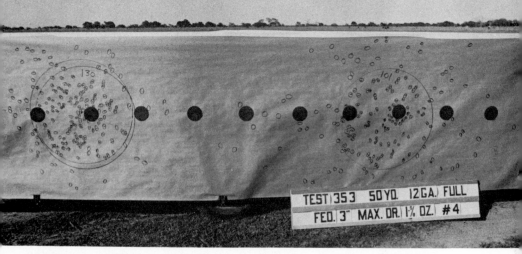

TEST 353   50 YD.   12 GA.   FULL
FED. 3" MAX. DR. 1⅞ OZ. #4

Magnum duck loads may kill farther than ordinary loads because they put more shot into the air and the odds are better more shot will strike within the area of the bird, but most of them deform a higher percentage of shot and thus lose efficiency. The pattern at left (64 percent at 50 yards) was made by a 3-inch magnum custom load created by Tom Roster using 1½ ounces of extra-hard Lubaloy copper-plated pellet cushioned with ordinary white household flour. Note how few flyer pellets surround the pattern even at that distance. The magnum pattern at right, however, with standard lead shot and no buffering agent spread much more, patterning only 46 percent. More revealing were moving tests (40 miles per hour) of the same two loads. Roster's handload lost only 7.4 percent due to stringing at that speed, while the standard softer, non-cushioned load lost 20.5 percent, stringing some of its shot 7 feet behind the bulk of the pattern.

lets were tested at Nilo. However, E. D. Lowry analyzed the Patuxent tests where 6's seemed to do better than 4's, and he still shows the statistical preference for 4's. All I know is that over decoys, 6's will wrap up a duck like a tamale. I've killed plenty of greenheads at 40 yards with 7½'s too, but it is difficult to argue with tests on real ducks, and also with tests on penetration boxes, both of which agree small shot just lose too much penetration to be efficient on birds the size of mallards at longer ranges. For teal over decoys 7½'s are fine, and 6's are a fine choice for those backup shots after the birds flare. For small ducks in general I believe 6's are better than 4's. But for mallards (upon which the only really scientific tests have been done) 4's seem to be the best, particularly in the 12 gauge.

The standard 12 gauge with high-brass duckloads and No. 4 shot shows a significant drop off in efficiency between 45 and 50 yards. At 45 yards, high-velocity 4's are killing 83.9 percent, but at 50 yards they'd dropped down to 69.9 percent. The big 3-inch 12-gauge magnum loads (Super-X Double X with grex) at 50 yards, however, are still maintaining a 91.5 percent efficiency. This rather long-range lethality could be misleading, however, in that such performance cannot be expected of all loadings. Only one brand, the Super-X Double X Winchester at this writing contains ground plastic (grex) insulation of the shot which permits it to throw highly efficient patterns with minimal loss of density to shot stringing or flyer shot. New super loads, however, are being developed by other manufacturers and the new era of highly efficient shotloads is just beginning.

Handloading authority Tom Roster has produced custom handloads that consistently crowd 100 percent patterns at 40 yards and show impressive killing patterns at 60 yards from even a relatively light 1¼-ounce payload.

Roster's theory, to which I wholeheartedly subscribe, is that the important thing is not how many pellets are thrown into the air in the hope that some of them arrive within the pattern circle, but the launching of nondeformed pellets that will fly straight and remain in the pattern. In order to do this, he has cut down on total pellets (his 3-inch 12-gauge magnum loads contain only 1½ ounces as compared with 1⅝ or 1⅞ ounces in factory loads) yet the Roster loads consistently put more pellets into the pattern at 60 and 70 yards than did factory magnum 10-gauge loads. His 10-gauge loads, better still, showed killing capability at 70 yards, which I have never seen duplicated by any load of any kind.

The secret was using extra hard shot (Winchester copper-coated Lubaloy) packed with common household flour to fill in crevices and equalize pressure around each pellet and prevent pellets from moving against each other and deforming at ignition.

This is the same basic principle used in the Winchester Super-X Double X magnums (which use grex plastic powder rather than household flour) but Roster takes the process a step farther by increasing wad cushioning effect within the shell and thus reducing pressures that deform shot.

If there is a problem with such loads, it is perhaps in the fact that discussing killing ranges out to 60 and 70 yards may encourage excessive skyblasting by shooters who may have little idea how far those ranges really are.

Many shooters believe they can consistently kill waterfowl at 60 to 70 yards with common high-velocity lead loads, and discussion of loads far superior to these may too often be translated into shots at ranges where excessive crippling results.

The fact is that standard loads will not consistently kill, without excessive crippling between kills, at such ranges.

Lowry computed for me the average ranges at which a hunter firing No. 4 lead shot from a full-choke barrel could expect to bag at least 80 percent of the mallards he shot at when the bird was perfectly

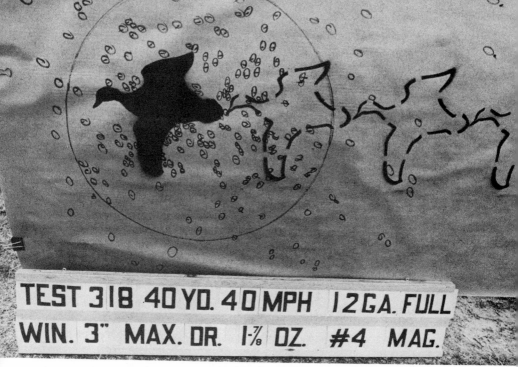

TEST 318 40 YD. 40 MPH 12 GA. FULL
WIN. 3" MAX. DR. 1-⅞ OZ. #4 MAG.

The deadliest long-range factory-loaded duck downer for the 12 gauge is this 1⅞-ounce load of No. 4's with powdered plastic buffering, the Super-X Double X Winchester, which gets a computer rating near 70 percent clean kills at 60 yards. But in ounce-for-ounce efficiency, the short Magnum Super-X Double X load with 1½ ounces of shot patterned slightly better. This shows again that even with hard, plastic-buffered shotloads, the larger magnums deform slightly more shot. The most pattern-efficient load tested was a non-magnum handload with only 1¼ ounces of shot.

centered in the pattern using as the statistical basis the Nilo Lethality Model derived from the test shooting of 2400 mallards.

Thus computed, a 20 gauge with 1-ounce high-velocity factory lead load turned up to have a clean-killing range of 38.5 yards, a 16 gauge with 1⅛-ounce load 40.9 yards, 12 gauge with high-velocity 1¼-ounce load 43 yards (about the same performance or slightly less could be expected from the 3-inch 20-gauge with factory 1¼-ounce loads), the non-buffered 12-gauge standard magnums 46.1 yards, the 12-gauge magnum 1⅞-ounce load 48 yards, the 12-gauge Super-X Double X grex-buffered standard magnum with 1½ ounces 50.5 yards, and the heaviest grex load, the 1⅞-ounce 3-inch Super-X Double X 53.5 yards.

Remember that these are not maximum killing yardages, but maximum *consistent* killing yardages, based on 80 percent kills when the gun is perfectly pointed. If 100 percent efficient killing were computed, ranges would be even shorter. If the shooter is satisfied with killing, say, 65 percent of the time on perfect shots, and crippling the rest, longer range figures would be shown for each gauge and load.

Certainly a stray clump of shot may strike a bird and kill it stone dead at 70 yards, but the same shot, fired exactly the same way with the same forward allowance might cripple or miss many birds before it killed another one.

Despite modern technology the shotgun remains a relatively close-range weapon, with or without steel shot. The consistent clean-killing range of a steel shot load of No. 4's (1⅛ ounces) is about 44 yards and the heaviest new steel loads (3-inchers with 1½ or 1¹⁵⁄₁₆ ounces) should kill with 80-percent consistency at roughly 50 yards. This final figure is mine, not Lowry's, because his computations were made before announcement of the 3-inch magnum steel loads.

These ranges seem short, but they are based upon as much valid statistical data as is presently available. An actual 40-yard kill (bird struck in the air at that range) is usually considerably different than an "estimated" 40-yard shot where the bird may fall 50 to 60 steps away due to its momentum. Stepping off yardages to downed birds is often misleading, and ducks and geese killed overhead almost invariably seem farther away than they actually are.

In researching this book every U.S. brand of magnum shotshell has been patterned, tested for shot stringing, and for penetration. Most patterned poorly. One series of tests of nonbuffered Federal, Remington, and Winchester 1⅞-ounce 3-inch magnum loads revealed an average pattern density (from a 30-inch barreled full-choke pump) of less than 65 percent with a great deal of shot deformation and stringing evident on the moving pattern board. Some of the cartridges went as low as 55 percent on the moving target, while the Super-X Double X magnums in either 2¾-inch or 3-inch case patterned between 70 and 85 percent, the best patterns generally coming from the 2¾-inch load of 4's in terms of percentages. But the 3-inch Super-X Double X magnums (with more shot) put the most hits into a 30-inch circle whether moving or still, despite a slightly lower percentage of density. The 1⅝-ounce 3-inch load often put as many hits as the 1⅞-ounce load and with significantly less recoil. The reason is the same as why grex-insulated super loads patterned so much more efficiently; they deform less shot. In general, the heavier the load the more pellets are deformed due to inertia of the heavier load at ignition. I have tested improved loads by other manufacturers designed to equal, or perhaps surpass, the efficiency of the Super-X Double X, and one test run of handloads has definitely done so. The answer is merely preventing excessive shot deformation.

But when extra-tight patterns are delivered, is this not more a handicap than a help to the average shooter? What about the blessings

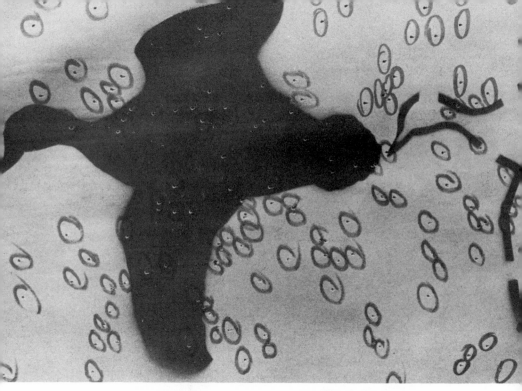

This closeup of the center of a Super-X Double X 3-inch Magnum load of 4's shows a distinct overkill situation. This can be remedied, and the shooter given more pattern spread and permissable error in pointing, by using a more open choke. Modified choke, with the most efficient duckloads, kills cleanly with more even pattern fringe, and may actually pattern heavy goose loads (No. 2 shot or larger) as well or better than a full choke. But when open chokes are used, they should be used with the most efficient loads available; open chokes and deformed shot create long, inefficient shot strings.

of margin for error contained in shells that throw less efficient, more open patterns? Well, many shooters need all the margin for error they can get, but they cannot have it without giving up efficiency at longer ranges. Nor can they have a great deal of margin for error, with a full-choked gun, without strewing some deformed pellets into the air that may or may not hit some duck not even being shot at.

These deformed shot tend to go wide of the rest of the pattern, usually trail the central shot string, and are not dependable either in placement around the pattern or in penetration once they reach the duck. Deformed pattern-edge shot, tested in a penetration box by "fringing" rather than centering the load, revealed losses of around 15-percent penetration, and some pellets lost 30-percent penetration compared with the non-deformed pellets in the center of the pattern. Efficient loads, such as the Winchester Super-X Double X, had good fringe penetration.

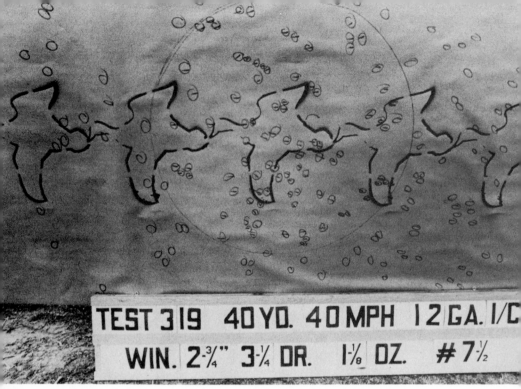

TEST 319 40 YD. 40 MPH 12 GA. I/C
WIN. 2-³⁄₄" 3-¼ DR. 1-⅛ OZ. # 7-½

No. 7½ shot have poor penetration at long range and are particularly susceptible
(as are any small shot) to excessive deformation unless extra-hard shot are used.
This inexpensive upland load strung out its load as shown, but not much worse
than more expensive, high-velocity No. 7½ loads which patterned poorly in every
brand tested. The best No. 7½ loads the author tested were Winchester and Federal pigeon loads, 3¼ drams equivalent and 1¼ ounces of shot, their superiority
stemming not from velocity, but primarily shot hardness. For shooters who like a
low-recoil, 12-gauge load, a 3-dram No. 7½ trapload is superior in patterning
to game or upland loads in that shot size. Again the difference is in shot quality.

It seems clear to me that the way to obtain more margin for error
for the waterfowl shooter is not to open up patterns with soft, easily
deformed shot, but to encourage the close-range shooter to use a more
open choke.

In tests made with some experimental loads containing extra-hard
shot, barrels choked modified consistently gave more margin for error
than full chokes and soft shot. Moreover the hard shot had a significant advantage: since fewer of them were deformed, the fringe retained better penetration capability. This means that the shooter using
a slightly more open choke, say modified, and highly efficient loads
can enjoy the best of both worlds—more margin for error and more
penetration of the fringe pellets in instances where he does not center
the bird in the pattern.

There is still another side to the story, that of shot stringing and potential secondary crippling of ducks or geese other than those particular ones that were shot at.

Waterfowl, as any hunter knows, often fly in formation or stack up just before they make the last pass into the decoys in such a way that a number of birds may be relatively close to each other. Some of the deformed pellets from an inefficient or soft-shot load may strike a bird several feet behind the front pellets. The bird may not show it at the time, and he could recover. He could also die later and become one of those unexplained statistics that have prompted the U.S. Fish & Wildlife Service to list crippling as the number-one factor in loss of waterfowl.

It would seem that the conservation-minded waterfowl hunter would be better off using the most efficient, least-deforming lead shotshells he can buy, even if those loads cost slightly more than regular

The author's favorite duck load until the advent of grex-buffered loads was Federal's No. 5. Note the relatively even pattern fringe despite the tightly choked full-choke gun used. Most full-choke patterns are over-dense in the center and ragged on the fringe. No. 5 shot offer a compromise between the long range penetration of 4's and the dense patterning of No. 6, and many hunters may find they pattern better than either of the two in a tight barrel. The author believes a ground-plastic-buffered duck load with 1¼ ounces of shot in No. 4 or 5 shot would be a winner, offering magnum pellet counts within the 30-inch circle but without magnum recoil.

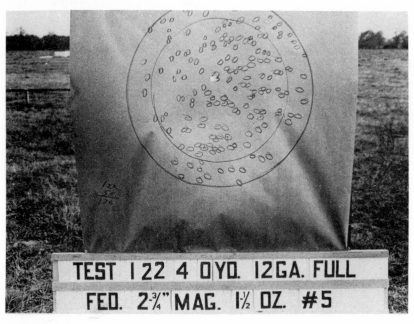

TEST 345 40 YD. 12 GA. MOD. CK.

WIN. XX 2¾" MAX. DR. 1½ OZ. #4

Here's a method for obtaining added pattern spread while retaining good center-pattern density: a highly efficient load and modified choke. The advantage over a similar pattern from a full choke using soft, easily deformed shot is that the non-deformed fringe shot penetrate better. Whether non-deformed shot are achieved by extra hardening or plastic insulation, the important thing is efficiency not only of center pellets, but of those fringe pellets that give the shooter his margin for error.

loads. And for long-range shooting (anything over 45 yards) the most efficient possible load (12 gauge or even 10 gauge) and the full choke become critically important to clean killing.

With every load tested the percentages of efficiency drop drastically at 60 yards and even the Super-X Double X 3-inch Magnum is bagging only 69.4 percent of the birds perfectly centered in its full-choke pattern. This indicates considerable chance for crippling, and the 20-gauge load of 6's—such as the man in the Stuttgart cafe so firmly believed would kill as far as any 12—is bagging only 22.7 percent of the birds it hits.

Certainly any one of the loads tested is capable of killing a duck stone dead at 70 yards or more, if a lucky clump of shot happens to strike in precisely the proper spot. But this is luck, not skill, and certainly not sportsmanship.

Nash Buckingham, that literary gentleman and duck hunter from

Predicted Percentage Bagged – Mallards at Center of Pattern

Range/Yards	12 Ga. Super-X 1¼ oz. + No. 4	12 Ga. Super-X 1¼ oz. No. 6	16 Ga. Super-X 1⅛ oz. No. 4	16 Ga. Super-X 1⅛ oz. No. 6	20 Ga. Super-X 1 oz. No. 4	20 Ga. Super-X 1 oz. No. 6	12 Ga. 3" Super-X Double X Magnum 1⅞ oz. No. 4
30	100.0	100.0	100.0	99.8	99.5	99.3	100.0
35	99.2	98.8	98.9	96.8	95.1	93.4	100.0
40	94.4	92.2	93.2	86.5	83.7	79.4	99.7
45	83.9	79.0	81.8	70.6	68.3	61.9	97.6
50	69.9	62.7	67.3	53.9	53.0	45.5	91.5
55	55.7	47.3	53.1	39.4	39.9	32.4	81.6
60	43.0	34.5	40.7	28.2	29.6	22.7	69.4

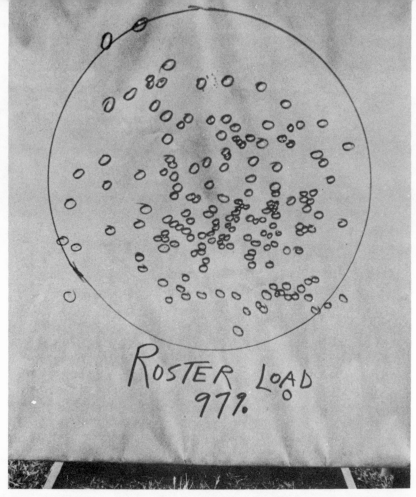

The near ultimate in pattern-density efficiency is this flour-buffered handload of 1¼ ounces of No. 4 copper-plated shot loaded by Tom Roster. The true excellence of such a load lies in its tight pattern and very short shot string, the lack of flyer pellets to cripple game. That's exactly what Nash Buckingham was after when he loaded his old double with the tightest-shooting copper-plated shot of his day.

an earlier era, once wrote of shotguns and waterfowl: "Don't send a boy to do a man's job." I believe that states very well the case against the all too common idea nowadays that it is more sporting to use a little gun. Buckingham hunted during a time when great numbers of ducks were available, and he had the time and means to shoot at thousands of them in his lifetime. He was in every sense of the word a sportsman.

But even over decoys, Buckingham normally used a 3-inch 12 gauge loaded with No. 4 copper-plated shot, the tightest patterning, most efficient load of his day. If the ducks were too close, he let them get out a bit before pulling the trigger. If they were not in clean killing range of the big gun and the big shot, Nash just didn't shoot.

18

FORWARD ALLOWANCE

The easiest way to hit flying game is to swing the barrel through the bird as if to paint it out of the sky.

That rash recommendation comes after more than twenty years of taking the trouble to watch directly over the shoulders of some of the world's finest shots and that is how most of them do it. Precisely when they pull the trigger depends upon distance, speed of target, and angle, the judgment of all three being one of the main reasons for moving the gun barrel through the target at the last instant before firing. It's like giving the mental computer a last-minute readout on all the variables.

I suppose this could be called the swing-through system, because most shooters start their movement of barrel with the target, then swing through it. But to be really precise in long-range pass shooting, it helps to actually start behind the bird, because the gun is then forced to speed up to pass him and in doing so provides added insurance against slowing or stopping the swing. The momentum of the gun will keep it moving even if the shooter fails to follow through consciously.

Fred Kimble, believed by some shotgun historians to have been the greatest duck shot of all time, must have used the swing-through system. Certainly I did not watch over his shoulder because he did his market hunting in the 1800s, but I've read everything I could find about him or by him on the subject of forward allowance. That infor-

Starting the barrel behind the bird and swinging through him to judge angle and speed is the best insurance against aiming or stopping the gun. The barrel speed required to pass the target provides additional forward allowance, thus reducing the lead the shooter must see ahead of the bird.

mation, compared with shooting in the field and testing on crossing targets at known speeds and yardages, convinces me that Kimble used the swing-through system—or some derivation of it—because he had to in order to hit ducks with the leads he said he saw ahead of the bird.

In *The Shotgunner's Book* by Col. Charles Askins, Kimble is quoted as saying that his most common lead on mallards was one duck length ahead of the bird's bill at 40 yards, at 60 yards two duck lengths. Unfortunately he didn't mention what the duck was doing at the time, whether cruising over the treetops or hovering over decoys, but if the duck happened to be passing at the rather common mallard speed of 35 miles an hour, the only way Kimble could have killed him would have been to swing past him rather swiftly.

The reason I can say that is that for months I have been shooting at life-sized silhouettes of ducks (including mallards with measurements taken from real ducks) and the only way I can hit one while holding the gun one duck length ahead of his bill at 40 yards and 35 miles an hour is with the same swing-through system I use hunting.

Computers show that a shot load leaving the muzzle at 1,235 feet-per-second requires a forward allowance ahead of a duck crossing at 40 yards and 35 miles an hour of about 6.2 feet. Judging by the loads he was supposed to have used, 1,235 fps would have come close to the correct velocity for comparison, and if Kimble saw a one-duck lead, and the duck was the same as our mallards nowadays (about 24 inches), somehow or other he had to make up the difference in required forward allowance.

He did it, I believe, by taking advantage of his gun's lock time. His eye perceived the distance ahead of the bird to be one duck

This is the sight picture, barrel swinging with leading duck, used to test the sustained lead required at various speeds and yardages. On this shot, the load struck the fourth duck from the front. Thus a three-duck forward allowance would be required for a sustained-lead shooter. A swing-through shooter would need from one half to one third less to hit the same duck.

length, but with the gun swinging fast, by the time the trigger finger responded, ignition occurred, and the load left the barrel, the barrel was pointed farther ahead of the bird than Kimble realized. That is the beauty of the swing-through system. It provides built-in lead, added allowance, overthrow, or whatever one wants to call the phenomenon of shooting farther ahead of a target than the eye realizes.

This phenomenon can be tested by simply shooting at the ground. Start a fast swing from left to right and pull the trigger when a predetermined spot is reached. The load will not go to that spot, but will impact beyond it in the direction of the swing. This does not mean that you have sprayed the shot, nor physically overthrown the load past the point where the trigger was pulled. It means there is a tiny delay between the message sent by mind to trigger finger and the actual pulling of the trigger, another tiny delay between pulling the trigger and falling of hammer, another tiny delay of primer ignition of the powder charge, and then the elapsed time required for the load to get out of the barrel. Throughout this process, the fast moving gun barrel has been moving. And it requires very little movement to make a decided difference downrange. One degree of barrel movement translates to about 25 inches at 40 yards. This is part of the theory of Robert Churchill, who claimed no such thing as forward allowance is necessary; the shooter should simply point at the target and swing fast.

One great competition shooter of Kimble's day claimed he could swing his gun so fast he needed absolutely no lead ahead of a duck at 40 yards. Adam H. Bogardus, who was by no means a shy fellow, often took out ads in newspapers proclaiming himself to be the greatest shooter of all time. So it is not surprising that he might consider himself able to hit crossing ducks at 40 yards by pointing at them.

Perhaps he could do this, and maybe Churchill could, too. But I certainly wish they were alive today so I could watch over their shoulders as they fire at my moving duck target at 40, 50, and 60 yards. Several of the best shooters of my acquaintance have tried that target, some with the firm conviction they never consciously lead a crossing duck. But their average pattern placement as revealed by pellet holes in the target crossing at 40 miles per hour—at a precisely taped-off 40 yards—revealed they were hitting from 1 to 3 feet behind the duck when they fired just as the barrel passed the bird.

I have tried the same thing myself, at various speeds and yardages, in some cases using the full Churchill drill of pointing the left hand at the target as the gun is mounted, swinging as fast as I possibly could, in effect literally lurching the barrel past the bird's bill, and the best I can do is hit slightly behind the duck at 40 miles an hour and 40 yards.

Now at 25 to 30 yards or so, and 25 to 30 miles per hour, this fast swing will indeed hit the bird with virtually no observed lead if the swing is fast enough. But I found it more difficult to concentrate on fast swinging than simply to see a little daylight ahead of the bird.

English writer Gough Thomas shrugs off Churchill's no-lead theories with the observation that it is simply impossible to move the gun fast enough for long-range hits on fast moving objects. Before him, Major Sir Gerald Burrard wrote: "The truth of the matter is that with shotguns a big forward allowance will always be necessary . . . we must face facts as they are and bow to the inevitable."

Having studied the various theories of forward allowance and marveled at how the Churchill system could circumvent laws of physics, it was revealing to try it on the moving target. From those tests I have decided, at least to my own satisfaction, that the works of Thomas and Burrard on the matter of forward allowance are full of plums of wisdom and that Churchill on this subject was full of prunes.

In attempting to determine how much a fast-swing system can reduce lead at long range, I first had to determine what smooth swing or sustained lead forward allowances would be at given yardages. To do this I would swing with barrel pointing at the lead duck on the target and fire while swinging along with it as the target passed. At 40 yards and 40 miles an hour, the loads struck between 6 to 8 feet behind point of aim, which translates into 7 foot or more lead ahead of a bird crossing at that speed with a smooth swing at target speed. Then, by swinging fast as I usually do in duck shooting in the field, I could cut the observed lead about in half. But as distances became longer, even

Although a fast swing worked fairly well at 35 yards, long ranges required seeing a great deal of daylight ahead of the target no matter how fast the barrel was moved.

the fastest swing I could make required more and more daylight ahead of the bird.

For an example of how much forward allowance we're talking about—say with the gun swinging smoothly the same speed of the bird at 60 yards—I had to hold on the rear bumper of the car to place the center of the pattern on the middle of the target 12 feet behind the bumper! And in case you wondered about some of the many stories you've heard of clean kills on ducks and geese at 70 yards, I've measured the sustained lead required for me with the target moving at 40 miles an hour and it is approximately 18 feet! The pattern, by the way, will have strung out well across my 16-foot board target at that range with most duck or goose loads.

Obviously birds do not all fly at right angles to the gun, nor are they all going 40 miles an hour. Tom Roster did some studies that convinced him that waterfowl fly around 35 miles an hour crossing country, and up to 50 miles an hour when they're really in a hurry or have a tailwind. Then he cranked the necessary data into a computer and determined the actual forward allowance required for birds crossing at 35 to 50 miles per hour and various yardages. Those tables, through special permission from Roster, are shown at the end of this chapter as converted into bird lengths relative to the waterfowl species size.

I was surprised at how closely my computations made on the moving target tallied with those of the computer; maybe more surprised at the consistency with which the human trigger finger can each time pull off a shot and place a pattern on a moving duck at essentially the same spot it did before with the same load. I had expected much more human error variance, but then I had not expected to get so much practice, either. Tests expected to take 1 month took 6. What really surprised me are memories of some long shots I've made at distances I was positive were beyond 60 yards, yet I certainly did not recall being 14 feet ahead of the bird.

Obviously what appears to be 14 feet at arm's length and how 14 feet of spread looks over a gun barrel at 60 yards are entirely different. At 60 yards, 14 feet may appear to be little more than half that; maybe to some shooters it looks even less. This is why I believe it is easier to estimate forward allowances in bird lengths rather than feet and inches. But even if the shooter knows the number of bird lengths and exactly the distance and angle of the target (which he never will out hunting) there remains more art than science to long-range waterfowling because human reaction times and trigger times vary widely.

The late Nash Buckingham wrote that he would envision "a moving spot out in front" of the bird and swing to it, touching off when he reached it. Although Buckingham referred to a spot, he was not a spot shooter. He was a swinging shooter, because he specifically referred to the place he pulled the trigger as "that moving spot out in

A shotgun is not aimed at moving targets, but must be pointed and kept swinging; the "aim" here was used to show where gun was pointed to put pattern 10'9" back on the target. Such long leads cannot be made by simply swinging faster; at least in the author's tests, no one could do so. The sight picture with a swing-through lead at this yardage at 40 miles per hour was approximately 4 mallard lengths (96 inches).

AIM   LEAD 10'9"   59

TEST 46 B 60 YD. 40 MPH 12 GA. FULL
WIN. XX 2¾" MAX. DR. 1½ OZ. # 2

Geese at this distance should not be skyblasted; they are more than 70 yards away, and at this crossing angle shot-strings are long and patterns relatively inefficient no matter what the gun or load.

front." Years of experience had taught him just where that "moving spot" has to be at the angle, speed, and distance of the bird.

Certainly there are other systems of shooting that may work for some. The so-called sustained lead, as advocated by skeet and trap champion D. Lee Braun, simply amounts to starting out in front of the target and staying there, measuring up and if necessary correcting the distance in front, continuing the same steady speed of swing, and firing. This works very well at skeet, fairly well at trap, and may be the easiest way to learn to shoot these American-style games. This is particularly so at skeet, where the path of the targets and their speed are known and the shooter can get locked into his gun, put the barrel out in front the required distance, and start swinging the minute he sees the bird emerge from the house. With this system it is easy to keep the barrel ahead of the target.

But skeet shooting and field shooting are different things, and calls to mind an incident by no means disrespectful of the shooting talents of the great D. Lee Braun. Lee, as we called him, was a friend of mine and a longstanding friend of one of the greatest all-around shots of all time, Grant Ilseng, and he once came down to hunt ducks and geese with us in the marsh country of the Texas coast near Anahuac. The snow and blue geese were flying by the thousands; trouble was they were way up there, and Lee was having a tough time. For one thing, his feet were mired in the marsh, and his sustained-lead system required a lot of distance out in front of the bird. He was trying to measure sustained lead, which had to be around 8 to 10 feet,

Forward allowance for the incoming, rising bird is easiest achieved by starting beneath him, swinging fast, blotting out the target, and continuing the swing. If the bird is close, no observed lead is necessary; if he's high, some daylight between gun and bird becomes imperative with most shooters.

while looking back out of the corner of his eye to see what the goose was doing back there. Often the goose would see Lee just about the time that long, long lead had been computed, and would flare back with the wind without getting touched. Ilseng, a swing-through shooter, was starting with the geese, painting the barrel fast through them, seeing (as he told me) about four goose lengths ahead of the bird as he fired.

It was very much like watching an artist paint birds out of the sky. We came in with the limit, although I cannot say who got all those geese. I do know that Lee took a lot of joshing that day.

Now had Lee Braun, one of the greatest shotgun shooters of all time, wanted to master goose shooting in a Texas marsh, he would indeed have mastered it. But he concentrated on making a living with his shotgun as a professional for Remington Arms Company, and as a instructor primarily devoted to skeet and trap where he was all but unbeatable. One of my prize possessions is a copy of his book *Trapshooting with D. Lee Braun* which he autographed and personalized with a little notation that means a lot to me.

But the story underscores why I like Ilseng's (or Fred Missildine's) swing-through system best; they cut down the daylight I must see ahead of a duck or goose at long range.

On birds that suddenly appear—say a duck that comes whipping past the blind while you're looking the other way—the swing-through system is almost automatic. You're behind that bird to begin with; you frantically try to catch him with the barrel, pull out in front, see some forward allowance in that split second, and pull the trigger. The odds are that that bird will fall. But then along comes a lumbering goose or duck that you have watched grow from a tiny dot on the horizon. When he is finally within range, you carefully estimate the yardage, mount the gun, measure up the same lead you saw on the previous bird whipping past the blind—and miss.

How can that be when the forward allowance seemed perfect?

The main difference is that the first bird caught you off guard and you began your swing from behind. This meant the gun was accelerating fast as it passed him, and you could not stop it if you wanted to during the interval of reaction time and lock time. But with the bird you've watched all the way in, the tendency is to start partially out in front of him, swing slower (because you want to be precise about it) and slow the swing as you shoot. The difference in a continued swing and a slowed swing translates into several feet at 40 yards. The way around the problem, I believe, is to force yourself every time to start out behind, swing the gun through, (not yank it ahead, just pass him) and see a little more daylight ahead than you think necessary.

In long-range pass shooting, birds appear slower than they are, particularly geese which seem even slower because they are big. Watch a jet passing high overhead; it will barely seem to be moving. Thus, the longer the range the greater the optical illusion as to the speed of target. Always swing past a goose far enough to center the pattern on his head rather than his body. If you misjudge his speed, the extra allowance often provides enough error margin to center the pattern in the body. If you're perfect it should still kill him, because there are invariably plenty of pellets behind the front portion of the shotstring at long range.

In experimenting with speed of swing (relative to leads obtained) I asked my wife to drive the moving target past at varying speeds, keeping records on each run and the actual speed the vehicle crossed the shooting position. Since I would not know target speed, I would have to estimate it, the same as in the field. Several times, on a target run that I suddenly realized was faster than I'd thought, I would accelerate the gun to gain added forward allowance, and those were times I best centered the bird. The times my pattern went behind the bird were almost invariably those in which I tried to be too careful, or thought I might be a little too far ahead of the target.

Since I've been making the same hits and misses in field hunting most of my life, I'm inclined to believe the moving target told a fairly accurate tale of what happens to many shooters. However, it must be remembered that a shooter cannot swing as suddenly, nor follow through as perfectly, with his feet mired in marsh mud. Nor can he do so in a duck boat, or sitting in a blind, or on his knees in a rice stubble. Thus, any demonstration of methods of forward allowance must be taken with the shooter's position in mind, or maybe with a grain of salt. I have seen advocates of the fast swing move rather deliberately when standing in mud. They still hit birds, but they did it more deliberately. Otherwise, in yanking the barrel around too abruptly they'd probably have fallen flat—and I've seen, and done, that too.

Thus the shooter must make allowances for shooting conditions as well as speed and distance. He'll need a little more lead when conditions force a slower swing. But never slow down, look back, and try to measure up to see how far ahead you are. That's the easiest way to miss.

I've heard and read statements to the effect that the same lead can be used at 60 yards as 35 yards because what appears to be 3 feet of lead at 35 will actually be much more than that at 60. This can be easily proved by propping up a yardstick on the ground, backing off, and looking at it over the gun. The farther back you go, the shorter the stick will seem to be.

But this is an optical illusion directly consistent with distance, whereas the shot load's speed is not consistent with distance but is slowing up much more rapidly at 60 yards than it was at 35. Therefore, if one sees what appears to be the same forward allowance at the two yardages, it would seem to me that the load would have to hit behind the target at 60 yards due primarily to changes in its time of flight.

I tried this out on my moving target, and had others do the same. Firing was done at markers that had been put out in advance at distances from 35 to 60 yards, but the shooter did not know the exact distance. Target speeds were kept standard at 35 miles per hour. On the longer shots, even though we concentrated on swinging faster when the yardage was longer, we shot behind unless we saw considerably more daylight ahead at long range than short range. This system may indeed work for some shooters, but I have never observed

The late Norman Clarke demonstrates the English system for dealing with fast incomers such as driven grouse or pheasant. Weight is shifted to rear foot, gun shouldered quickly, and trigger pulled as the bird is blotted out by the barrels. Since the faster the bird the faster the swing required to catch him, the system is somewhat self compensating. But on very high, fast overhead birds, such as waterfowl, author prefers seeing some lead in addition to the fast swing.

anyone in the field hitting long shots consistently who was not pointing his barrel well out in front of the bird. I have thus become convinced that I must go on shooting the same way I always have, seeing a great deal more lead ahead of a bird at long range than I see at close range.

When I perceive a bird is really a long way out, at the very edge of clean-killing range, I try to get the gun out in front of him a little farther than I believe necessary, trying to force myself to remember that the shot are slowing down out there. I was taught that system by a one-time market hunter who believed the shot load slowed so fast the lead had to be doubled between a 40-yard bird and a 60-yard bird. In those days I had much more faith in ammunition than I do today, and I doubted the old man's theory. But I could not doubt his ducks, since he killed more of them than I did. So I tried more lead, a lot more than I figured I needed, on the long crossing shots and ducks and geese started falling.

In looking at computer readouts of actual required leads at various speeds and yardage, it seems the old man was closer to correct than I had imagined. The computer claims a forward allowance of 6 feet is required for a crossing target at 35 miles per hour, and a forward allowance of 10½ feet at 60 miles per hour. While 10½ feet is not double 6 feet, it's pretty close. And when you add to that the natural tendency to slow the swing a little while trying to measure up a longer lead, the old man's computations could have been quite close. Obviously they were, because birds quit flying and fell when he shot.

The old man did not condone pass-shooting ducks or geese at long range except in certain situations where he was reasonably sure they could be retrieved. Over open water, or an open field, he would do it. But not in the marsh where a long bird might be very difficult to find if not dead. I believe he was right about that, too.

The conscientious shooter will have studied his gun and loads, have a good idea of what they can do and he can do, and will be in a situation (ideally with a good retriever) that permits recovering the occasional gliders or long cripples that eventually crash a long way from the blind. Just standing and shooting at anything that flies over, trying to guess whether the bird is 60 or 100 yards, is the sort of skyblasting that costs all waterfowl hunters in terms of crippling. And I have no intention of contributing to it by suggesting that any shotshell load, even the 10-gauge magnum, will consistently kill (without crippling as well) at 70 to 80 yards. My moving-target tests show that the finest loads made will string out pitifully at 70 yards and will not have the density they show on the stationary target. Also, the long shotstring at that distance is likely to hit other birds in flight with stray pellets.

No matter what fancy shooting system is employed, it is difficult to center birds in the pattern at long range, and the longer the range the more difficult it becomes. Most of the hunters I have observed over a lifetime of hunting some of the finest duck and goose country in America are pretty good at 35- to 45-yard shots; beyond that they miss a lot and cripple. And no amount of computer studies can make long-range shooting a simple thing.

The computer's estimates, for example, relate to targets crossing at a 90° angle. This is a quite common angle in long-range pass shooting, and certainly the one requiring the most forward allowance or lead. But not all birds fly at 90° angles, particularly birds that have just been shot at. Second or third shots into a flight of mallards, pintails, or geese may require much less lead because the birds often flare backward with the wind, or climb, or vary their speed and angle in several ways. A bird just starting to climb requires very little forward

The fast swing and follow through is often impractical, even impossible, with one's feet mired in marsh. A fast incomer here could send the shooter backwards into the mud. In this case it is better to take incomers out front rather than overhead. Shooting from a duckboat, on one's knees, or mired in mud requires more gun control with the arms and is usually more effective with a slower, more deliberate swing and more forward allowance. This gives the shooter a better likelihood of maintaining his balance.

Forward Allowance Calculated in Bird Lengths (by Species) Crossing at 90°

35 Miles Per Hour

YARDAGE	20 YD.	25 YD.	30 YD.	35 YD.	40 YD.	45 YD.	50 YD.	55 YD.	60 YD.
Teal	2.2	2.6	3.4	3.8	4.5	5.3	6	6.8	8
Mallard	1.5	1.8	2.3	2.6	3	3.6	4	4.6	5.4
Pintail	1.3	1.5	2	2.2	2.7	3	3.6	4	4.7
Scaup	2	2.5	3	3.5	4	5	5.6	6.3	7.4
Lesser Snow Goose	.9	1.4	1.8	2	2.5	2.9	3.3	3.7	4.3
Greater Snow Goose	1.1	1.3	1.7	1.9	2.3	2.6	3	3.4	4
Canada Goose	.96	1.1	1.5	1.6	1.9	2.2	2.6	2.9	3.4
Western Canada Goose	1	1.2	1.6	1.7	2	2.4	2.8	3	3.7
Lesser Canada Goose	1.3	1.5	1.9	2	2.5	2.9	3.4	3.8	4.4

50 Miles Per Hour

YARDAGE	20 YD.	25 YD.	30 YD.	35 YD.	40 YD.	45 YD.	50 YD.	55 YD.	60 YD.
Teal	2.8	3.8	4.7	5.6	6.5	7.7	8.8	10	11
Mallard	1.9	2.5	3	3.8	4.4	5.2	5.9	6.7	7.4
Pintail	1.7	2.2	2.7	3.3	3.9	4.5	5.1	5.9	6.5
Scaup	2.6	3.5	4.3	5.2	6.1	7.1	8.1	9.3	10.2
Lesser Snow Goose	1.5	2	2.5	3	3.6	4	4.7	5.4	6
Greater Snow Goose	1.4	1.9	2.3	2.8	3.3	3.9	4.4	5	5.5
Canada Goose	1.2	1.6	2	2.4	2.8	3.3	3.7	4.2	4.7
Western Canada Goose	1.3	1.7	2.1	2.6	3	3.5	4	4.6	5
Lesser Canada Goose	1.6	2	2.6	3.1	3.6	4.2	4.9	5.5	6

These allowances are for a smooth sustained lead based on computer readout of mathematical lead in feet. Swing-through shooters can reduce leads one-third to one-half depending upon speed of swing.

allowance; in fact, if the wind is strong you may need to point over him and even behind him slightly, because he can actually move backwards in the air for a short distance flaring back out of trouble.

Such things are learned only by practice, and I am reticent to even mention computers or sustained leads in the same sentence with ducks or geese. Yet there are laws of physics that cannot be circumvented, and the same computer expertise that put men on the moon can be used to accurately compute where a gun barrel must be pointing to hit a crossing object. Some shooters can attain that point by swinging fast, some by swinging more deliberately but farther ahead. It doesn't really matter how the allowance is achieved so long as it *is* achieved.

Sometimes it seems almost ridiculous to swing the gun so far ahead of a distant bird, as if you are purposely trying to miss him in front. If that's the way it seems, then try to miss some long-shot gander by shooting in front of him, and see how hard he falls.

19

THE FINE ART OF WATERFOWL SHOOTING

The fine art of waterfowl shooting is a fading one, and most of the old masters are gone. We may never see such artists with duck guns again, because any art is perfected with practice and modern laws do not permit such feats (on wild birds) as those of market hunter Fred Kimble, who in 17 days of hunting in early 1872 took 1,365 ducks and 5 brant.

The oldtimers accomplished such feats with relatively primitive guns, mostly muzzle-loading single shots. But with the skies full of game, they perfected the whole of waterfowl hunting. Not only did they know what they were doing, they knew what ducks could be expected to do. Kimble, before witnesses, dropped 57 straight ducks on the wing without a miss, and he probably made longer runs than that. A sensitive man, who handled his violin almost as well as his shotgun, he may well have been the best of them all.

There were many more masters of the waterfowl gun who, because of where or how they lived (often outside laws they could not understand) never achieved reputations beyond the backwoods areas where they hunted. As a boy, I was privileged to hunt with two such men, both getting on in years but still capable of remarkable skill at taking waterfowl. Fortunately they were also full of tales of earlier days, complete with lessons for a wide-eyed youngster who preferred their lessons to algebra class on a good duck morning.

These men, like Kimble, were not just duck butchers in overalls.

They were intelligent men who had chosen their way of life in the flooded timber rather than walking behind a plow or clerking in a store. Times were hard but they loved every moment of it, I believe, until the day they died. Most of the great ones were market hunters at a time when this was a legal and well-looked-upon occupation.

One old gentleman, whose name must remain anonymous due to family considerations, continued market hunting long after laws were passed against it. He saw no reason not to—where he hunted there were plenty of ducks. He carved his own duck calls and with them he could speak mallard about as well as any susie. I have watched him converse with ducks on the water 10 yards away, when any mistake by the man with the caller would have exploded mallards like quail.

One morning we were standing knee deep on a flooded pinoak flat, calling and sloshing water under the trees to make ripples as if a lot of ducks were there and suddenly there was a great swishing sound and the sky was literally black with mallards, hens calling, drakes geezing, dropping in around us with wings back pedaling to slow their splash into the icy water. How many ducks we could have killed, emptying two guns into that melee of wings, would be impossible to estimate. But the old man didn't like shooting ducks that way; he liked calling ducks, decoying ducks, and then taking them as they climbed out of the timber with his shiny-worn old Model 97 Winchester pumpgun.

Make no mistake, though, the old man was thinking duck strategy as much as sportsmanship when he failed to shoot into that swarm. One shot and every duck there would have been spooked from that particular slough where we'd set out decoys. As it was, they came trickling back in small bunches and singles, working beautifully to the call. It was one of the greatest days of my life, not only because of the great numbers of ducks but because the old man was in a particularly good mood and took time out to teach me some things.

One of them was how to watch decoying ducks as they lined up coming down through a hole in the timber, and at the instant two crossed or were in perfect line, swinging and leading them both for a one-shot double. This was an old trick of market hunters requiring split-second timing and considerable knowledge of the flight characteristics of ducks. But it can still be done. Many guides in the deep-marsh country of Louisiana and in the flooded timber around Stuttgart, Arkansas, can do it quite often.

Don't believe that? Neither did some contestants in the North American Duck Shooting Championship at Center, Texas, in 1972, when in the first round of competition (game-farm mallards flighted in pairs over a blind in the timber) I managed to kill both my birds with one shot. Whispers of "accident" and "luck" emerged from the gallery

A concentration of mallards takes wing from a woodland slough. Rarely will a hunter stalk this near, and a long shot taken into such a flock may cripple several birds for every one killed. Instead, permit the birds to leave and then set up decoys. Chances are good the ducks will return in small flights and decoy well. If shot when flushed from such a spot, the chances are they will be spooked from it the remainder of the day.

behind the judge's table. But after I had managed to do the same thing over again every day of competition, several times in side-bet shooting after the main event each day, some shooters began asking how that trick is done.

The answer, of course, starts with trying to do it, studying the flight speeds of birds in the air so as to anticipate when one is catching up to pass the other. Mallards and pintails often cross each other as they swing back and forth with wings cupped to lose speed. Decoying teal, swift little birds plenty tough to hit normally, usually offer one split second in their decoying procedure when doubles or triples can be made. They will pass low over the decoys downwind, then suddenly whip back and hesitate almost in a wad before dropping in. A shot at that instant may take several birds, but it really isn't recommended unless shooting is slow and a hunter wants to fill out his limit in a hurry. A couple of times, without intending to, I've finished my limit prematurely on teal when the intention was to wait for mallards or pintails.

As much of an art as the shooting is reading the birds, being able to estimate what they'll do and when they'll do it. Diving ducks, such as scaup, bluebills, redheads, and canvasbacks, will often come barreling past in a relatively straight line of flight, even though the hunter reveals himself by sitting up or standing to shoot. Thus, it is fairly safe to take the first bird as soon as the bunch is within good range, leaving more time for second and third shots as the flight passes. But on puddle ducks such as mallards, pintails, gadwall, widgeon, and black ducks, an entirely different strategy is required. Raise a gun to shoot just as a flight of mallards enters range and they may flare backwards with the wind and climb out of range before even a second shot can be fired.

Veteran waterfowl guide Morgan LaFour has hunted the Trinity River bottomlands on the Texas coast for some 50 years. Although never a market hunter, LaFour was an artist at waterfowl shooting until his eyesight began to fail in the late 1960's. At the time of this photograph, about 1961, he could consistently kill two crossing ducks with one shot as they worked the decoys.

In winning the North American Duck Shooting Championship of 1972 the author makes a double on mallards using the swing-through system. Note the follow through on the second bird and the relatively short distance the first bird has fallen before the second is dead in the air. The gun was a 26-inch-barreled Winchester 101 over-under (improved cylinder and modified choke).

This is the most common mistake of inexperienced waterfowl hunters, and one way to avoid it is to set a stake or a lone decoy as a marker about 40 yards in all directions from the blind. Don't shoot at any duck beyond that marker, and for that matter don't shoot at any mallard or pintail until you know he's within range; let him come as close as he will.

The toughest decision is judging whether the birds will make one more pass nearer the blind or whether they'll take a look at the decoys and go on their way. Here the oldtime market hunter had the advantage. He had enough experience to judge the birds and enough confidence in his calling and decoy setup to wait them out. And he also didn't have to worry so much as we do now about some other shooter close by firing just in time to spook the decoying birds.

Modern shooters for the most part do not take advantage of the chances they have to learn waterfowling. There is no law against putting out decoys when the season is closed and simply watching ducks work them. Much can be learned that way. Pintails, for example, may seem to be leaving the scene, going straight downwind and well past the decoys, when they have actually made up their minds to come in.

They make that characteristic last long swing downwind and then whip back bellied up over the decoys. When a pintail is losing interest in a decoy spread (which many of them will) he shows it by hanging high with cupped wings and looking down on the blocks, refusing to lose altitude. He is the one, if ever he comes within range, you'd better take when the chance occurs because he is most likely to drift off elsewhere. But any flight that approaches the decoys low, or loses altitude rapidly, should be permitted to let work until they are set up for multiple shots, rather than firing at them too soon and letting them flare back out of range.

Once birds are close over the decoys, it is best to pick out one of the trailing drakes (shoot drakes only, if possible) rather than the front bird. Take the front bird and the more distant birds are likely to flare out of range by the time you get around to them. For another reason, your partner probably will have picked one of the front birds, usually

In typical diving-duck fashion, a flight of redheads comes barreling over blind despite hunters obviously visible to them. Once divers have made up their minds to swing over the decoys, they are likely to keep coming even after first shots are fired and thus first birds can be dropped well out front leaving easy second or third shots as they pass.

the most obvious one in the bunch. It is very common for two men in a blind to shoot the same duck, winding up with just that one well-ventilated carcass while the rest of the bunch gets away.

The secret of getting several is for both men to pick trailing birds on their respective sides of the blind, take care to drop them, then mop up on the nearer birds which will by then have stabilized to provide relatively easy straightaway climbing shots.

It sounds more difficult to take the longer birds first, but is actually easier. The pattern has more chance to spread and more margin for error on the longer bird (provided he is within range to start with) and the close birds aren't as easy as they look anyway. The nearer a duck or goose is to a hunter rising to shoot, the more erratic the bird's evasive movements are likely to be. That bird is much more spooked than one farther out over the decoys. And since a spooked duck can make some very erratic moves, and the hunter's pattern at close range is quite small, it actually becomes easier to take one of the more distant ducks.

In pass shooting geese that are bucking strong frontal winds, let them pass over and shoot only when they're past the blind. Then, when they flare back with the wind as they invariably will when shot at, they will still be in range.

I often reverse the firing sequence of a double or over-under, firing the tight barrel first at one of the trailing birds in the bunch and leaving a climbing shot for the open barrel on the closer birds.

I used this tight-barrel-first technique throughout the aforementioned North American Duck Shooting Championship, and was fortunate enough to set a record that still stands: 37 mallards out of 40 shots, all birds fired at as doubles. Since these were game-farm mallards flighted in pairs toward a waterhole some distance beyond the blind, they did not stop to climb as wild ducks would have and it was imperative to drop whichever duck of the pair seemed inclined to go wide out of range, then quickly turn and get the closer bird. This was not easy, because the blind was located in a stand of tall pines, and most ducks were flying slightly higher than the treetops while a few were dodging in and out through the trees. I watched a number of very good shots, who obviously had not hunted many ducks in timber, take a close easy bird while letting the second, already the more distant one, either flare out of range or go behind a screen of limbs.

But the most common miss made by duck and goose hunters today is what would seem to be a very easy shot—the duck or goose that can be seen coming from some distance away, giving the shooter plenty of time to get ready. This bird will be missed more consistently than the one that suddenly appears from the side of the blind forcing the shooter to make a quick swing.

Limit filled, hunter watches pintails and widgeon over the decoys. Much can be learned about when (and when not) to shoot by observing the decoying character-istics of the various species.

Hunter in pit blind remains motionless to let low-flying Canada geese pass over decoys. They are bucking a strong wind (note decoy in foreground almost blown over) and to shoot at this point would mean most of flight would flare back with wind out of range.

The reason the "easy" bird is so often missed is that the shooter tried to take dead aim on him, and although he may be conscious of seeing a relatively long lead ahead of the bird, he's likely to stop his swing and try to perfectly measure up the bird. Stopping, or even slowing, the swing is fatal, not to the duck but to the chance the shooter had at that bird.

The slower a bird appears to be coming, such as a big Canada goose lumbering along straight for the shooter, the more likely the tendency to aim rather than swing. Actually that big goose may be moving as fast as a teal; he just looks slow because he is so big.

The way to avoid stopping the swing on any seemingly easy shot at waterfowl is to force yourself to start either with the bird or behind him and swing the gun past him. This is particularly important on high, incoming birds that seem to be barely moving against the wind.

Such birds may be moving slower in ground speed, but the wind resistance slowing them is also drifting the shot load. A 15-mile

The most commonly missed waterfowling shot comes when shooter attempts to aim rather than swing at big birds that appear to be barely moving. The trick is to start behind the bird and swing through smoothly. As it is more difficult to swing a heavy gun from a kneeling position (or with feet mired in the mud) marsh hunters often do better with lightweight guns they can swing with arms and shoulders.

crosswind will drift No. 2 shot 26 inches at 60 yards, 11.5 inches at 40. Number 4's drift 10 inches at 40 yards, 22.5 at 60. No. 6 lead and No. 4 steel drift 11 inches and 12.7 inches respectively at 40 yards, 25.4 and 28.8 at 60 yards. So additional lead is needed on birds hovering into the wind.

Start behind (in this instance, behind would translate to beneath the incomer) and swing right through him until you achieve the proper lead. Never lead a goose or duck by his "body" but lead as if you were trying to put the full load into his head. This provides added insurance your pellets will arrive at the front end of the bird (where he can be easiest killed) rather than tailing him and possibly crippling. Very few ducks and geese are missed in front; most shooters really have little idea of how much forward allowance is required at long range.

The late J. R. (Jimmy) Reel of Eagle Lake, Texas, was one of the originators of the white-spread technique of attracting geese and ducks to large numbers of white rags spread out on rice-field stubble to simulate concentrations of feeding snow geese. A lifetime guide and past master of calling as well as shooting, he is shown calling geese for Olympic trapshooting silver medalist Tom Garrigus.

The reason such old masters from the 1800s as Fred Kimble and Adam Bogardus wrote that they saw shorter leads ahead of ducks than my moving target tests indicate may partly have been in the speed of their swing, but more likely in the relatively slow lock time of their black-powder percussion guns. As the fast-swing shooter passes the bird, his barrel continues moving faster than the bird, and the slower the lock time (delay between the pulled trigger and the departing load) the farther out front of the duck the barrel has moved when the load leaves it. Thus the forward allowances the oldtimers saw and the leads they were actually obtaining through their system of shooting were probably entirely different distances.

However they did it, they did it very, very well.

20

UPLAND GUNNING

Certain gauges and barrel lengths are often referred to as best for doves and quail, others for pheasants and grouse, with size and toughness of game the overriding consideration as if one were selecting an elephant gun. But shooting conditions are more important, and the gun effective on Dixie quail may have little in common with one suited for prairie quail or pass-shooting doves.

I learned that a long time ago, losing a gentlemanly wager in the process. A group of competitors at a live-bird shoot in Mexico were talking hunting, and I made some comment that my 28-gauge quail gun made up for whatever it lacked in firepower with greater speed at getting on game.

Bill Price, one of the fastest guns around, suggested weight is not always that significant a factor in speed of handling and that such theories, projected far enough, could mean a toy popgun with cork and string would be a good quail gun.

"I'll take you and that 28 gauge hunting in the high plains country," he suggested, "and I'll bet you'll be wishing for more gun."

Two weeks later we put down the dogs at dawn 60 miles north of Amarillo, Texas, with an icy Panhandle wind howling across the buffalo grass. The low, rolling ridges contained very few trees; and it seemed the only thing between us and the North Pole was a barbed-wire fence.

Bobwhites rarely hold well to dogs in high winds, and the first

In prairie shooting, a great deal of open space may separate hunter and bird. Bobwhites take advantage of what little cover they have, getting some sort of bush between gun and game, and in prairie winds quickly attain distances not commonly considered quail range. There were 15 birds in this covey, but camera (and hunter) got a clear shot at only one. Larger gauges and more choke work best in open country like this, where wind is the major factor.

covey came roaring up 15 yards ahead of Price's pointers. In a split second they had flared off downwind, picking up speed like jets, and before my second shot they were out of range. Price made what I considered to be an incredible long second barrel kill and the score was instantly two to one in his favor. After that it got worse. The little 28, which had killed like lightning in my native piney woods timber, seemed to be spitting sleet instead of shot.

There was nothing wrong with that 28, custom-bored skeet in one barrel and improved cylinder in the other, except that the conditions where it had worked so well were entirely different than those on the bald, wind-howling prairie. Price was shooting a 20-gauge bored improved cylinder and modified and I'm not sure he wasn't shooting 3-inch magnum 7½'s in his top barrel. Before the day was over, I was indeed wishing for more choke, more gun, or both.

Quail supposedly are not really fast birds, normally attaining only about 25 miles an hour. But like O. J. Simpson, they get it all at once. Give them a 40-mile tailwind and they become a bird of an entirely

different feather—mostly tailfeather. Doves vary even more in gun re-quirements. Floating in cautiously over a waterhole they can be taken cleanly with small gauges and open chokes. But cruising high over a feeding field, a tightly choked 12 gauge more commonly associated with pass shooting waterfowl becomes a very fine dove gun.

Pheasants also sometimes require a lot of lead. At the 1975 "One Box" pheasant hunt at Broken Bow, Nebraska, I talked (the night be-fore competition) with a gentleman who assured me he had killed many, many pheasants and that by far the best combination was a skeet-choked 12 gauge and No. 7½ shot. Seems he had been doing quite a bit of practicing on game-farm pheasants at a shooting pre-serve. The next day the wind blew and the pheasants flew and I was lucky enough to get my limit without missing a bird. I was using No. 6 high-brass loads with the full-choke tube screwed into my Perazzi Mirage over-under 12 gauge.

Every shot in that event is recorded by judges, and I made it a point to find out how the man with the skeet gun fared. To put it in a nice way, he had not seriously reduced Nebraska's pheasant popu-lation. Yet I have hunted pheasants near Lethbridge in Alberta, Can-ada, when a skeet gun would have been just fine; birds were sticking tight along canal banks in heavy cover and often wouldn't flush until almost stepped upon. Pheasants will often do that, and in such cases I believe it is easier to try and center the bird's head with a gun with

Typical Southern quail country—piney woods with grass savannas—where the 20 gauge, or smaller, is perfectly adequate for gentlemanly bird shooting. Ranges are seldom long, and open chokes are best.

some choke and range than to gamble the next cock won't come cackling up at 40 yards.

One of the most important tricks to taking pheasants is remembering that the bird's bulk is mostly tail; to hit him low is almost certainly to cripple. A tail-shot cock pheasant, or any other pheasant that comes down with his head up, is likely to disappear and never be seen again unless you have a good dog and a great deal of knowledge of pheasant hunting—they'll run like ostriches and can hide under a pencil.

I've found exactly the opposite shooting technique applies to woodcock, quail, and ruffed grouse in heavy cover. There you can't very well concentrate on the bird's head because you'll be doing well to see the bird at all, and you either shoot at what you see or forget it. Blink once and he's out of sight behind the brush. This is fast, close gun pointing where a skeet shooter's beautifully executed swing and follow through may merely bang his gun barrels against a tree.

I have never advocated spot shooting because it is a poke-and-punch sort of thing rarely dependable on anything but a straightaway. But on close-cover woodcock I probably spot shoot to some extent be-

Pheasants sometimes flush underfoot, sometimes at the outer edge of shotgun range. With large shot and fairly tight choke, it is easier to permit a close bird to gain a little distance before firing (or concentrate on a head shot) so as not to ruin the meat than, because of inadequate pattern, to cripple birds that jump at longer range.

cause I just try and get off some kind of shot in the general direction the bird seems to be going. Sometimes that will turn out to be a tree, but it is remarkable how many birds fall when shot through what seemed to be dense foliage. Shot pellets get through somehow, and I've observed that the most efficient woods hunters do not stand around computing sustained lead.

No matter how open the barrel may be, this sort of shooting usually puts the hunters into an overchoked situation. And the best constriction I've found is none at all. One afternoon in Louisiana our party put up over 100 woodcock, and I cannot remember ever having cursed a firearm so severely as I did the lightweight little 20 gauge that kept connecting with vines, limbs, and tree trunks more often than birds. In theory, this was a fine upland gun. It had 26-inch barrels bored improved cylinder and modified and was being used primarily because I was doing some field testing of that model.

I liked the feel of it, and killed I believe every quail I shot at that afternoon. The quail were mostly in grassy openings alongside a little

There's a woodcock in this picture, but neither camera nor hunters picked up the fleeting shape clearly or quickly enough. In such cover a timberdoodle or quail can be gone in a wink, and the problem is getting gun on bird, not range nor penetration. For such cover, the author favors no choke at all, cylinder barrels.

bayou and all we got were relatively open shots because the singles would go on across the flooded bayou where we couldn't get to them. But the woodcock were right along the water's edge in thick brush, concentrated along a ridge by high water on either side. That was why we found so many woodcock in one small area and also why I nearly wore out the barrels of that little gun on tree trunks.

It didn't take long for a decision to be made. I'd buy the gun rather than send it back, and did anybody have a hacksaw? I knew the risks. Just whacking off a few inches of barrel is safe enough at producing broad, even cylinder-bore patterns because it effectively removes all choke. But many gun barrels are not the same wall thickness a few inches back of the muzzle that they are at the end, and if the barrels are not bored perfectly concentric, or maybe had been bent or regulated at the muzzle, there's a good chance patterns will not converge perfectly after the tubes are shortened.

I took that chance, bobbed off the barrels to 22 inches, and they shot to point of impact well enough for the job to be done. Since then I've killed a great many close-cover quail and woodcock with that gun. It is no longer a beautifully balanced firearm. It does not swing so much as it pokes. I would not use it on crossing doves or open-country quail. But it is very good for shooting around trees.

In a lifetime of fooling around with shotguns I've bobbed off quite a few barrels, and circumsized some, trying to retain a little choke by leaving a half inch or so of the start of the choke constriction intact. Most of the time this has worked. When it didn't, I've had to back bore or jug-choke the gun to get acceptable patterns and sometimes wound up getting rid of the gun to someone who needed a poker more than I did.

I once cut back the barrel of a beautiful-handling little Ithaca

Never gamble with an expensive gun by cutting off the barrels; impacts may not be true and balance often will change sufficiently to ruin the gun for anything other than close cover spot shooting. This fine old Parker 20-gauge double should be left as is, although boring out some choke can help for Southern-style quail shooting.

Above:
For larger upland birds such as pheasant, prairie chicken, and open-country grouse, modified choke in a 12 gauge is a fine compromise that can be made to pattern improved cylinder with brush loads but tighten to full with extra hard shot trap or pigeon loads.

Opposite:
For shooting a wide variety of game in Mexico, including tough wild pigeons, this shooter's gun has Baker choke tubes which screw into barrel to change choke. Exterior twist-type chokes are OK, but shooter must test to see which settings produce the patterns desired; markings cannot be completely trusted.

Model 37 Featherweight 20-gauge pump to 22 inches, trying to create an even faster gun. It turned out to be a fast gun indeed, but one so out of balance and so quick that when a quail got up I'd swing past him, stop and try to get back, and usually miss. I never could shoot that gun again. The moral is that the makers of firearms have some vague idea of how shotguns should balance, and it's wise to think twice about the type of hunting to be done before making radical changes.

Unfortunately, standard borings often fall short of being ideal for upland gunning. For all-around upland hunting, from quail to pheasants, I suppose I'd probably pick an over-under with one barrel bored

improved cylinder and the other improved modified (almost full). The English, of course, learned that years ago and many of their guns for rough shooting (what we'd call walk-up hunting) are bored quarter choke and three-quarter choke, which translates into just about improved cylinder and improved modified. For large upland birds modified is a good all-around choice. For closer quarters, and particularly if the gun is a 20 or 12 gauge with considerable pattern density to work with, a gun bored skeet in one barrel and modified in the other is deadly indeed. These borings can be obtained by opening up one barrel of a common improved cylinder/modified gun.

For the one-barrel man, improved cylinder is hard to beat. Many upland shooters try to compensate for the single barrel's single choke by adding a variable choke device, the most common being the twist-type, which supposedly will provide anything from wide open to extra full. There is nothing wrong with this except that the devices do not always deliver the choke spreads indicated.

By twisting and shooting, each time checking the pattern, the shooter should determine where that particular device must be turned to give the pattern desired. When this is determined, mark the spot with fingernail polish or a scratch or something to show where the "sweet spots" are. Some shooters use different colors of nail polish. Line up the red marks and you have improved cylinder, the white marks mean full, etc.

One other word of advice about adjustable chokes of this type; many guns do not shoot straight after having one installed. This is no fault of the device but of the gunsmith who installed it. Due to differences in barrel wall thickness or other factors a barrel cut back for variable choke installation may be shooting a foot or more off center unless the gunsmith checks it for alignment and preferably shoots it to determine impact. It is the rule rather than the exception that adding a choke device will raise the front sight and tend to lower impact.

If you're considering such an installation, first shoot the gun to see where it impacts. If it's OK, inform the gunsmith that you know where it shoots and that when the job is finished you'll shoot it again to check him out. He may offer to correct the impact if the installation changes it; if he doesn't do so, take it to another gunsmith. An off-shooting gun is to be avoided like a case of colic.

Another thing the short-barrel shooter needs to know is whether he is getting full velocity and penetration from his ammunition. Various loads contain various powders, some of which burn faster than others. This may be no big deal in a 30-inch barrel that offers plenty of time for slow-burning powders to be consumed. But go back to 24 inches or less and in the late afternoons you may find you're using the equivalent of a flame thrower. When the gun is throwing out a long

Special brushloads, so-marked on the box, broaden patterns as shown. New special skeet loads without the shot collar also open patterns at close range. But the most effective pattern spreader is the square (cube) shot used in Europe. Possibly they will someday become available in the U.S.

blaze of fire at the muzzle it is not burning its powder completely. Some flame throwing can be expected; it's just a part of shooting a very short barrel. But it can be minimized (and penetration improved) by finding out which loads do the best job.

Matching loads to conditions is a big part of the secret of getting more upland game. Say you have an improved-cylinder barrel and you want it to throw the broadest possible pattern for close cover. Try using a brush load (which has separators in its shot column to distribute the pellets more rapidly). Best of all for this are square shot loads—that's right, little cubes of lead—which really open up in a hurry and can convert a full-choke gun to about improved-cylinder performance at 25 yards. They're called Desperante loads and unfortunately are available only in Europe. The well-known gun writer Roger Barlow provided me a few for loading and testing.

In general, the inexpensive field loads sold in this country contain soft, easily deformed shot that spread faster because they deform more pellets. This is fine for quail or close-range game of any kind because shot stringing doesn't matter much at close range, certainly not so much as pattern spread. Heavier powder charges tend to open up patterns quicker than light loads.

Federal offers special loads (designated T-22) in No. 7½, 8, and 9 shot that do not have plastic shotcup wads and thus open patterns quite quickly. Although they also deform more shot pellets, the advantage in close cover is significant.

But say you want your improved-cylinder barrel to pattern as tightly as possible for pass-shooting doves or maybe those wild-flushing prairie quail that happen to be the common variety in some parts of Texas, Oklahoma, and Kansas, three of the best bobwhite states I've hunted.

The tightest, most efficient-patterning upland loads currently available are traploads and pigeon loads. In many guns you'll get about a 20 percent tighter pattern than the common upland load in the same shot size. Traploads are available only in 12 gauge and come in 1⅛ ounces of No. 7½, 8, or 8½ shot. Pigeon loads have 1¼ ounces of 7½, or 8. For doves I like 7½'s, because the larger pellets are less affected by wind drift and have sufficient shocking power to put down birds that might be feathered with 8's. I've taken a great many doves, many of them with 8's from open-choked, small gauge guns, but over the years, I've settled on 7½ if I'm using 1⅛ ounces or more of shot. For quail in ordinary conditions, a No. 8½ trapload first, followed by 8's, is a fine combination. For wild-flushing quail in high winds I often use 7½'s; for thicket birds, brush load 8's.

I lean toward larger shot than may be generally recommended for many upland situations because I've learned that prettiness at the pat-

Jump shooting, even with birds as small as doves, often requires tight patterns and good penetration. An excellent choice is 3¼ x 1¼ 7½'s in hard shot 12-gauge pigeon load, which patterns much better than standard high-velocity loads but has equal penetration at 50 yards.

tern board does not always prove out on birds. If dense distribution were the whole story, I'd shoot nothing but 9's. And indeed many shooters swear by them. But I've found they put too many pellets into the flesh of birds I plan to eat, feather too many going-away birds due to lack of penetration, and are more susceptible to wind drift than 8's or 7½'s.

A friend of mine who hunts quail in some of the most fabulous hunting country in America, the south Texas brush country, uses a .410 with No. 6 shot. His theory is that one or two 6's will instantly put down a quail that might flutter off into the brush when hit with several 9's. He also doesn't like small shot in his teeth, and says the 6's will drive on through and lodge against a bird's breastbone. I have never fired at a quail with No. 6 shot, but the man knows what he's talking about. He and his friends (who started out using 9's years ago and worked up to 6's) annually harvest well over 1,500 quail from his shooting lease and in the process possibly have learned something about shooting quail on that lease. Admittedly they have a problem different than most other shooters in that their birds must be shot very quickly while flying across openings in the brush (called sen-

Waterhole dove shooting is usually best with relatively open chokes; the birds aren't far but tend to be erratic when they see the shooter and are not always easy to hit. Author favors improved cylinder, No. 7½ or 8 shot.

In this situation quail must be dropped dead instantly or likely will be lost in brush beyond the open "sendero." Note trail of feathers left by the fast-moving bird centered by .410 load of No. 6 shot, a rare combination but one that works at close range due to little gun's shot deformation and quick opening of pattern.

deros) and if the bird is not dropped instantly in the opening he becomes very difficult to find in the dense, thorny brush. Dogs sent into such brush to search for cripples run the risk of rattlesnakes, so these shooters have a situation requiring sudden death to quail, usually at short yardages and with quick shots.

If the .410 seems a great handicap, note the illustration in the chapter Choosing Chokes and Loads that shows that at very close range a 3-inch .410 pattern is often larger than that of a 12 gauge. This is true because the little gun generates more chamber pressure (13,000 psi compared with around 11,000 for the 12 or 20) and deforms a lot of shot that quickly spread. The pattern may be as full of holes as a

Different dove-shooting situations require different loads; the top shooter needs a tight pattern because bird must fall instantly in the opening or be lost in brush. The shooter below, in shade at a waterhole, has a clean area around him where winged birds can easily be found and he can thus utilize benefits of broader pattern without losing cripples.

Around the world, versatility has made the 12 gauge the sportman's top choice. Here Spanish secretario shows red-legged partridge taken with improved-cylinder doubles, the most popular choice from Scotland to Spain for driven birds.

rusty bucket beyond 25 yards, but at quick, close range it gets the job done.

For dove shooters looking for a little extra range for really high-flying doves or wild-flushing quail, one of the finest and tightest patterning loads available is the pigeon load, containing 1¼ ounces of shot and the equivalent of 3¼ drams of powder. Federal Cartridge Company for some years had the tightest patterning load of this type; although marked "field load," it also carries the pigeon-load notation elsewhere on the box. The reason it is good is that it contains very hard shot, while most field loads contain soft. Therefore I would recommend it for long shots, but not in close-range upland situations where more pattern spread is needed. Remington has made 3¼ x 1¼ loads with extra-hard nickel shot that are great performers. Winchester in 1976 put on the market a new and highly efficient pigeon load offering extra hard 1¼ ounces of No. 8 or No. 7½ shot, and I would far rather shoot such loads—if I had to take my pheasants or ducks with 7½'s—than the standard high-velocity load. Patterns are tighter and penetration is often actually slightly better at 50 yards than with the high-velocity loads, due to the fact the hard pellets stay round and fly with less atmospheric resistance than deformed pellets. Also, the faster

In Botswana, Africa, the author's versatile Perazzi over-under (with inter-changeable choke tubes) took doves, sand grouse, ducks, and geese from same waterhole.

a load is started, the faster its percentage of velocity declines. At 40 yards, the high-velocity loads I've tested penetrate farther than the pigeon load; at 40 yards they were about equal with the pigeon load or slightly better. Recoil is less in the pigeon load.

Because of the many options of factory loads, including everything from brush loads to tight-patterning traploads and pigeon loads, the 12 gauge remains the most versatile of all upland guns. And if weight is a problem, there are 12 gauges that heft and handle about the same as ordinary 20 gauges. The 12-gauge Franchi autoloader (non-gas) weighs a little over 6½ pounds as does the Ithaca Featherlight pumpgun and the Franchi over-under. The Ithaca "XL" model autoloader is gas operated and weighs only very little more than the Franchi long-recoil action. Such guns, with short barrels, carry and handle more like standard 20 gauges but have the load options of the 12.

Certainly the 20 gauge is lighter in the same makes and models (the Franchi non-gas autoloader weighs about 5½ pounds) and 20's in almost any model seem to have a little better balance and quicker handling, plus trimmer looks, than comparable 12's.

Most versatile of the 20's are doubles and over-unders with 3-

inch chambers. I hunt a great deal with standard 20-gauge loads, but in a back pocket someplace there are usually some 3-inch magnum 7½'s in case a little more range or "authority" is required. Fortunately most modern two-barreled 20 gauges come with 3-inch chambers.

Whatever your choice of an upland gun, just remember that shooting conditions, not toughness of game, are likely to be the important factor—unless you're hunting elephants.

21

TRAP AND SKEET

A young cafe waitress one morning noticed the padded shoulder of my shooting shirt and asked the reason for it. When I told her I was on my way to a trapshoot, she stiffened and became quite cool, perhaps envisioning the blasting of some poor creature in a trap.

Somewhere in my files is a clipping from an antihunting publication quoting statistics on how many skeet shooters there are in America, the tone of the article seeming to imply "skeet birds" may be going the way of the passenger pigeon.

To me these were classic examples of the general lack of public understanding of the use of sporting firearms in general, and the games of skeet and trap seem particularly misunderstood even by a large segment of the nation's hunters.

How many times have you heard some hunter say that the reason he doesn't bother with clay targets is that he can beat "any of them hotshots" at ducks or quail?

Maybe he can, maybe he can't. So what?

Skeet and trap are great off-season fun, and shooting a shotgun can do nothing but help the field performance of any shooter no matter how good he may be. Compared with the prices of everything else nowadays, target games are relatively inexpensive, particularly when friends pool resources and acquire reloading equipment to reduce ammunition costs.

Since the clay-target games would each require a full-length book for adequate instructional discussion—and since there are some fine books that do just that—this chapter will hit just a few high spots. I will, however, provide the names of publications I consider to be the best on the subjects: *Score Better At Skeet* and *Score Better At Trap* by Fred Missildine (Winchester Press), and *Trapshooting with D. Lee Braun* and *Skeet Shooting with D. Lee Braun* (Remington Sportsmen's Library).

Now then, for the many who may not know, those clay targets thrown by hand devices are not skeet nor are they trap; they are clay targets thrown by hand devices. Many shooters erroneously refer to such practice as skeet.

Skeet is the game requiring two houses to launch targets, a high house and a low house, and the average distance of shots at targets passing at 50 miles an hour between those houses is 21 yards. Trap is the one in which all the targets come out of one house, but the shooter does not know exactly at what angle. Handicap trap requires a shooter to fire from yardage longer than 16 yards, that being the distance from which singles and doubles are shot.

If you have never seen either game (and believe me I had not until I killed many a mallard, dove, and quail) it might be worth visiting a gun club just to smell the powder burn. You also might get interested enough to try one or the other, and if so could get sufficiently hooked to become eventually a better all-around shot.

Why there is much controversy around sporting-goods stores over whether some skeet or trap champion could beat ol' so-and-so at doves or quail I'll never understand. That is sort of like arguing over whether the current champion at the Indianapolis Speedway could beat some backwoods mail carrier at driving in deep mud or snow. The clay-target games, like driving or anything else, have become highly specialized. So, for that matter, are the various forms of hunting. I've seen terrific quail shots who can't lead ducks worth a darn.

Both skeet and trap are to some extent trick shooting, in that once you learn the trick you can certainly smoke a lot more clay than when you first walked out on the field attempting to shoot as you would at real birds. For this reason, no good field shooter who fares poorly his first round of either game should give up and go home. Nor should any sharpie at skeet or trap come to believe he must automatically be better on birds than the man who follows bird dogs all season.

For one thing, the clay target games contain optical illusions.

Trapshooting is an optical illusion in which the target appears to be going almost straight away but really is rising quite swiftly. And that is why special stocks are needed for shooting trap really well; the higher stock (or lately, the bent-up barrel) provides some built-in compensation for the optical illusion inherent to the game. No matter how great the field shooter, if he must hold high over every fast-rising trap target, blotting it out with his gun in order to make a hit, he's at a disadvantage with shooters whose guns are set up so the bird can be seen and broken at the same time. But often the addition of an inexpensive cheek pad to the comb of the field stock is sufficient to make it a trapstock.

A dove at 50 miles an hour is flapping his wings pretty regularly; he lets you know he's moving on. So does a teal or bluebill or bandtail pigeon. But a skeet target sort of sneaks out of the house looking as big as a basketball (or maybe for beginners more like an aspirin). The illusion often is that the target simply cannot be going as fast as the required forward allowance in front of it indicates. This is particularly true of the long stations (positions 3, 4, and 5) where sustained leads of 3 to 4 feet in front of the target will break it. Otherwise you have to swing to beat sixty, pass it, and still see some daylight ahead. Most shooters, when they finally break a target from one of those stations, estimate the distance to target to be around 30 yards or more. It is actually 21 yards to the center crossing point, but the speed is roughly 50 miles an hour at that point—another couple of optical illusions.

American-style trapshooting as seen from the mouth of the traphouse. The clay target, always going away from the shooter, is launched by a single machine at varying angles. The trapshooters are shooting from 16 yards behind the trap, which is standard distance for singles competition. At handicap, depending upon scoring average and ability, shooters may be required to fire from as far back as 27 yards, meaning their targets must be broken at 50 yards or so. With every yard of increased distance, the game gets tougher.

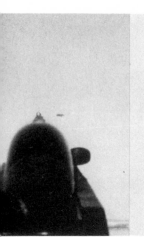

With a movie camera mounted on his gunstock D. Lee Braun smashes one of the toughest targets on the field, low house 4. Starting out ahead of the target (left) he then pulls ahead to establish what he sees as 4 feet of forward allowance ahead of the target (center) which is shown breaking (right) as the ejected hull is thrown from the autoloader. It is difficult for many shooters to visualize forward allowances ahead of targets; the actual lead ahead of this target was 4 to 4½ feet (as Braun saw it) but it does not look that way over the gun barrel. For this reason, the book Skeet Shooting With D. Lee Braun, *precedes each over-shoulder visual lesson with a view of a measuring device showing precisely how three feet, two feet, etc. actually look over the barrel at skeet yardages. (Sequence photographs from* Skeet Shooting With D. Lee Braun, *courtesy of Remington Arms Co.)*

I believe the biggest mistake made by the beginning skeet or trap shooter is in equating his first score with his ability. The guy who so casually smokes 25 straight has done it before, a lot of times probably. I've seen shooters who couldn't break 10 targets out of the first 25 turn out to be champions once they realized how to equate the optical illusions with their field-shooting experience.

The second biggest mistake, I believe, is made by the shooter who is not serious about taking up championship skeet or trap but who tries to learn to shoot precisely the way the current champions do, with a rigidly mounted gun. It's all in what you're after. If you are interested in improving your field-shooting and game-hunting skills, forget locking into the gun at skeet. Drop the gun to the position you'd approach a pointing quail dog and take your shots as you would in the field. You may not break quite as many targets, but your hunting skills should increase significantly. But even if you do shoot skeet locked in, your field shooting also will improve to some extent.

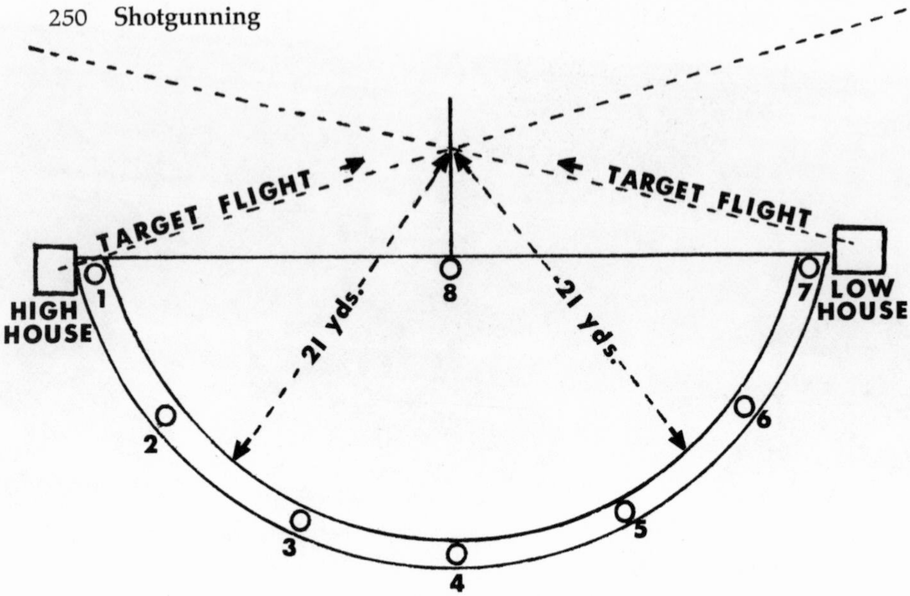

Above:

As seen from above, this is the basic layout of a skeet range for either American-style or international-style skeet. Note that the targets do not go straight across between high house and low house, but at a distinct angle. The longest distance from any station to the crossing point of the target is 21 yards, and average target speed in American skeet is about 50 miles an hour, for international, 60 miles per hour or more. The shooter begins each round at Station 1. Singles and doubles are fired from Stations 1, 2, 6, 7; all others offer one high-house target and one from the low house.

Opposite:

Many things can be done with a skeet field that will aid field shooters. This illustration shows a small tower containing a rotating trap machine installed above the high house to throw targets higher and at wide and unknown angles. From the various skeet stations, tower shooting becomes a most difficult game of great benefit for practicing for doves, ducks, etc.

The international skeet and trap games contribute more, I believe, to field-shooting proficiency than do American skeet and trap. Both international games are shot as the standard form of skeet and trap virtually everywhere else in the world, despite the fact that both games originated in America. They are more like field shooting in the following respects: At international skeet you can't shoulder the gun; it must be down at waist level with stock touching hipbone and must stay there until the target emerges from the house. And believe me those international targets do emerge! They are moving almost one-third faster than American skeet targets, and they do not necessarily appear

when the shooter calls pull. There is up to three seconds delay; you may get the target instantly or it may come three seconds later. This is great for nervous indigestion and also for learning to be death on game birds.

International trap permits shouldering the gun and has no delay mechanism as does international skeet. But its targets are faster, wider, higher, lower, and harder than American trap. International targets may go sizzling off very high, seemingly straight up when you first see one climbing into the breeze at about 100 mph, or they may be grass cutters a few inches off the ground. They can go hard right or left at such acute angles and so fast that many American trapshooters, accustomed to holding a high gun, never see the low-angle targets. This has happened several times on squads where I've been competing; I saw it in a NRA Zone Championship in Florida and another at DeWitt, New York—good American-style trapshooters literally not even seeing a target until it hit the ground 75 or 80 yards away.

But fun! You get two shots at each target, and if you break it with the second barrel the hit scores just the same as it would if it had been hit by the first shot. Which, of course, makes it more like field shooting where a grouse or quail counts just as dead if hit by the first barrel as the second. The ability instantly to correct and place the second shot is one of the major differences between the more deliberate pace of American trap and the stand-on-tiptoe-and-pray excitement of international. The speed of the targets and the extremely long second-barrel shots so beautifully executed by Olympic-caliber shooters makes international trap almost as much fun to watch as to shoot.

International skeet is also a great game to watch, particularly when contestants face Station-8 targets hurtling straight toward them and with only a split second to mount the gun and pull the trigger. This shot is so fast that even experts at it occasionally are unable to get gun completely to shoulder. But most are good enough that they can break the target virtually from the hip if necessary.

Unfortunately there is still relatively little international skeet or trap being shot in America, but it is gradually increasing. One reason international trap has been rare is that the original I.S.U. (International Shooting Union) trench layout under Olympic or world-competition rules required 15 target machines in an underground bunker, an in-

The quail walk game is started with gun down in hunting position and shooter walking slowly toward the center of the field from each shooting station. The puller may release singles or doubles at any time he desires, trying to catch the shooter offstride. This is not only fun but excellent practice at quick gun mounting and instant judgment of target—the same qualities required in field shooting. Here the author smokes a high house after walking past Station 8.

Above:

International skeet requires the gun butt at waist level (butt visible below the elbow) with no movement until the target appears. This may be instantly or up to three seconds after the call of "pull." Here 1976 All-American team captain Ricky Pope of Trinity University is shown winning the U.S. Intercollegiate Championship in 1975 with 98 x 100, a very good score at international. Pope is one of this country's most promising young clay target shooters, deadly at skeet or trap. At the collegiate championships he broke 97 x 100 at international trap to tie for that championship as well.

Opposite:

Here's something few U.S. shooters have ever seen, a full-house bunker layout for international trap, as used in Olympic competition. The top photo shows shooters at their stations; there is no visible target house as at American trap, only a ground level roof from which targets emerge at more than 100 miles per hour, some wide, some almost straight up, some at grass level. The middle photo shows the 15 traps in clusters of 3 beneath each shooting station; shooters fire from 17 yards behind the lip of the roof. The lower photo shows the expensive machinery and manpower and why so few true international layouts exist in the U.S. This one is at Lackland Air Force Base.

stallation cost that could be afforded by very few gun clubs. Most of the bunker traps in the U.S. are on Armed Forces bases, and not all of those are used much anymore.

But changes have been made in I.S.U. rules which now permit a single machine that can duplicate the angles and speeds of the 15-target trench. With the single machine, the game becomes less expensive to play. But it is not quite the same, and there has been much controversy over the fact that U.S. teams to the Olympics and World Moving Target Championships have in recent years been selected at tryouts conducted with single trap or wobble trap setups only to be confronted by the full 15-trap layouts where gold medals are won or lost. This has been compared with picking a U.S. equestrian team by having contestants try out on cow ponies.

Fortunately the U.S. Army has an excellent full trap bunker layout at Fort Benning, Ga., and it is from this facility, and one previously in use at Lackland Air Force Base at San Antonio, Texas, that most of this country's medal-winning trapshooters have come, including Don Haldeman who won the gold at the 1976 Olympics.

That's the good news about U.S. Olympic hopes at trapshooting; the bad news is that most of the military bases that once fielded strong trapshooting teams no longer have budgets to train such shooters. Nonetheless, one-trap wobble machines are showing up at public and private gun clubs around the country, and there is at least hope the international style of shooting will catch on in this country. Winchester-Western in 1976 announced a new and improved single-trap machine able to throw as hard and at as many angles as the 15-trap bunker machines. That machine was badly needed.

Why international skeet has not caught on faster in the U.S. is a matter of conjecture. Only minor modifications (like tightening the trap spring, using harder targets, and plugging a delay timer into the pull cord) are required to shoot international skeet on an ordinary American skeet range. The shooting stations and distances are the same. In fact, international skeet rules as the game is played almost everywhere else in the world are very similar to the original skeet rules that initiated the game in America. Years ago American skeet rules required a low gun position, but the rules were gradually relaxed to permit the rigid, high-precision stances of today.

My suggestions to shooters out to win at American skeet is to learn to shoot with the gun mounted the way most everybody else does. But if you want to improve your field shooting, and perhaps get a head start at a game where trophies may come easier to newcomers because the competition is not yet quite so grooved in, international seems a great way to go. The field-shooting advantages are obvious; nobody walks through woodcock woods or quail cover with gun rigidly mounted all day long. And the more practice at fast, accurate gun mounting a shooter can get from skeet, the more it will help him on birds.

For the casual or beginning shooter at trap or skeet, here are a few basic tips that can sometimes get lost in more complicated discussions.

The original gun position, relative to the house from which the bird is launched, is very important. Often a shooter first trying trap-shooting will start with his gun pointing at the top of the traphouse, which means that with targets rising fast and high he has a lot of catching up to do. Watch the targets. If they are flying high, it helps to start the gun well above the top of the house (many top shooters hold the gun horizontal to the ground, at eye level where little upward movement is required). Trap targets are likely to make abrupt jumps upward in a headwind. Skeetshooters can experiment with bringing the gun back nearer the house; the nearer the house the more they have to chase the target and swing with it. Starting farther from the house gives a jump on the bird but can lead to poking rather than

The Grand American Championship at Vandalia, Ohio, lasts more than a week and attracts more competitors than any other sporting event in the world. It is the World Series of trapshooting. Nearly 20,000 shooters, supported by score-keepers under umbrellas toe the line in various events, and trap ranges stretch for more than a mile.

Clay-target shooting, particularly skeet, is changing with the times, possibly for the better. These youngsters at the National Gun Club at San Antonio, Texas, during the intercollegiate championships took advantage of the Texas sun and had a great time cheering on their teams. Although bikinis around shooting ranges are not conducive to total concentration, the kids took it in stride and shot scores as sizzling as the scenery.

swinging. Practice will show where your gun position works out best to suit your shooting style and reflexes.

Whatever the system, it is vitally important that there be consistency of gun position, because only then can there be a consistent series of movements to break the target. Many new shooters are not even aware of where they start the gun, and thus start out with a distinct handicap.

Another vital factor is where the shooter looks for the bird to appear. Many top trapshooters mount the gun with eyes focused on the spot just above and beyond the traphouse where they will first catch a glimpse of the "streak" of the departing target. This is faster, I believe, than waiting in some vague way for the target to appear somewhere over the end of the barrel. By concentrating the eyes just beyond the traphouse, the two-eyed shooter can in effect see "through" the gun and it does not distract him. One-eyed shooters usually have to hold on the traphouse to prevent the target being blotted out by a high gun.

Many trapshooters, observing the latest trends toward ultra-high

Dan Bonillas of Los Banos, Calif., one of the greatest trapshooters of all time, set in 1975 more all-time records than any shooter in recent history. He believes in complete familiarity with one gun and does all his trapshooting with the same Perazzi MX-8 "combo," which consists of a full-choked single barrel (shown) for singles and handicap and a set of over-under barrels for doubles, which fit the same receiver and fore end. He also standardizes on loads with Winchester paper-hulled Super Target Trap ammunition, which he says provide low recoil and high pattern density in his barrels. Note the high step-up rib which permits a relatively straight stock without excessive elevation of impact. Bonillas prefers a sight picture almost flat down the rib rather than the upswept view provided by a high-combed stock and/or bent-up barrel preferred by some other modern champions.

shooting guns (barrels bent up, extremely high stocks, etc.) have the impression that this is the only way to go. But the shooter who has set by far the most records of any in recent history, Dan Bonillas, shoots a relatively "flat-stocked" gun without a bent barrel. Each shooter must find the equipment and shooting system that works best for him; too much attempting to copy the local champion may be a mistake.

Reading the manner in which a target breaks can be a great aid to the shooter in correcting or perfecting his pointing. If the target often breaks in three rather large pieces, there is an indication it is being hit low. Obviously if the front end or tail end is knocked off, either too much or not enough forward allowance is being applied. When a trapshooter sees the top of his targets consistently breaking, he may try lowering his gun position slightly and then begin smoking them.

Although most trapshooting champions use full choke, even for close 16-yard targets, the average new shooter will fire better scores with a modified barrel because it gives him more margin for error. If he is a new shooter he won't have to worry about 27-yard handicap targets where the full choke is at its greatest advantage. Modified barrels break handicap targets back to 22 or 23 yards with smoking authority.

Skeet shooters using small guns such as the .410 and 28 will probably find they can break more targets with the gun weighted for more forward balance. Remington makes special weights for its 1100 skeet guns that simply screw on to the same threads as the gun's original magazine cap. Lead tape (which can be found in many golf pro shops) is an easy way to weight barrels of any gun; simply apply strips of it to the underside of the barrel.

Hunters who have no serious interest in trapshooting other than to practice for hunting season may find they can score better (and actually obtain better practice) by adding ⅛ to ¼ inch of moleskin to the stock comb. This will help compensate for the optical illusion of the rising clay targets, an illusion that is not so pronounced in rising game birds, whose body angle and beating wings tell the shooter more clearly the speed of ascent.

There are thousands of tips for clay target shooting, the best of which can be had only by spending some time around a trap or skeet field. My experience has been that it is well worth the time.

22

COMPETITION

Shooters have always been highly competitive, and whether the object is the Grand American Handicap or beating the guy next door, all of us at one time or another experience the pangs of pressure. Some shoot best when the chips are down; others choke and miss shots they normally would hit. For the latter, shooting under pressure produces symptoms similar to stage fright. Palms perspire, pulse rate increase, breath gets short, and just as a speaker's voice may quiver or break when he stands up before an audience, a shooter's nerves and muscles sometimes refuse to cooperate when he needs them most.

I certainly am no psychologist, but I have observed many shooters. And I firmly believe a part of the difference is in the shooter's basic personality. If he tends to be self-confident, even cocky, he is likely to believe he can win and may very well do so. Confidence is the greatest weapon against choking. Some have it naturally, others must develop it.

Veteran competitors know that just looking cool and deadly, relaxed and ready is one of the best weapons they have. At the Mint Handicap in Las Vegas one year, a new trapshooter named Richard Smith of Dallas, Texas, tied for the big money with 99 x 100 and was in a shootoff for the championship. On one station he reached for a shell, dropped it, bent down and picked it up, turned and laughed at some friend in the crowd, kissed the shell, and then called for the target. He smoked it a few feet out of the house. If that distraction unnerved anybody it was the other shooter; Smith won.

Although new to trapshooting Smith is a veteran live-pigeon shooter who knows every trick of the trade of gamesmanship. I'm sure he did not drop that shell on purpose, but I am equally sure he determined to let the accident unnerve his opponent rather than himself. The foundation for that capability is the understanding of what pressure really is, and is not. Many shooters suffer pressure when they should be feeling the exhilaration of being ahead of the game.

I've observed shooters nervously pacing around the scoreboard, confronted with the fact that all of a sudden they are leading the race or are tied for it, and thus the feeling of pressure increases. It should be exactly the other way round. The man feeling the most pressure should be the one just behind the pace. If he misses, he's out of it. The man in front at least has a little cushion for error. And the very fact he is out front means he is shooting better than anyone else. He is proving he can do it. So he should be feeling stronger, surer. And if he isn't, he should go over into a corner and have a little talk with himself.

To new shooters, the presence of a crowd may add to competitive pressure; veterans may be stimulated by this element of major shoots. Here Noel Winters, 1975 world skeet champion, is cool and confident. Note how his left hand holds the fore end lightly for relaxed control. Winters used Purbaugh tubes (inserts in end of barrels) in his Krieghoff to shoot the same gun in .410, 28-, 20-, and 12-gauge events.

When a top trapshooter toes the line, nothing matters but the target if he is to win consistently. Here shooters at the Mint Handicap ignore sand blowing into their faces from a short desert windstorm. Shooting conditions are a part of the luck of the draw; the shooter who worries about being unlucky enough to shoot in rain or wind merely adds a more serious handicap—poor mental attitude.

I recall one youngster at a live-bird shoot who was literally sweating through his shooting jacket. He was tied with one of the best shots in the world, and faced a sudden-death shootoff. "Of all people," he groaned, "and all places. We'll be shooting it off on ring one, and I got three bad pulls there last time I shot."

My advice to him went something like this: "You can't shoot that other guy, so there is no use thinking about him. You can't shoot the puller, so there is no use thinking about those bad pulls. What you can shoot, and must shoot, is the bird. And that is what you should be thinking about right now. Are they flying high or low, hooking with the wind or driving? You should be down there on ring one watching and planning exactly how you will kill that first bird rather than talking to me."

He did not win. But he killed his first bird, got over his sweat to some extent, and simply was beaten by a better shooter.

Concentration on the job to be done is a wonderful antidote to pressure. If a shooter is concentrating properly, he may not know he has won until the shooting stops. All he is thinking about is making sure his gun is in the right place, that he is shooting with proper timing. The crowd, the other shooters, are just out there somewhere in the edge of consciousness.

I believe the word concentration has been written so much in interviews with skeet and trap champions that it has become misinterpreted by many new shooters. Concentration does not mean the champions think of nothing else from the time the shoot starts, nor does it mean they are so buried in concentration they don't see what's happening around them or hear things. They have developed the ability to concentrate totally at the time they are shooting; then they can turn it off and relax in between.

The mind will accept only so much concentration. Too much of it

On the firing line there is tendency to feel the whole world is watching, but it is evident here—at a columbaire pigeon shoot—that others are more likely socializing or worrying about their own score. Although the most difficult, columbaire is the least formal of all shooting sports.

It is wise to arrive at the shooting field, equipment ready to go, at least 15 minutes before your skeet or trap squad is to shoot. This provides eyes time to adjust to the light, gives the shooter time to study how targets are flying on that field, and have mind and body prepared for the concentration ahead. A last-minute dash to the field, with squad waiting, has cost many a target in the first round.

is tiring and will eventually dull the shooter's capabilities. The most common example is the new shooter who starts concentrating the night before the shoot, turning and tossing in bed, mentally going over the targets he must hit the next day. But birds hit the night before do not count on the scoreboard, so there is no use in lying awake shooting at them. The top guns will be relaxing trying to think of something else.

Too much relaxing, of course, can also be a bad thing, especially if it involves the overuse of alcohol the night before a shoot. This tends to produce jumpy nerves and can affect timing and reflexes the day after. Loss of sleep is one of the worst things for shooting performance, particularly after the shooter passes his 20s. Some shooters use mild sleeping pills to insure a good night's sleep if they feel too keyed up before a big shoot.

In European-style box pigeons, the moment of truth comes when the shooter faces a row of boxes, one of which will produce a speeding, dodging bird which must fly only to the boundary fence to be lost whether hit or not. Here the shooter favors a crosswind from right, holding his gun slightly in that direction, realizing that a bird from the boxes at left will be out of range very quickly downwind.

No matter how it is accomplished the shooter can deal with competition better if he is fresh and rested and if he confines his concentration to when it counts. There is no need to go into some kind of trance before the shoot starts. By saving full concentration until it is needed, all power is there; the mental battery hasn't been drained by leaving the switch on between rounds.

One of the most effective forms of concentration is studying how the bird is hit or the target breaks and working to perfectly center the next one. Just tell yourself you're merely working on your game, which is indeed what you're doing, and if you get sufficiently absorbed in that you don't have time to develop fears of losing.

Apprehension, or fear of missing, is the principal reason for poor performance. Some shooters may tell themselves that it's just a game, the championship doesn't really matter, or things of that sort. But it is impossible to fool one's subconscious mind, and it's better to be honest with it. You want to win. The way to do it is to hit with every shot right in the middle, and take them one at a time. The shooter who goes into a round of trap or skeet thinking that he must have "this 25" to win is kidding himself. What he must have is the next target, then the one after that.

The champions understand pressure, and use it to advantage. The adrenaline the body pumps under stress is strong stuff; it prepares muscles, eyes, and nerves for the utmost challenge. Cutting the edge off that with alcohol or sedatives is throwing away one of the advantages nature provided.

The sensation generated by the thrill of being out front of the pack is possibly the greatest advantage a shooter can have. At the World Live-Pigeon Championships in Mexico City I shared a cab every morning with Bueford Bailey, the great trapshooter from Nebraska who is also a terrific hunter and pigeon shooter. Somebody mentioned that another shooter, who had not missed, must really be under pressure, and Bailey laughed.

"I'd sure like to be under that kind of pressure," he said. "I'm one down."

There was a feature article about Bailey in *The American Shotgunner*, a magazine for and about shotgun shooters, in which the story was told of a year at the Grand American in which more than 40 shooters tied with 200 straight for the Clay Target Championship of America and somebody asked Bailey what he thought his odds were of winning

Some of the most beautiful gun clubs in the world have been built around the sport of pigeon shooting, which dates back to England in the 1700s. This one is at Mexico City, where shooters in the lounge overlook the competition while those at the bar watch the world championships on closed-circuit television.

An Italian professional in the world championships points gun to sky for a moment of intense concentration before lowering it to box level. Note the rib chalked white to show up against the ground. The man at right is holding a microphone that will electronically release a bird from one of the boxes the instant the shooter calls "pull"; results are instantaneous in any language.

against all those tough shooters. "Better odds than when the event started," he answered, and went on to win it.

That was a most significant remark relative to competition. Bailey was sharp enough to take mental advantage of the fact that instead of the hundreds of shooters he started out to beat in that 200-target race, he only had 44 left.

Live-pigeon shooters may face more pressure than exists in any other shooting sport. The birds are more difficult to hit than clay targets, and each bird counts more. Each one in a 25-bird pigeon shoot is the equivalent to 8 targets in a 200-target trap or skeet event. Certainly in any sport it does no good to miss one, but just one flyer can really mean the difference between champagne and soda pop afterwards. The shooter must be absolutely on his tiptoes in readiness, because he has no idea which direction the bird will go. Also, no matter how perfect his lead and swing may be, if the bird makes a sudden directional change at the instant the trigger is pulled, a miss results. A fair comparison of that in terms of pressure might be a golfer in a sudden-death playoff confronted with controlling not only his stance and swing but the possibility that at the last instant the ball would move over a foot.

Pigeon shooting permits two shots at each bird for that reason, and the shooter must be in total concentration, with instantaneous reflexes, to get the second shot off in time should the bird make a move on the first one.

In his book *The Golden Age of Shotgunning,* Bob Hinman wrote: "Box birds, flyers, live birds—whatever name you call it—pigeon shooting has always been the aristocrat of shotgun sports. Today, it's where many big-league trap and skeet champions end up after collecting all the titles and silver they desire." He went on to say that pigeon shooting is a big-money game, which it is, and if there is anything that can contribute to pressure, money seems to be it.

In the Golden Days Hinman wrote about so well, pigeons provided the toughest test of a shooter, just as they do now. In fact, the

Before entering the ring, each shooter inserts a plastic chip into an automatic selector mechanism that will choose which box will open for his bird; nobody knows which it will be.

After winning the high over all Grand Prix of the Americas at pigeons in 1976, the author is congratulated by 1975's world champion, John Tirelli of Bologna, Italy. The trophy shown is a bronze buckle engraved by famed gun engraver Frank Hendricks.

first Grand American Championship was fired at live pigeons. The predecessors of the modern clay pigeon consisted of attempts to duplicate the flight of live birds, and years ago glass balls filled with feathers were thrown from mechanical traps in an attempt to simulate a game that was thriving in England back in 1793.

Pigeon shooting remains the biggest shotgun game in Europe, at least as far as money is concerned, and is better understood there than here. Europeans seem to take the pragmatic view that it is no more cruel than hunting birds in the field, or perhaps shooting pigeons at field trials for dogs as is widely practiced in the U.S. The pigeon shoot amounts to a field trial for hunters; no mechanical target can duplicate difficult flight characteristics of birds. Since the birds provide food utilized primarily by the poor, and give work to trappers (who are often acquired by municipalities to help control pigeon populations and the diseases they carry) even the non-shooting European tends to view the pigeon shoot as a means of reducing damage to buildings and the transmission of diseases at no cost to the taxpayer. The birds would have to be controlled anyway, as the budget of many U.S. cities attest,

Oddsmakers on every bird create a roar of conversation in several languages at the world live-bird championships, adding to the pressures of sudden-death shoot-off in Mexico City.

because they are so prolific and because of the health problems. Outbreaks of parrot fever and encephalitis have been traced to pigeons in some cities.

In Italy, magazines cover pigeon shooting much the same as publications in the U.S. cover trap and skeet; large crowds watch the competition. In Spain, King Juan Carlos personally presented trophies to winners of the 1976 world championships.

Despite these attitudes elsewhere, the relatively little pigeon shooting done in the U.S. is kept discreetly quiet and the potential for making money at it is very small. There are no touring professionals, such as those in Europe who compete for thousands of dollars, automobiles, and other prizes on a touring circuit similar to the golf and tennis circuits in America. These European professionals are the modern masters of the shotgun—at least at the sort of shooting for which the fowling piece was originated—and their shooting techniques vary a great deal from those used by U.S. skeet and trap experts.

The hunter, who also expects to shoot live birds rather than clay targets, can perhaps learn much from them. Guns, for example, are balanced almost perfectly between the hands, even slightly barrel light

A columbaire, or thrower, goes into an overhand windup with grace and power; a split second later the bird was gone; missed with both barrels. The row of flags in the background marks the perimeter of the 100-meter scoring ring.

in some instances, rather than with the weight-forward balance preferred by clay-target champions. Stocks are normally straighter and higher at comb than U.S. hunters prefer, but the European professional has learned a shooting style whereby the gun barrel is kept below the bird to provide a better look at the sudden turns, twists, and reversals of direction only live birds can accomplish. The likelihood of head raising is reduced, and there seems little doubt that this is the best of all shooting styles if it can be mastered and used in the field. But most U.S. shooters would have to learn to shoot all over again to be able to hold below every bird with a high-shooting gun.

Perhaps the greatest lesson from the live-bird profession is the art of dealing with pressure and competition; pressure is the name of this game. With hucksters yelling the odds (in Europe they bet on every bird at a major championship) the shooter stands on the firing line feeling very much in the spotlight. If he hits, there may be no applause from the crowd because the oddsmakers are usually giving 8 or 9 to 1 that the shooter hits, and they win. But if the shooter misses, a great roar goes up, because the oddsmakers have lost and everybody else wins. At Mexico City I got so mesmerized listening to my own odds go up that I missed the 21st bird in the 25-bird world championship. And there was nothing to blame but one brief lapse of concentration.

Pigeon shooting today consists of two basic competitions, columbaire, in which the birds are thrown by hand, and box-pigeon or flyer competition, where birds are released from devices called boxes, which in effect are miniature traphouses containing one bird each. These boxes are in a small circle surrounded by a low fence and the shooter does not know from which one of the boxes the bird will come. The bird must fly only 17½ yards to be clear of the boundary, and with a strong wind can be at the fence before some shooters get off the first shot.

The reason live birds are used, rather than some form of mechanical target, is that they are so totally unpredictable and difficult. Whereas it may be possible to predict the potential winners of a trap or skeet shoot, where targets fly with some similarity, it is impossible to predict who will win a live-bird shoot until the last shot has been fired. A certain percentage of birds are virtually unkillable by virtue of erratic moves made the instant the trigger is being pulled. The competition is toughest of all at the columbaire-style shoot.

The difficulty of any shooting game can to some extent be assessed by how many targets are required to separate the field. Nowadays, it takes 200 or more targets to do that at 12-gauge skeet or 16-yard trap, but only 100 at .410 skeet or handicap trap, because these latter contests are more difficult.

Box pigeons require 25 birds to separate winners from losers. But columbaire (hand-thrown) pigeons require only 10 birds. Very few 10 straights are recorded. The game came from Spain, flourished along the Mexican border, and now also exists quietly in many Southern and Southwestern states. Numbers of shoots are relatively small, usually 1 or 2 per year in a given area. The scoring ring is big, 100 meters from the shooter's position to the boundary fence, but the bird launched by a professional columbaire is so incredibly fast and erratic that the finest skeet, trap, and flyer shooters do very well to average 7 birds out of 10.

The international organization TAPA (Tiro Al Pichon Association) compiles averages of its members, selects All-American teams each year, and sets rules and regulations for competition. Of top shooters chosen for the 5-man All-American team each year, averages of 80 percent are extremely rare and shooters with 60 percent are classified in the masters division.

Here competition becomes a three-headed monster; the shooter is competing against his own nerves, the bird, and with another man who is exactly like a baseball pitcher in that his reputation rides upon how many strikeouts he throws. The art of hand throwing pigeons, with graceful windup and delivery much like the form of a discus thrower, was brought here by a maestro from Valencia, Spain, named Pepe Manuata. Since then, American throwers have developed other styles and I believe are better than the maestro ever was.

Perhaps the significance of all this, which may be fascinating to some shooters and utterly boring to others, is that the competitive side of shotgun shooting reaches its peak as numbers of targets remaining

This bird has been thrown discus style by maestro Pepe Manuata. The feathers in ring are carefully chosen tailfeathers, plucked to help turn the birds in the direction the columbaire desires. The bird's flight is not impaired by the loss of the feathers, and in effect is helped to get away. This shooter also missed, even though when stopped at a 1,000th-second shutter speed, the shot appears easy.

to be shot are reduced. The columbaire pigeon shooter, who will have only 10 birds per day to determine his fortune, feels intense pressure from the very first shot. The skeet or trap shooter capable of breaking scores in the high 90's may not really begin to feel pressure until the final 25.

At this point, champions are separated from chokers. This is really a strange situation when one thinks about it, because in effect the most pressure should be on the first shot. If that one is missed, the shooter is in immediate trouble. Yet if he has continued far into the shoot without a miss, he should be feeling much more sure of himself; he has had all those other targets to practice on getting ready for the final targets. The two greatest all-around shotgun competitors I have known are Joe Devers and Grant Ilseng. And they have both told me the same thing—that the last bird should be the easiest. "If you get that far," Ilseng said, "you can darn sure hit one more."

23

THE SHOT STRING STORY

How does a shotgun's load arrive at its target? Is it strung out in a long line, or pancake shaped as shown by hits on a stationary pattern plate? Or, as one of my erudite friends puts it, who gives a damn? My tests indicate we should all give a damn. With some loads, shot can string out sufficiently at distant crossing angles to cripple not only the bird being shot at but one several yards behind. Yet the most quoted of all early shotgun writers, Major Sir Gerald Burrard, conducted tests back in 1923 that convinced him shot stringing was not really much of a problem.

Few students of Burrard have studied the Major's test reports more earnestly than I have, and what he actually said was that he lost as much as 30 percent of his pattern density on crossing targets at 40 yards from shot stringing. These were pellets that simply did not arrive at the target along with the bulk of the pattern. Thirty percent was in fact his average loss with improved-cylinder barrels at that yardage; the average density loss, with full-choke barrels, was 13 percent at 40 yards. These are significant losses in shotgun performance, particularly when a load is already nearing the line between killing and crippling.

But the Major said that not many shots were taken at directly crossing birds (in driven-grouse shooting that is not even cricket) and he figured 35 yards to be a good long shot anyway.

Burrard wrote that despite the loss in pellet density, he found very little elongation of the pattern across his target, an armor-plated Model T Ford, at which he fired from distances of 30 to 40 yards and mostly at 30 miles per hour. He did make a few tests at 40 miles an hour, this being, as he wrote, "the maximum the car could attain with regularity."

He computed from his observations that the actual length of the shot string in midair (or the main bulk of it) was about 4 feet, 6 inches at 40 yards while improved cylinders showed a string length of about 5 feet, 6 inches at the same range. These computations conflict in many ways with more modern tests. Winchester technicians photographed full-choke shot strings at 40 yards with ordinary hunting loads, and found them to be about 11 feet long. Even discounting the front 5 percent and rear 5 percent of the string, which are highly inconsistent, the length remained over 9 feet. That's roughly twice as long as Burrard figured. With all due respects to most of the pioneering research done by the Englishman, he was apparently quite wrong in some of his surmises. And one of the first to prove him so was a brilliant young American engineering graduate from Cornell named John Olin.

At the same time that Burrard was studying shot strings, Olin was working to obtain a patent on an instrument known as a flightometer, to be used in determining the length of shot strings. That patent was ultimately issued to Western Cartridge Company of East Alton, Ill. The basic patent claim was: "A method of determining the stringing of a loss of shot which consists in causing each shot to pass through a stationary target and a target moving at a known speed, measuring the time intervals between successive shot by the respective distances the moving target moves during the intervals between passage of said successive shot."

Olin found that shot strings of the 1920s were irregular and some were as long as 25 feet. He recognized this to be an imperfection and was many years ahead of his time in realizing that pellet deformation was the principal culprit. He went to work on the problem from two directions. One was development of progressive-burning powders, designed to launch the shotload with less traumatic passage through forcing cone and barrel (and thus less deformation). The other way was to increase hardness and resistance of shot to deformation by coating them with a plating of copper.

Olin applied for a patent on progressive-burning shotshell powder in 1923, and it is apparent Burrard knew Olin was working on copper-coated shot as well. In fact, Burrard took some potshots at Olin in his book *The Modern Shotgun*. "The most extravagant claims are sometimes made that a particular brand cartridges has a much shorter shot string than others," Burrard wrote. "I have explained the impossibility of

John Olin, honorary chairman of the board of Olin Corporation (parent company of Winchester-Western) was an early student of the shot-string effect. His experimentations into shot stringing helped give impetus to his development of progressive-burning powders and extra-hard copper-plated shot, both of which contribute to less shot deformation and a shorter shot string.

preventing pellet deformation by giving the pellets a thin coating in copper, in itself a soft metal, and will not refer to it again." While Burrard was writing this, Olin was succeeding in shortening shot strings by using extra-hardened shot coated with copper.

Olin had already succeeded in developing a progressive-burning powder (in 1922) but a long battle over patent rights delayed issuance of the patent until 1933. In the meanwhile, the original short-shot-string shell had been born. It hit the market in the late 20s and was called "Super-X."

Olin was also proceeding with his work on harder shot, and in 1926 Lubaloy shot (copper coated) was announced. It further shortened shot strings and increased pattern efficiency. But then, as now, the general public seemed little aware of the full importance of shot stringing and Lubaloy shot never attained the general acceptance and usage it possibly should have. This shot remains available today, and is currently the hardest lead shot available in sizes large enough for maximum range waterfowl loads.

During his 60-year career with the ammunition business, Olin remained deeply concerned with shot-string performance, and insisted that with any new load introduced by Winchester-Western, shot-string tests be made. Beyond any doubt, John Olin was the father of the high-performance, short shot-string load in America. But long before he or Burrard had made any tests, another Englishman, R. W. Griffiths in 1887, had been working on the problem.

Griffiths used a rotating circular target 12 feet in diameter which turned 318 revolutions per minute behind a stationary, thin paper target. The non-moving target would tell him how the pattern looked stationary, and as the pellets struck the fast-whirling wheel behind it, he could measure, by their placement, roughly how far behind the main load the stringing shot were. He estimated from all this that the main bulk of the shot charge flies in a comparatively compact mass, with the remaining 10 percent stringing out into a tail roughly as long again as the distance from front to rear of the main bulk of the forward shot cloud.

Griffiths may have been quite correct in his computations with the loads he had available then, but like Burrard he failed to grasp what he had almost learned—that shot stringing is not a standard situation but a very complex one that varies widely with shot size, shot hardness, and shot deformation from various gauges and barrel configurations.

In 1928, P. Quayle, of Peters Cartridge Company, became the first to photograph a shot string through what was then called spark photography. Although there were no strobes then (he actually used an electrical spark) his findings closely match those made with the most

At short range and slow speeds, stringing of shot proved of little consequence. The ducks on the target are used to measure forward allowance, to provide a relationship when closeup photos are made of shot strings.

sophisticated modern equipment today. Quayle estimated that the length of the string, front pellet to back pellet, at 40 yards was 12 feet, just 1 foot longer than Winchester's modern strobe measurement of the total length of a standard modern hunting load.

When Winchester later photographed shot strings of its Super-X Double X grex-insulated loads, the shot string was found to be considerably shorter. With some chokes the string was only about half the length of the other loads. The point is that the state of the art of shotshell manufacture now permits loads with very short, highly efficient shot string. Yet most shooters are not aware of it and may be using loads with strings more comparable to those of 1928.

For some close-range forms of shooting, such as skeet, an elongated shot string from a large-gauge gun can be an advantage, in that it gives more margin for lateral gun pointing error on birds "over lead." But for long-range shooting, or medium range with small gauges and light shot charges, excessive stringing of shot can rob the heart of the pattern of the pellet density required for clean kills.

Apparently the first man to study shot stringing in a direct, easy-to-observe manner—by firing at a moving target—was an Englishman named H. A. Ivatt, who fired 4 shots at a passing train in 1890. His purpose actually was to study forward allowance for a moving object, but since the train was only doing 11 miles per hour, Ivatt learned little that was startling to him except for one thing: The pellets hit the side of the train in a circle almost as round as if fired at a stationary target.

What happened to that elongated shot string indicated by Griffiths' revolving wheel and proved by Quayle's photographs? There could be no doubt shot do string out in the air. But there was much mystery as to the time of arrival of pellets relative to the distance apart the pellets might be in flight. Burrard quickly perceived that the difference was in the relation of load speed to target speed. Otherwise, Ivatt's train at 11 miles per hour should have shown an elongation of shot string just as did Griffiths' revolving plate, which was whirling at the equivalent of 125 miles per hour.

Another Englishman, W. Webster Watts, had tried to find out more about this in 1907 by laboriously raising a heavy steel plate to the top of a tall tower. His idea was to cut loose the plate and let it fall like a guillotine, shooting just before it reached the ground. This, he reasoned, would truly prove how a shot string arrives at a fast moving object. Unfortunately the target was small, fell very fast, and Mr. Watts mostly missed. He put enough pellets on the plate to indicate a few things, but apparently nobody was willing to hoist the heavy plate up again to find out what they were.

I believe I know how the man must have felt, because I have fired hundreds of tests at moving targets on a ranch airstrip near my home, and things have not always gone well. My target is plywood bolted to a frame welded to an old boat trailer to create a patterning area 16 feet long by 4 feet tall. Over this is stretched heavy brown wrapping paper providing a surface that reflects with absolute certainty where each pellet arrives on the moving target. For visual reference, scaled-to-size silhouettes of birds and clay targets are stenciled on each target, to help in analyzing forward allowance and also to make photographs of the patterns more easily interpreted.

Watching that moving monster coming at me the first time, throwing up a plume of dust as it neared my shooting position, was both thrill and apprehension. The towing vehicle was the family station wagon driven by my semi-brave wife Sandy. And for fear stray pellets might strike the car, I shot at the rear area of the target. Unfortunately, the forward allowance for that load with the target moving 40 miles per hour at 40 yards was about 7 feet, and I mostly missed.

After that, things went about as well as could be expected.

On the first shot testing Ithaca's giant 3½-inch, 10-gauge magnum, a tire on the tow target collapsed. With that repaired and better protected we tried a 50-mile-an-hour skeet target with a 28 gauge, and just as I swung on target and pulled the trigger, dust, paper, and debris exploded into the air as if I'd fired James Bond's antitank gun. When the debris settled, it became obvious a weld had popped loose on the target frame, dropping the forward end of the plywood into the dirt at 50 miles an hour.

With the demolished target replaced, we tried another run just as the ranch's prize Brahman bull became belligerent toward the string of stenciled ducks crossing his territory and came trotting across the line of fire. Fortunately the test was only a .410 skeet load of 9's—but it may have been history's first gun-test report in which the bull manure preceded publication.

Perseverance prevailed, and gradually our efficiency at changing the 16-foot-long strips of paper improved. My knowledge of precise aiming points began making possible two or more pattern tests on the same 16-foot paper sheet. This also, however, took some doing. It is difficult to force oneself to hold and swing perfectly on the rear of one's own station wagon and pull the trigger there. But this was where the shot had to be fired, swinging the gun at target speed, to place the pattern upon the front portion of the pattern board in many tests.

These details may do the reader little good, but they may explain why some of the photographs of tests have some pellets circled and some x'd. In making multiple-shot comparisons, it is necessary to circle each shot before the next test is made because patterns often overlap. By circling pellet holes from the first shot, the next test can then be made and identified another way, as with x's.

To graphically show the difference between a moving pattern and a pattern shot with the target stationary with the same load, barrel, and distance, we first made a moving run and I placed the shot toward the front of the target, thus making sure the tail of the shot string didn't miss the board. Then we circled every pellet hole, drew a 30-inch circle around the tightest part of the pattern, counted the pellets in it, and with our electronic calculator obtained the percentage of pellets at the center of the moving pattern. Then the target was turned around, returned to firing position, stopped, and a stationary shot made. By counting the pellet holes in the 30-inch circle representing the tightest area of the stationary pattern, and subtracting from that the percentage of the moving pattern, we could roughly estimate the loss of central-pattern density due to shot stringing of that load, choke, and size of shot. If properly placed, the two patterns could be side by side for easy visual comparison.

We never did, however, lick the cow problem. The rancher was feeding his cattle from a trailer that must to them have looked something like ours, and the herd kept following us, getting in the way of our target runs. We wound up establishing two shooting stations, each taped off from 20 to 70 yards and marked off with stakes. If the cattle crowded us on one shooting station we'd drive as fast as we could to the other end of the airstrip and shoot from there until the herd arrived.

If some of our assumptions seem more hastily drawn than those

TEST 104 50 YD. 12 GA. FULL
WIN. 2-¾" 1½ OZ. #2

Each pellet is circled for photography, then a 30-inch circle drawn to determine percentage. The pattern at right (91 pellets) was fired with the target moving at 40 miles per hour; the pattern at left (92 pellets) was shot with the target stationary. Due to its efficient, short shot string, this grex-buffered load had very few flyer pellets.

produced with slide rules and computers, it must be remembered that there are no bovine ballistical problems in factory testing laboratories. Also there is no wind in the environment where most factory test patterns are made.

It may be that air currents generated by our towing vehicle slightly increased the effect of shot stringing by reacting on deformed pellets more than would have been the case in a dead calm. Theoretically crosswinds merely move patterns rather than disrupt them. Our stationary tests in general showed slightly lower pattern percentages than those achieved with laboratory pressure guns.

But then, hunting is done outdoors, with ordinary guns and barrels, and very often in wind. So we just did the honest best we could with what we had.

Right away we began observing some perplexing things. Our tests indicated that anyone who breaks 100 straight with the .410 at skeet apparently has Providence on his side. There were holes in some of the moving patterns big enough to put a clay target through sideways, and some would have admitted a China saucer. Yet when loads from

Measuring total spread, then bulk of spread, tells about the efficiency of the load. Inefficient loads invariably had a much greater spread moving than stationary, even when there was little difference in center density. At longer ranges center density suffered increasingly.

the same box of shells were fired at the target stationary at the same distance (21 yards being the distance a skeet target crosses the stake in the center of the skeet field) they produced fairly good patterns, normally dense enough to break a well-centered clay target.

It became obvious that the shooter may not have the pattern efficiency on a crossing target he thinks he has, and that stationary pattern boards can lie. After testing high-efficiency waterfowl loads, magnums, traploads, virtually every other type of shotshell load produced in America, it became obvious that shot stringing is indeed an important factor in how far and how cleanly a shotgun can dispatch game. In poor loads with soft shot and a high percentage of deformed pellets many of the pellets simply do not arrive in time to strike along with the main bulk of the pattern. This can create gaps or holes in the shot string not evident in ordinary pattern tests and can weaken the effective density of the central pattern at the instant it strikes the bird.

The old idea that a long shot string is an advantage may be true at very close range and steeply crossing targets (such as 12-gauge skeet) because at 21 yards there is still adequate pellet density almost

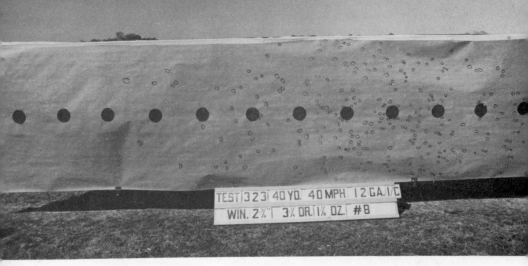

Open chokes, combined with soft shot, produced the highest loss of density due to shot stringing. The center of this pattern contained only 76 pellets in a 30-inch circle; total spread was slightly more than 12 feet. By comparison, hard shot trapload of 8's had much shorter string, and a center density of 163 pellets.

anywhere along the shot string to break a fragile clay target. But most of this advantage would come to the shooter who fires too far in front of the target (one of the rare types of misses).

In field hunting, the stringing of shot is of little importance at close-range quail, woodcock, etc., but appears critically important in long-range dove and waterfowl hunting.

The loads that kill game farthest and cleanest are those with the shortest, most efficient shot strings. The most important single factor is perfection of the shot pellets. If they are hard enough, or cushioned enough, to remain round through the pressures of firing and pass through the gun's forcing cone and choke without being deformed, these pellets will produce a highly efficient pattern with a short shot string.

I have fired many tests of hard shot loads from 40 yards at the moving target doing 40 miles an hour that produced patterns so perfectly round it was impossible to discern (without counting pellets) the moving test from a pattern fired with the same gun and load with the target sitting still. But pellet perfection isn't the whole story. Things change drastically, even with the most perfect shot loads, when either target speed or range increases. The longer the range, the more time pellets have had to separate, and also the more the load has slowed down relative to target speed. At 70 yards, with the most efficient loads made, shot are strung almost the length of my 16-foot board.

The best patterns are made with very hard shot (high antimony

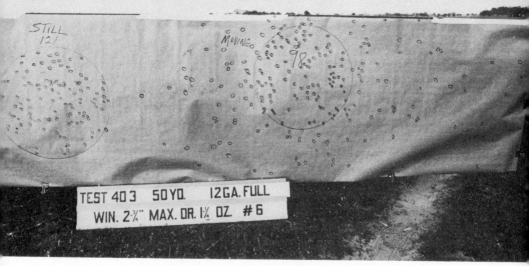

No. 6 high-velocity load at 50 yards lost 9 percent of its pellets to stringing at 50 yards and 40 miles per hour. Pattern at left was shot with the target stationary at same yardage.

count), plated shot (copper or nickel), steel shot, or lead shot protected from deformation by a buffering agent such as powdered plastic. The shortest strings of all were made during tests of steel shot and with buffered or cushioned extra-hard lead shot. Steel, being harder than any lead pellet, does not deform. Pellets arrive at the moving target at so nearly the same time and velocity that moving target patterns with steel shot at 40 yards are often better than those fired with the target stationary. I cannot fully account for that, except that there may be more variation from one shell to the next than the difference in moving or still targets at that range.

Some high-brass, high-velocity, supposedly long-range lead-shot hunting loads were found to contain such soft shot that they strung out halfway across the board at 50 yards. As a general rule, the smaller the shot the more the stringing, possibly because it is easier to make big shot hard than to make small shot resist deformation.

The worst loads were soft, small shot in some of the less expensive field loads when fired from relatively open-choked barrels, some of which strung out as much as 12 feet at 40 yards! Perhaps it should be pointed out that although a 12-foot shot string might seem a great advantage to the poor shot, there is no such thing as a free lunch. Whenever pellets are robbed from one area of pattern to increase string length, pattern density must suffer.

As a general rule, open chokes lost a higher percentage of density from shot stringing than did full choke when the loads were of soft lead shot. But when very hard shot were substituted, there was little difference in percentage of loss between open and tight chokes. This possibly explains why Burrard found an average loss of 30 percent from improved cylinder but only 17 percent from full choke. In Burrard's day, shot pellets were quite soft.

I have been purposely vague in discussing percentages of loss of density due to shot stringing (unlike Major Burrard's detailed charts) for several reasons. Burrard tested only one gauge (12) and only one size shot (No. 6) and his fastest crossing speeds were 40 mph. Thus he had relatively simple data that could each be given five or so tests and then translated into charts and graphs. Unfortunately, in doing it this way, Burrard missed some of the most important aspects of shot stringing, such as variances in shot size, gauge size, magnum or non-magnum loadings, hard or soft shot, some combinations of which did not even exist in Burrard's day.

My tests were done with every shot size from 9's to 2's, every gauge from .410 bore to 12, every choke from cylinder to extra full, and virtually every load available in every gauge. That alone took months because of all the variables of distance and speed. Thus, I could not do a sufficient number of repeat tests of each one for statistical reliability. Some comparisons, if they seemed to show an unusual result, were repeated until an average of five tests could be taken. Many tests were duplicated only once or twice if the results seemed consistent with others similar to them. Some tests were repeated 10 times or more to check load variation.

To determine the significance of pellet loss due to stringing, it is necessary to compare the percentage produced by stationary shots with those produced by the moving target at the same yardage. Some moving-target patterns may look quite good, having evenly distributed clusters of pellets, but in trying to find the best or heart of that elongated string of shot it turns out none of the clusters are close enough together to quite get into the same 30-inch circle, thus the pattern percentage comes up much poorer than another pattern that looks similar but has clusters of shot close enough together in the shot string to produce a high pellet count in the 30-inch circle. This difficulty in estimating differences between moving shots and stationary shots increases with distance and/or speed. But we tried to circle every pellet and measure the length of total spread and bulk spread.

With one heavy magnum load for the 12 gauge at 50 yards and 40 miles an hour we found differences between moving and stationary targets of 33 percent, but the next set of shots (one still, one moving) showed a difference of only about 8 percent. It is difficult to determine how much of the difference is due to variation of the shell and how much difference is due to shot stringing, wind deflection, etc. So all we have is several hundred targets worth of indications.

Cameras, computers, and extrapolations can go so far. But variables of barrels, chokes, forcing cones, shot hardness, etc. turn up in actual moving target testing that would blow a computer's mind.

The moving target changed my own mind about several things. I used to assume that the more pellets I could get into a load, the better were the odds of more of those pellets striking the bird. So in the 12-gauge magnum I often used 1⅞-ounce super-magnum loads. But some of the worst patterns and highest losses of density due to shot stringing seen on my pattern board have come from the supposedly long-range heavy magnum loads. Such loads, without benefit of extra-hard shot or some buffering agent, actually put fewer pellets into a 30-inch circle than loads containing fewer shot but which were better buffered and more efficient. It was, for example, quite common for the Super-X Double X Winchester short magnum with only 1½ ounces of shot and with grex insulation to put more No. 2 pellets into a goose silhouette at 60 yards than the heaviest 3-inch magnum load of 1⅞ ounces without a buffering agent. Tom Roster, who had already perceived this, loaded for me some super-duper handloads in a short 12-gauge case (2¾ inch) with only 1¼ ounces of shot buffered with common household flour that put more hits into a goose silhouette than standard 10-gauge loads!

The moving target showed quite clearly that the longer and heavier the payload of shot packed into the case of a cartridge—relative to the size of the bore—the greater the shot deformation and poorer the pattern percentage on crossing targets. This is why the 3-inch .410 (which is in effect an elongated mini-magnum) strings shot much more erratically and with less efficiency than the same shotload fired from a 28 gauge. The 28 gauge has a larger bore relative to the length and weight of the shot column being pushed through it. For the same reason, a 10 gauge (with a shotcup wad comparable to those now in 12-gauge loads) can be made to handle 1⅞ ounces of No. 2 shot (or even 2 ounces or more) more efficiently than can a 3-inch 12 gauge which must push a whole lot of shot through a relatively small hole, deforming a high percentage of them in the process.

It can be done, of course, if the shot being pushed are cushioned enough or are hard enough to prevent excessive deformation. Dramatic proof of that came in tests of Remington's 3½-inch, 10-gauge magnum loads which went on the market in 1976. This is a much-improved load over previous 10-gauge fodder, because it contains a power-piston shotcup wad. Other 10-gauge loads, I'm sorry to say, were still in the dark ages at this writing, throwing mostly pitiful patterns from a tight full choke.

Actually the improved Remington was not as good as it could have been because the shotcup was half an inch too short, made to fit either 3-inch or 3½-inch cases. It seemed obvious in patterning that either barrel or choke deformation (or both) of the non-protected half-inch of shot was producing flyer shot. So I experimented with a simple form of buffering agent, ordinary household flour mixed in with the shot load. (I am not suggesting anyone else do this. I did it because I had available pressure testing by Remington's lab to make sure I was not getting excessive breech pressures. Adding a buffering agent slightly raises pressures unless other compensations are made.)

I took the precaution of removing about 15 pellets or so from the load to make more room for the flour and also to remove a little payload weight to avoid building excessive pressures through the addition of the filler material. Several such flour-buffered loads were fired at the moving target at the same yardages and speeds I had tested the original factory load. The difference was dramatic. At 50 yards and a speed of 40 miles per hour, an Ithaca "Mag 10" autoloader with full-choke 32-inch barrel (with flour-buffered Remington load) put a goose-getting 117 pellets in the 30-inch circle at the center of a compact, short shot string, a density that should kill the largest Canada goose without a quiver. But the same gun and load, without flour buffering, put only 76 pellets in the center of its pattern; enough to get a goose, but showing a more elongated, ragged pattern.

We slowed the target vehicle down to 35 miles an hour, more like the crossing speed of a non-spooked goose, and fired more tests with

At left, shotload emerges from power piston wad a few feet from muzzle, at right starts to string out into what will be 11-foot string at 40 yards. Note the heavy concentration of pellets in front; lagging pellets in rear and those seen beginning to veer away (top) probably will not arrive at distant crossing target in time to contribute to the central pattern produced by front pellets. These characteristics were observed with all loads other than those of extremely hard shot (steel) or shot protected with cushioning or buffering powder.

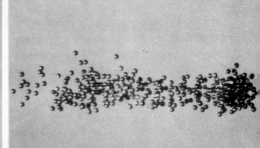

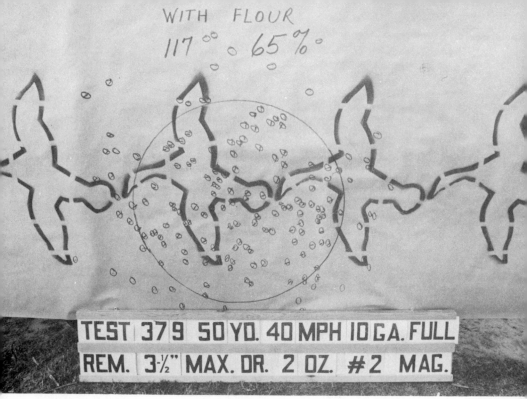

Extremely short string and high efficiency was gained by buffering standard Remington load with household flour. This moving pattern was almost as good at 50 yards as the original load averaged stationary at 40 yards.

10-gauge loads without flour. They averaged 78 pellet hits, indicating the five miles per hour made little difference. The factory load was still below the performance of the flour-buffered load even at a slower speed. Then we moved to 60 yards, fired at the target doing 40 mph, and the flour-buffered load hung in there with 70 well-distributed hits in the center of the moving pattern. But the non-flour load was fading fast, putting an average of 40 pellets into the center of the pattern. The flour-cushioned load was thus 43 percent more efficient at 60 yards, whereas it had been 35 percent more efficient than the non-buffered load at 50 yards. These differences were not nearly so evident at 40 yards, and may not be at any yardage in the future since Remington has apparently improved the factory load since my tests.

Tests with a number of loads, including the best of them all, Tom Roster handloads, showed that the longer the range, the more the superiority of the buffered loads was evident. In some load comparisons there might be really little difference at 40 yards, but at 60 it was more like daylight and dark. Winchester's grex-buffered loads of No. 2 shot in 3-inch 12-gauge magnum were about 50 percent more efficient at 60 yards than were 3-inch 2's without buffering.

Despite the efficiency of the buffered loads, every load tested began to string shot significantly between 50 and 60 yards. At 60 yards, one test of the 10-gauge magnum load (without flour) showed a total spread (from first pellet to the last across the board) of 10 feet, 6 inches with the target moving at 40 miles an hour. A still test showed a total spread of 8.1 feet. However, these were spreads between widest flyer pellets; the bulk of the load spread was about 4.5 feet.

If this sounds extreme, one test of a non-buffered No. 2 3-inch 12-gauge magnum load at only 50 yards showed a maximum spread of 12 feet and 8 inches! This was an extreme spread, with flyer pellets at both ends, but at the most dense area of that pattern only 39 pellets could be counted in a 30-inch circle. That's a 23-percent pattern, since there are 168 No. 1 pellets in the 1⅞-ounce load. Yet at the same yardage and speed a 2¾-inch grex-cushioned load of 2's containing only 135 pellets put 75 hits into a 30-inch circle with a maximum shot spread of 5 feet, 1 inch.

This performance, considering the fewer shot in the short-magnum load with grex, really shows the difference in both shot stringing and pattern efficiency related to the buffering or cushioning of shot. It also points out graphically that many of our old ideas about how to get the most pellets into a long-range bird were wrong. It is not the number of shot to start with, but how carefully they are kept spherical in the process of getting to the target. If reducing the number of shot to make room for cushioning ingredients or lowered breech pressures is required, it certainly proves worthwhile in terms of shot stringing and thus in terms of actual pellets arriving at the target.

If you are at this point adequately convinced of the value of buffering or cushioning agents, the natural question is whether powdered plastic "grex" is available for handloaders. The answer now is no. But you can use common wheat flour (which is heavier and thus adds weight and increases pressures) or you can make your own powdered plastic filler material by grinding up ordinary plastic egg cartons. This is soft stuff and converts into "meal" quite easily when ground between two strips of coarse sandpaper. It is lighter than flour, but flour seems to do the best buffering job because it is more dense.

Obviously the larger the case, the more room there is for buffering material and the more opportunity to cushion the pellets and launch the load rather than blasting it out and deforming more shot. This is clearly indicated in comparing performance of the big 10-gauge 3½-inch magnum load of 2's (buffered with flour) with the same number of pellets in a 3-inch 12-gauge load of 2's (buffered with grex plastic). In adding flour to the 10-gauge load, I removed 15 pellets each time to make more room for the flour and to help hold down pressures. Since 2 ounces of No. 2 shot normally contains 180 pellets, taking away 15 of them left a pellet count of only 165 in the shell. This is

Magnum loads in all brands, without buffering, showed long shotstrings and large losses of density due to stringing. This 1⅞-ounce load of 4's spread nearly 13 feet at 50 yards, the result of the combination of relatively soft pellets with deformation accentuated by the heavy load.

almost exactly the same number of pellets in a 3-inch Winchester magnum 1⅞-ounce load of 2's (168 pellet average).

Although the Super-X Double X Winchester load was by far the most efficient of any 3-inch 12-gauge factory load tested at long range, it did not compete with the larger case capacity and more importantly, larger bore, of the big 10 gauge. The 12 magnum put an average of 45 of its No. 2 pellets into a 30-inch circle at 60 yards at 40 miles an hour. The 10 gauge averaged closer to 70 pellets. I believe the difference here was more in bore diameter (the larger bore handling the shot better without deformation) than in quality of shot or buffering agents. In general, the shortest shot strings are obtained (all other things being equal) when relatively light loads are pushed out a relatively large bore rather than when very heavy loads are pushed out a small bore.

But no matter what bore, buffering, or balance, by 70 yards with the target crossing 35 to 40 miles an hour, the problem of shot stringing is acute. The best flour-buffered 10-gauge load of 2's had an extreme pellet spread averaging around 11 feet at that distance, with the bulk of the pattern covering around 6 feet. There were several spots up and down that string of shot capable of cleanly killing a goose, but there were several other spots capable of crippling him and obviously there was also the possibility of some of those stray shot hitting other birds.

And then, there was the very good possibility for missing the whole bunch, because the smooth-swinging lead at target speed at 70 yards and 40 miles an hour came out the same with the 3-inch 12 gauge or the 10 gauge. That forward allowance was approximately 18 feet!

Given the pattern and forward allowance required at 70 yards, it would seem the odds of getting geese at that range are very poor, which they are. But many geese are downed, and by some shooters fairly consistently, because of other factors. For one thing, not all shots are taken at 90° angles, as our target tests were done, and a goose can be killed farther at a 45° angle because the loss of pellet density in the center of the string is proportionately less as the angle decreases.

I believe this is one reason so many hunters miss the first shot at high geese, that shot being taken usually as the birds pass almost directly overhead or to the side at approximately 90°. Then, the hunter often makes a kill on his second shot, because at that time the goose has slowed forward motion and started to climb, often the angle changing to a mild quartering angle rather than an acute crossing angle as the bird flares away. This reduces pattern density loss due to shot stringing because it reduces both speed and angle.

The old idea that a bird can be killed farther crossing (by running into more pellets as he crosses the shot string) has not been proved out by my moving board. If this were true, the stenciled ducks on that board would contain more pellets after being shot crossing than when shot stationary. Yet the opposite has been the case.

The reason I believe a bird can often be killed farther at a crossing angle than going straightaway is that more of his vital areas are revealed to the load and less penetration is required. A lot of penetration is required from the rear. To put that another way, it's a long way to the heart via the rectum.

Obviously on a long shot with some pellets ranging 8 to 12 feet behind the front pellets, a bird far behind the one being shot at may fall. But the bird did not necessarily fly into the shot string. More likely, the bird and some late pellets happened to arrive at the same place at the same time. Much more likely the allowance for the bird being shot at was just about perfect for the bird two or three back in line. Lack of adequate forward allowance, even more than stringing of shot, is what so often gets the duck flying several feet behind the drake intended.

24

THE FUTURE LOOKS HARDER BUT BRIGHTER

A nationwide steel-shot controversy crystallized when the National Wildlife Federation, claiming an estimated 3 million waterfowl a year were being lost to lead-ingestion poisoning, produced a series of widely published news releases (entitled "Get the Lead Out") which in effect chastised the arms industry for "foot dragging" in developing a suitable nontoxic substitute for lead shot.

The industry returned fire with statements that even if lead shot were eliminated, steel shot would damage guns and could increase crippling losses by 2½ to 3 million birds a year. In other words, a trade off.

Waterfowl mortality from lead poisoning losses had been extrapolated from areas and conditions in which ducks and geese were primarily feeding on corn. But later studies of birds in many other areas, where the diet contained more vegetable matter, indicated that toxicity of lead pellets was not nearly the problem originally believed. Since great numbers of birds winter in California, Texas, Louisiana, Arkansas, and other areas where cold-weather stress and corn diet are not significant, early estimates of lead-ingestion losses became highly suspect.

At the same time, careful statistical evaluation of estimated increases in crippling from steel shot revealed some divergence from reality. The steel loads tested contained 1⅛ ounces of shot (less efficient than the present loads that can be made at present) and com-

SPHERICAL STEEL
SUPER X 1 1/8 OZ. No. 4

LEAD WITHOUT GREX
SUPER X 1¼ OZ. No. 4

LEAD WITH GREX
WW XX 1¼ OZ. No. 4

Steel pellets, recovered from a soft material, show why they performed comparably with ordinary lead pellets in tests on live ducks. The hard steel remained spherical and traveled through atmospheric resistance with less drag than the lead pellets, which deformed at firing. But lead pellets have highest sectional density. Grex-insulated lead pellets from a Super-X Double X magnum show why they outperform either steel or common lead; they combine the advantage of sphericity plus high sectional density.

parisons with lead loads such as the Super-X Double X plastic-buffered magnums indeed showed more crippling from steel. But when compared with loads that are in more common use (the super magnums being used only by a small percentage of the nation's hunters) the figures become much different.

When compared with the standard high-velocity 12-gauge loads containing 1¼ ounces of lead shot, steel loads of 1⅛ ounces have been found to compare closely in killing efficiency, up to approximately 45 yards. Beyond that distance, the best lead loads are clearly superior to the best steel loads, including the newest steel loads developed. In 1976, the development of more shot space, by the elimination of wadding or the use of a rolled crimp, increased the number of steel pellets that can be loaded—thus offsetting some of the disadvantages of the less dense steel shot pellets.

At Nilo Farms, Ill., in 1972–73, 2,400 game-farm mallards were shot under scientifically controlled conditions, with kills and cripples at various ranges recorded to produce voluminous data for a computerized lethality model to be used for predicting shotshell efficiency with any load of lead or steel.

Ballisticians chose to compare highly efficient lead magnums containing 1½ ounces of shot to steel loads of 1⅛ ounces, in an effort to determine the relative efficiency of lead and steel pellets of nearly equal velocities, pellet counts, and patterns.

Winchester ballistician Rod Van Wyk attempted to make clear more accurately the differences between lead and steel performance in his comments to the U.S. Fish & Wildlife Service Environmental Impact Statement on steel shot—comments that unfortunately never received the attention or understanding they deserve.

Van Wyk explained that a No. 4 steel shot load of 1⅛ ounces would slightly outperform (in duck killing) the most comparable lead load of 1¼ ounces of No. 6 shot if the duck is centered in the pattern—but would do so only at the expense of extremely tight patterns, which reduce the margin for error by the shooter.

This means simply that the big problem of steel shot (within 40 yards where common lead loads of 1¼ ounces are consistently clean killers) is not adequate pattern or penetration (as has become the general public misconception) but that of centering the duck within a tighter pattern.

One of the big problems in understanding this is that previous conceptions of shot sizes must be discarded in comparing an entirely new shot material with a long-familiar one.

Because steel pellets are lighter for their size (having lower density), comparisons of shotshell efficiency cannot be made on shot size alone, but must be made on *number of pellets on target* and the *energy per pellet*. For example, comparing No. 4 steel with No. 4 lead would be unfair to lead because there are 214 No. 4 steel pellets in a 1⅛-ounce load compared with only 152 No. 4 pellets in the same lead load.

Likewise it would be unfair to steel to compare No. 4 steel to No. 4 lead in penetration, because two sizes larger in steel compares much closer in energy per pellet (and pellet numbers) and the heavier pellets would penetrate much better.

So if we can for a moment forget old ideas of shot sizes and get it firmly ingrained that No. 2 steel has approximately the same number of pellets per ounce and about the same energy per pellet as No. 4 lead—and that No. 4 steel similarly compares with No. 6 lead—we are beginning to understand something about realistic comparisons of the two shot materials.

When lead/steel tests were conducted on live mallards at Patuxent, Maryland, in 1969, U.S. Fish & Wildlife Service technicians, working in cooperation with shooting industry ballisticians, found that steel shot in a 1-ounce load seemed capable of killing mallards almost as effectively as 1¼ ounces of lead shot up to 40 yards. At 60 yards the steel load bagged 28 percent of ducks compared to 38 percent bagged with lead 6s. Over all yardages in the Patuxent tests, lead shot was superior to steel shot.

It seemed contrary, however, to the laws of physics that lightweight, low-density steel pellets could perform so closely to lead loads

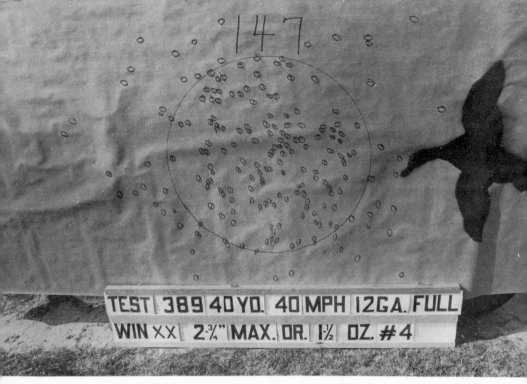

This beautiful pattern of No. 4 lead from a Winchester Super-X Double X standard magnum tells the story of shotshell efficiency; there is virtually no stringing evident, and density would insure an instant kill. There was no attempt to hit the duck shown; pellet holes are too difficult to see against the black. The bird's size (24 inches long) is merely a reference to show spread of pattern.

containing 20 percent more payload weight and pellets of much better density. This was certainly contrary to downrange ballistics tables (then believed as gospel) that years before had been compiled by SAAMI.

These tables, which had been produced with mathematics rather than downrange testing, computed velocity and retained energy of lead pellets at various distances. When the steel-shot issue arose, ballisticians took these lead tables, substituted the poorer density of steel, and computed tables for steel shot that indicated that steel pellets would lose velocity and penetration very rapidly, and would perform very poorly.

But ballistician Ed Lowry, who had participated in the Patuxent tests and had been baffled by them, did some computations of his own. He found that for some reason steel pellets were utilizing their kinetic energy more efficiently than lead pellets. He suspected the difference lay in a highly significant aspect of projectile ballistics known as "form factor."

Three basic factors affect the performance of shotshell pellets, the original velocity, the density (weight) of the pellet, and its "form fac-

TEST 337 40 YD. 12 GA. FULL
2¾" 3¾ DR. 1 OZ. #4 STEEL

This 1-ounce steel load patterned better at 40 miles per hour than stationary, an indication that there was more variation between two shells from the same box than loss of shot to "stringing." A number of steel-shot tests showed this peculiarity, although at long ranges even steel starts to string slightly.

tor," which is what sort of shape it presents in flight to atmospheric resistance.

Lowry suspected that the extremely hard steel pellets were retaining their roundness better than lead, thus traveling through atmospheric resistance at a higher degree of efficiency then their density would indicate.

To investigate the mystery, SAAMI funded a grant to Winchester-Western for tests of both lead and iron pellets, to be made by firing pellets downrange and measuring their deceleration. Their retained velocity could then be more accurately computed into retained energy.

From those tests several things became obvious. The original SAAMI tables had been wrong. They had not taken into sufficient consideration the firing deformation of lead pellets, which reduced both velocity and penetration capability downrange.

Thus, computations of iron shot ballistics, based on these original lead shot tables, were *really* wrong, because steel shot did not flatten and thus had a 12 percent higher form factor than lead. This gave them considerably more downrange energy than had been previously believed.

Even at 50 yards, grex-buffered lead loads showed little stringing or loss of pattern density. Moving target at right had 74 pellets.

A new set of tables entitled "The Aerodynamic Performance of Lead and Iron Shotshell Loads" was completed by Lowry on Feb. 26, 1970, and turned over to SAAMI. Copies of this report, showing steel shot to compare quite favorably with lead, were issued to SAAMI members for their use, but the new findings were not incorporated in the SAAMI manual.

Table 1, at the end of this chapter, shows that steel pellets nearest in comparison by weight and number to lead pellets have slightly more retained energy than their counterparts in lead. And thus it might be surmised that the problems of steel shot are over.

This is not true, because steel presents a Pandora's box of problems not evident in the table. For example, No. 6 lead pellets are shown to have *less* retained energy than No. 4 steel, and since retained energy is a major factor in penetration it might be assumed the steel 4s would penetrate better. My tests indicate the opposite; the comparable lead pellet invariably penetrated better than the steel, although the difference was slight (about 4 percent) at 40 yards.

The difference is in the greater surface area presented to the penetration medium; steel pellets must be considerably larger to retain the same energy, and the resistance to penetration is thus increased for the same reasons that more energy is required to drive a blunt nail than a sharp one.

This does not mean steel pellets will not penetrate ducks; it simply means that more emphasis must be put on penetration in selecting

TEST 39 4 50 YD. 40 MPH 12 GA. FULL
REM. 2¾" 3¾ DR. 1¼ OZ. #4

Shot stringing and poor density were evident in all brands of non-buffered lead duckloads, the ones most commonly in use. Contrast this photograph with the previous one for comparison; it would be a killer or crippler as much by luck as by skill of the shooter.

the proper shot size to be used. No. 2 steel pellets seem to kill large ducks better than No. 4 steel, even though they have fewer pellets in the load. This had been purely my observation, since No. 2 shot were not tested on ducks at Nilo or Patuxent. But 3 years of field-shooting experience has convinced me that No. 2 steel does a better job on big ducks and that No. 4's are more suitable for smaller birds. Steel shot loads pattern very tightly. So there is little problem of too thin a pattern of the larger shot on large ducks at reasonable ranges, if the ducks are centered in the pattern.

But steel shot has many other problems. One such is that within the confines of a 2¾-inch shotshell, more No. 4 pellets can be loaded than No. 2. Hence, if energy-per-pellet is matched by substituting No. 2 steel to equal No. 4 lead, there are not as many pellets on target. For example, there are about 200 No. 4 pellets in the 1½-ounce, 2¾-inch lead load; but even with the new 1¼-ounce No. 2 steel load, there are only about 150 pellets. Both of these are maximum-capacity loads for the 12-gauge 2¾-inch shotshell case.

Because steel pellets are lighter relative to size, they are more susceptible to wind drift, and as they begin to slow down at longer ranges they become increasingly susceptible to pattern disruption by wind gusts. This, at least, was indicated on my moving target at 50 yards and beyond.

Because steel is so different from lead, there is at almost every stage of comparison between them some sort of good news and some bad news.

A major part of the good news about steel is its short, highly efficient shot string. In my tests on moving targets I got beautiful steel shot patterns at 45 yards that showed 1⅛-ounce steel loads putting more total energy into the 30-inch circle than 1¼-ounce lead loads launched at the same velocity. A glance at the moving pattern shows why. Steel pellets are so hard (and thus round) that they arrive at the target closer to the same time without significant loss of pattern density due to shot stringing.

Since lead loads at 45 yards frequently showed pattern-density losses from 6 to 8 percent due to shot stringing, that subject adds an entirely new dimension to comparisons of steel and lead, one that has not been cranked into computers from the Nilo tests. Ducks shot at Nilo were moving an average speed of 18 miles per hour on a special trolley to simulate flight and at this speed, shot stringing is of little consequence.

But at more realistic flight speeds for wild mallards in pass shooting (35 miles-per-hour up to 50 miles-per-hour) shot stringing becomes a factor of major importance, particularly at longer ranges. At 45 yards, due to the stringing effect of soft lead loads, 1⅛-ounce steel loads in many tests put more pellets and total energy into the moving target then a 1¼-ounce standard lead load. But this adds the vital human element of being able to hit such a fast-crossing target with the extremely tight, short shot string of a steel load. If hunters picked at random were required to stand on the range and shoot offhand at

These direct comparisons of steel and lead shot (the left pattern in each photograph was made with steel) show that on the moving target at 45 yards (top) the 1⅛-ounce load of No. 2 steel was putting more pellets, and more total energy, into its supertight full-choke pattern than a standard 1¼-ounce lead duck load of 4s. At this range, the steel 2s penetrated about equally with the lead 4s. But in the lower photo, made at 50 yards, the steel load had slightly less penetration than the magnum lead load, which put nearly twice the pellets into the pattern. Steel shot patterns seemed to suffer more from air movement across the target at 50 yards than did lead, but it must be remembered that the magnum lead load in the lower test contained 1½ ounces of shot, the steel load only 1⅛. New steel loads of 1¼ ounces would narrow the margin, but would not compare with the 1½-ounce grex-buffered magnum. In other words the best lead loads clearly outperform the best steel loads.

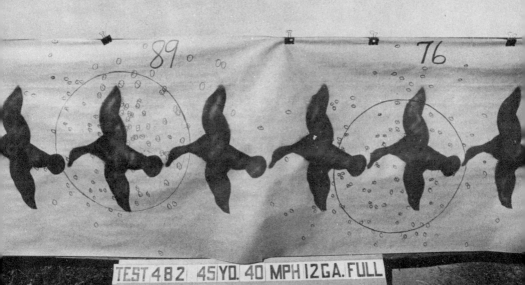

89   76

TEST 482 45 YD. 40 MPH 12 GA. FULL
WIN. 2-3/4" STEEL 1-1/8 OZ. #2 1-1/4 OZ. #4

5   107   8

TEST 472 50 YD. 40 MPH 12 GA. FULL
FED. 2-3/4" STEEL #2   WIN. XX   #4

crossing ducks (rather than using Nilo's mechanically programmed gun to fire at the precise instant required for a pattern-centering hit) the odds for bagging would probably go back in favor of the lead loads.

Thus the controversy over steel and lead is somewhat backwards to what was originally believed; the problem is not one of penetration (at least at ranges inside 50 yards) but one of margin for error for the shooter.

Beyond 50 yards, steel pellets on my moving target at 40 mph began to show fluctuating patterns which I am inclined to believe were the result of the larger, lighter pellets being more susceptible to wind effect generated by the towing vehicle, and air movement across the flat surface of the target. How directly this could be compared with gusty winds out hunting is difficult to say, but it was a factor that seemed to affect steel more than lead.

Turbulence created by the tow vehicle also undoubtedly had some effect of increasing shot stringing of deformed lead pellets, giving perhaps slightly more elongated strings and affecting the tests in this case in favor of steel. Nonbuffered 1¼-ounce waterfowl loads suffer more from stringing than does steel. More efficient lead pellets of high antimony content, or with some powdered buffering agent mixed with the shot load, show little more stringing effect than steel, because they retain their form factor better than standard loads.

Thus steel loads are not as good as the superefficient buffered lead loads, but the difference is slight when compared with standard lead loads. Unfortunately, steel has other major disadvantages that must be added to the equation. One is its high price (roughly 50 percent more than lead), which could be a hardship to lower-income shooters and could discourage purchase of duck stamps and creation of waterfowl-habitat revenues generated by excise taxes on waterfowl-hunting equipment. Waterfowl numbers have historically been more related to habitat conditions than to numbers bagged, and the waterfowl resource may be in more dire need of revenue for breeding and wintering habitat improvement than for protection from lead-ingestion losses as yet not clearly assessed.

Another factor directly relating to the future of all hunting is in shooter resistance to steel loads. Whether rightly or wrongly, public opinion across most of the U.S. seems strongly antisteel, a fact brought out in transcripts of public hearings held by the U.S. Fish & Wildlife Service. This could indicate resistance by hunters to obeying the law, and any such infractions would undoubtedly receive wide play in the news media. Difficulties in enforcing steel-shot laws may encourage attempts to circumvent them, particularly by hunters not convinced they are aiding waterfowl by using steel shot.

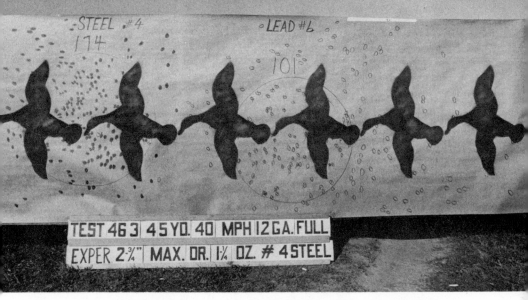

These patterns were both fired moving, and the difference in shot stringing by the common lead load (non-buffered) tilted performance in favor of the non-stringing steel shot. Using new SAAMI tables with figures based upon 50 yards (which should help lead, not steel), the total energy put into the 30-inch circle by lead 6's was 167.66 foot-pounds whereas steel 4's put 317.12 foot-pounds. The big difference is more pellet hits by the steel.

Perhaps the most important of all bad-news items about steel is the fear of gun damage.

Like the matter of penetration, this problem has been greatly misunderstood. But it persists as one of the principal reasons hunters are so suspicious of steel shot. My mail at *Field & Stream* magazine has contained many queries about steel loads, with shooters most often concerned that their barrels would be scored or scratched and the choke "eroded away" by the hard shot.

Due to the protection offered by extra-tough, extra-thick plastic shotcup wads, this is not really the problem. But there is a problem with barrel expansion behind the choke (and in some instances within the choke) due to the relentless peening of the hard pellets.

After interviewing spokesmen from all three U.S. manufacturers of steel loads, all having conducted hundreds of tests, barrel expansion does not seem to be a serious problem in a general sense. It is, however, a problem in certain barrels, especially those with excessive choke constriction (or undersized barrel boring) and in old and thin-walled double barrels.

The term "barrel damage" is a confusing one; some shooters view it as possible explosion of the barrel (which has proved to be highly unlikely) while others view even a .001-inch expansion behind the choke to constitute damage even though it may be impossible to perceive with the naked eye. Barrel damage is perceivable at approximately .005 in the form of a ring on the outside of the choke.

Philip H. Burdett, President and General Manager of Remington Arms Company, stated in 1973: "Most modern, American-made, quality shotguns can be used with steel shot without a significant reduction in their useful life." But, Burdett added: "Some evidence of choke damage may appear after a few hundred rounds, and lightweight double-barrel guns with thin barrels will probably be more susceptible to damage."

Federal Cartridge Company spokesman William B. Horn said in 1976: "With the majority of barrels we have found no real problems, although some which have unusually sharp, tight choke constriction did show expansion. In some instances this improved patterns and in some instances slightly reduced them."

Federal tested guns with modified and full chokes, all at 500 rounds each. Changes in modified barrels ranged from .001 to .004 inches (normally non-detectable by the naked eye) with virtually no change in patterning. Changes in full-choke barrels ranged from .001 to .015 inches. Some barrels showed no change.

Winchester spokesmen John Madson and Ed Kozicky in 1973 referred to barrel changes of test barrels that had fired 5,000 rounds of steel shot (these guns being Model 1200 12-gauge Winchester pumps) as being "cosmetic, not compromising safety or pattern performance."

Such tests are difficult for the average shotgunner to interpret because the barrels involved were simply referred to as "Barrel A," "Barrel B," etc., and no specific identification was made in most tests between one brand of gun and another. Yet the brand, the type of choke, barrel hardness, barrel thickness, and general quality are all of the utmost importance.

As a rule of thumb, doubles or over-unders with as much as 40-thousandths or more choke constriction would tend to be more affected by steel than would heavier barreled pumps and autoloaders, which as a rule have heavier, thicker barrels and full-choke constrictions of about 30-thousandths of an inch. Remington tested barrels of several of its pumps and autoloaders, one of which after 4,500 rounds of steel showed zero change; the most change experienced was .005, which was obvious to the naked eye but did not reduce the gun's patterning below full-choke performance.

However, during Remington's testing, some special barrels were purposely reduced in wall thickness, and these barrels after 500 rounds of steel showed changes up to .015.

Obviously if such tests were lumped together, dimensional changes could be said to range from .000 to .015, and that is a great deal of difference. Fifteen thousandths change is theoretically enough to change a gun's pattern from full to modified.

Thus a casual glance might cause the reader to deduct that such a wide range could mean that if he were unlucky, he might find himself owning a pump or autoloader that might change to modified from full after 500 rounds of steel. The truth would be that from a barrel of standard factory thickness, he could more realistically expect only a maximum change of .005 and continued full-choke pattern efficiency.

The point here is the complexity of interpreting the tests; in the only publication where such data is detailed (the U.S. Department of Interior's Environmental Statement) barrel tests are lumped together in anonymous Barrel A, Barrel B designations. It seems to me distinctly unfair to tell the gun owner that "some" barrels will be damaged, but not to make clear to him which barrels they are likely to be. Yet, certain members of the firearms industry claim that it is impractical for them to test and to certify that all shotguns of their manufacture now in use can be safely used with steel shot loads.

Again using the revised SAAMI tables on lead and steel shot retained energy (50-yard figures rather than 45 because the tables did not break down the yardages between 40 and 50), a comparison between steel 2's and ordinary non-buffered No. 4 lead duckloads shows 321 foot-pounds of energy delivered into the pattern by steel, 295.45 by the lead shot nearest to 2's in weight and numbers. Note the lack of stringing by steel.

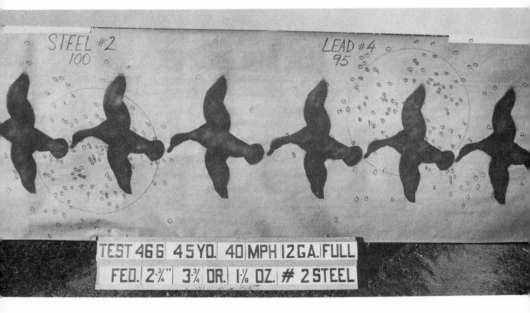

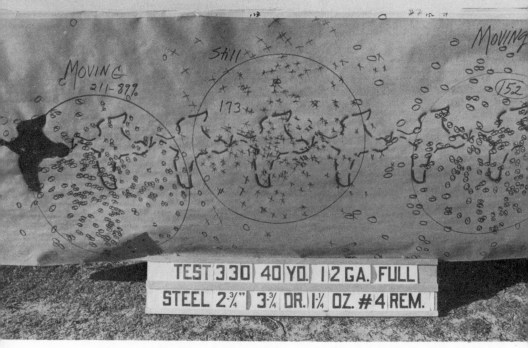

These tests of new Remington 1¼-ounce steel loads varied widely, probably due to test samples being factory handloads not yet in production; experiments are still underway. However, all gave adequate duck-killing density and penetration, and added pellets around edge of pattern provide more margin for error by shooter. Winchester also has a new 1¼-ounce steel load which did not arrive in time for tests for this book.

Winchester and Remington have already issued statements that their modern pumps and autoloaders are suitable for use with steel loads. Remington also has a Model 3200 3-inch magnum over-under with beefed up barrels designed for use with steel shot.

My own pattern and penetration testing of steel shot, though necessarily limited, has been conducted with two Perazzi over-unders, a Winchester 101 over-under, a Remington 870 pump, two Remington 1100 autoloaders, a Weatherby Centurion autoloader, a Weatherby Patrician pump, and a Beretta trapgun. None of these evidenced barrel damage that I could detect visually or in patterning.

My general impression from interviewing a number of factory spokesmen, makers of both guns and ammunition, has been that barrel damage from steel, with 1⅛-ounce standard loads, will be minor for most gun owners. Guns least likely to be affected are those modified or more open barrels. Tightness of the choke, tightness of inside barrel diameter, and thickness and hardness of barrels are the most important factors. The tighter the choke, and thinner the barrel, the more likely expansion seems to be.

William E. Talley of Winchester warned in 1976 that "too little is known about the entire matter of steel shot damage to gun barrels. For example," Talley explained, "it was believed back in the 20s, after extensive laboratory tests, that our then-new Super-X lead loads were perfectly safe. But when those loads were released to the public, some barrels were damaged because the progressive burning smokeless powder, which made those new shells such an advantage in improved patterning, also changed the pressure on the barrels beyond the chamber.

"These problems have long since been solved through technology," Talley said, "but they serve as an example of how the ultimate test is public use."

All steel shot-load producers have at one time or another singled out "thin-walled doubles" as potential problems with steel shot, and any fine Purdey, Holland, Parker, Winchester Model 21, or the like should not be used with steel shot until more is known about the loads. It may well be that future tests will indicate such guns in open chokes are ok, but I would not want to gamble on it now.

On the bright side of the steel shot ledger is the fact that breakthroughs were made in 1976 in production of more efficient longer-range steel loads; on the dark side is the question of whether these heavier loads will create more damage to gun barrels and chokes.

Remington achieved the loading of 1¼ ounces of shot (approximately 11 percent more than could be crammed into a 2¾-inch case previously) by changes in the base wad and other internal modifications of the case, which permitted retaining the standard modern crimp. Winchester took a different route, leaving its base wad intact but obtaining the 11 percent shot increase in the standard case by using a rolled crimp combined with a new top wad, which is heavier on one side than the other so that it moves aside instantly as the load clears the barrel and does not interfere with patterning. Both of these new loads add approximately 20 more pellets of No. 4s to the standard load, and 20 No. 4 pellets can produce considerably more density to the pattern and thus increase the odds of striking a vital area of the bird.

The additional 11 percent of shot load will increase density of No. 2 steel to make them even deadlier on big ducks, combining more pattern density with the high retained energy and penetration of the 2s. Tests of Winchester's new load show patterns in excess of 80 percent with 2s providing sufficiently dense patterns for mallard-sized birds at 50 yards.

Winchester also has a new 3-inch magnum steel load containing 1½ ounces of shot (an average of 68 more No. 4 pellets than the old standard case load) whereas Federal has a 1⁵⁄₁₆-ounce 3-inch magnum load.

Tom Roster, who has observed the use of steel shot on Federal refuges more hours and more scientifically than any impartial observer I know (he used rangefinders to determine the distances at which birds were being shot), says he has seen many ducks killed stone dead at 50 yards and beyond with steel 2s, even in the old 1⅛-ounce load. He said that postmortems on a number of these ducks showed that the steel pellets had gone completely through the bird at that range.

Roster's observations seem particularly significant because he is not a "steel-shot man" (and neither am I, although I've been called that for bothering to try and make impartial tests and tell the truth about them). Roster knows, just as I do, that lead is inherently the best shot material if properly utilized, and he has proved that by producing 100-percent 40-yard patterns in custom duck and goose handloads using buffered lead pellets. But he also knows, as I have written prior to this book's studies, that steel loads will kill ducks quite well.

Roster's observations with rangefinders on Bear River National Wildlife Refuge, where steel shot must be used exclusively, and my own three years of hunting the Texas ricefields and coast with steel loads, convince me that hunters are worrying unnecessarily about being able to bag their ducks with steel.

In the chapter entitled "How Good Is Your Duck Load?" the clean-killing capabilities of various gauges and loads have been compared by a computer. Twelve-gauge steel loads of 1⅛ ounces showed about the same effective range as 1¼-ounce high-velocity lead loads, and *more* range than the standard high-velocity factory loads in 16- or 20-gauge lead load. Thus the shooter who has been using common high-velocity loads (or 3-inch standard factory 20-gauge magnums) will not be handicapped in clean-killing range, although he may indeed to some extent be handicapped in ability to hit the bird with steel shot's tight patterns.

Shooters of small gauges have a big problem: no small-gauge steel loads are currently available, and handloading is not recommended until suitable components for it have been produced. Ordinary shotcup wads will not adequately protect the barrel from steel shot, nor will the same powders that work with lead shot burn properly with the lighter steel shot. Hunters who try to introduce steel pellets into lead loads risk increased chances of lodging a wad in the barrel and perhaps having the next shot blow up a gun. Proper reloading components for steel shot will undoubtedly be put on the market, and reloading writers such as Roster will work up suitable formulas for them. In the meanwhile, factory loads (expensive as they are) are the only sensible choice.

In the hunting of geese, particularly big, tough Canada geese, steel offers much more of a problem.

Despite the excellent showing by steel pellets in duckload sizes, they will not compete with the finest lead loads containing hard shot and a buffering material such as ground plastic. In the case of larger shot sizes, for long-range geese, steel loads fall well behind the best in lead. This pattern made at a full 60 yards by a standard case load of No. 2 Winchester Super-X Double X shows goose-getting penetration (all 25 boards of the penetration box were passed through by every shot that entered). The best steel loads of No. 1 shot tested penetrated only 23 cardboards at 60 yards.

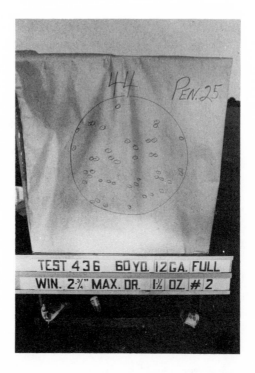

I believe more geese might be saved by exempting them from steel-shot regulations than by forcing hunters to use steel shot. The largest steel pellets now being loaded are No. 1s, and although these pattern beautifully (as much as 85 percent average with the new Winchester 1¼-ounce standard case loads) the No. 1s are not the equivalent of No. 2 lead in penetration. Size "B" pellets would have nearly equivalent penetration, but might also create more barrel-damage problems.

Even No. 2 lead in the heaviest magnum loadings is often not enough to bag big honkers cleanly at the long pass-shooting ranges where so much goose hunting must be done. Unless goose hunters take relatively long shots, in many cases they simply get no shots at all. And regardless of what is written here, they are going to take some long shots.

For a number of other reasons I believe geese should be excepted from steel-shot regulations.

Most goose hunting is done over land rather than water, and there has been no serious problem of birds ingesting spent lead pellets from vast land areas that are plowed under every year.

The reports on lead-pellet ingestion that I've studied indicate that the problem is primarily one of small pellets, the most common found

Table 1

Practical Comparison of Steel and Lead Pellets Based Upon Pellet Weight, Pellet Numbers in Load, and Retained Energies from SAAMI Tables on Shotshell Characteristics (Revised)

(All values are based upon full-choke 12-gauge guns with loads launched at muzzle velocities of 1,330 fps for lead and 1,375 for steel. Since heavier steel loads, including the latest 1¼-ounce loads for standard cases, are launched at lower muzzle velocities, their retained energy will be slightly less than for the loads shown in the tables.)

PELLET SIZE	PELLET NUMBERS PER OUNCE	ENERGY IN FOOT/POUNDS PER PELLET AT RANGE (IN YDS)			
		30	40	50	60
No. 4 Steel	188	3.32	2.46	1.88	1.43
No. 6 Lead	225	2.76	2.11	1.66	1.30
No. 2 Steel	122	5.45	4.14	3.21	2.53
No. 4 Lead	135	5.04	3.91	3.11	2.49
No. 7½ Lead	350	1.64	1.23	.93	.72

No. 6 steel would be the nearest comparison, but is not being made.

in gizzards of ducks and geese being No. 6 and No. 7½ with some 4s. Very few No. 2s are found in gizzards. It is possible that birds are less likely to mistake the large 2s for weed seeds or grit and there is also the simple numerical aspect. A goose hunter firing 2s is putting one-fourth the number of pellets into the environment as the duck hunter shooting 7½s. There are 90 pellets to the ounce of 2s, 350 pellets per ounce with 7½s, and 225 pellets per ounce in 6s.

But if federal laws do require steel for geese as well as ducks, which it now appears they will, the wise hunter will carefully weigh the stakes before he breaks the law.

It was not long ago, remember, that waterfowl hunting was challenged by a coalition of antihunting groups that attempted to ban waterfowl hunting nationwide. The hunter must retain his image as a conservationist; no group at present has better credentials in terms of contributions to the future of the waterfowl resources.

Ammunition available today, in both lead and steel, will kill farther and cleaner than any loads available to previous generations. And the new breed of extrahard lead pellets and super shells with buffered payloads offer shorter shot strings with much less chance for secondary crippling.

That's why I think the future of waterfowling will be "harder but brighter"; it will be harder in shot pellets, brighter in what these pellets can do to reduce lead-poisoning losses.

Out of the crucible of controversy has come the catalyst that accelerated shotshell development ahead of its time. The long-term winners will be waterfowl.

INDEX